How to Teach Your Baby and Teen To Drive

How to Teach Your Baby and Teen to Drive
Future Drivers Manual for Parents

by Ed Wooderson

www.DriverEdBooks.com

Published by Ed Wooderson

ISBN# **0982162308**

Library of Congress #

Copyright © 2010 by Ed Wooderson.

All Rights Reserved. No part of this book may be reproduced, stored in a retrieal system or transmitted, in any form, or by any means, electronic, mechanical, recorded, photocopied, or otherwise, without the prior permission of the copyright owner, except by a reviewer who may quote brief passages in a review.
Printed in USA.

My Purpose and Yours

The purpose of this book is very simple – to save the life of the child you have raised and whom you dearly love. This book could prevent your child or children from being killed at a young age in an auto accident – killed only because they lacked the knowledge and experience necessary to stay alive.

With an aging population in most western countries, it is of economic importance to stop the slaughter of teenagers and young adults by needless car accidents. For economic survival we need young people working, marrying and raising kids, not being killed or crippled.

Two skills are needed for driving a car. One is the skill of handling the mechanical things, such as the steering wheel, brake and gas pedals. The other skill needed is good observation of, and response to, road conditions and other drivers – all the things you need to know to stay alive. This includes such basic things as which side of the road to drive on, and less taught but very important things such as how far to look ahead.

Children can learn these survival skills, such as "reading the road," long before they get behind the wheel. The experience gained by being taught and observing while riding as passengers, will make them safer drivers in the future.

You wouldn't let a youngster learn to ride a bike without training wheels. Letting a child ride with training wheels lets them develop the actions needed to pedal and steer a bike. As the training wheels are raised balance is developed. Once the brain has developed the systems to steer, pedal and balance, the training wheels can be removed. Bike training wheels get kids riding bikes without skinned knees and elbows or broken bones.

The whole purpose of this book is to give you, a caring parent, the training wheels your future teenagers will need to learn how to drive safely and without broken dreams.

If your use of this book results in saving the life of your teenager from the needless slaughter taking place on our roads, then this book will have achieved its purpose.

Dedication

Mom, I dedicate this book to your wisdom and understanding.

As a teenager, you insisted that if I were too tired to drive, I should stop and take a nap. This I did, and Mom, you were right. I wouldn't sleep for long, because I would wake up stiff and sore due to the uncomfortable sleeping position. But once I slept for two hours I woke up in broad daylight much more alert.

Thank you, Mom, for granting me the freedom to make my own choices even though you didn't agree with my being out all night. Let's face it; I wasn't staying out all night to attend Easter Sunday's dawn church service.

Your wisdom and common sense approach to life gave me the know-how, I believe, that allowed me to get home safely every night. Mom, I hope that, because of you, other mothers and fathers will realize that orders and rules alone don't save lives. I hope they will learn that communication, one with another, builds respect and trust, just like you taught your children. And that teaching and advising me how to handle life is a much greater force than trying to control by imposing restrictions and "don'ts."

Thank you for that trust you had in me 50 years ago. My wish for you is that, in your sunset years, you will always be as alert and wise as when you guided me as a youth. May your faith in God and the love of your family never diminish.

Table of Contents

Introduction..7

Section One: Teach Your Baby to Drive

Chapter 1: Our Children's Future..........................15

Chapter 2: Making Confident Drivers 19

Chapter 3: Start Them Young and Make it Fun 23

Chapter 4: Roadwise 29

Chapter 5: Looking Ahead, Eyes Moving 39

Chapter 6: Following Distances 63

Chapter 7: Small Things Seem Farther Away 69

Chapter 8: Knowing the Machine 75

Chapter 9: Developing Senses & Judgment 83

Chapter 10: Braking.......................................95

Chapter 11: Defensive Driving............................101

Chapter 12: Set a Good Example...........................115

Chapter 13: Lanes and Passing............................127

Chapter 14: Trucks and Cars 131

Chapter 15: Teaching Games for Young Kids 139

Chapter 16: Help Wanted 145

Section Two: How to Teach Driving and Most Other Things

Chapter 17: How to Teach 149

Chapter 18: Driver Ed's Instruction Guide 177

Section Three: Teach Your Teen to Drive

Chapter 19: How to Teach Driving 181

Chapter 20: Behind the Wheel 195

Chapter 21: Lessons Plan 223

Chapter 22: Stick Shifts 231

Chapter 23: "Cars Kill Kids" Stops Here 245

Appendix 247

GLOSSARY 255

INDEX 263

Introduction

Start Now to Keep Your Children Alive Later!

Teach your Baby (and Teen) to Drive is a common sense approach to reducing the huge death toll of young drivers. By using the information in this book, you can teach your children vital driving skills while they are being passengers long before they are old enough to drive. By the time they do get their license they will be experienced at reading the road ahead and predicting what other drivers might do.

By the mid-90s, traffic accidents had become – and still are today – the #1 leading cause of death for four to twenty-four year olds. Too many teen drivers are far too dangerous on our roads – not only to themselves but dangerous also to others. Until the release of this book, experts had few ideas left, if any, about how to make teens safer drivers.

Passing more laws is not always the best way to make safe drivers. On the other hand, sometimes a new idea can change the way things are done, resulting in a new and effective approach to solving an old problem. *Teach your Baby (and Teen) to Drive* explains this new idea, an idea that could save the lives of many young people. It's an inexpensive solution to a deadly problem and as simple as using training wheels for drivers.

Research has shown that parental involvement in teaching car safety is the biggest factor in reducing the number of accidents teen drivers have. This book shows you how parental involvement can be started from a surprisingly young age.

Young people often start to learn sports and music at a very early age. Tiger Woods' golf outings started when he was only eighteen months old. By age twenty-one, Tiger had become an international celebrity because of his outstanding skills on the golf course.

If starting young is essential for athletic and musical success, then how much more important is it for your children to learn to watch the road from a very young age in order to later, as teenagers, to become successful drivers?

Your child's life may depend on developing these skills while you are in the car together.

The death toll among teenage drivers and their passengers (often young family members) is much higher than it need be. Having your children participate in and contribute to your driving, as described in this book, lets you work together as a team while applying these simple ideas.

This book includes a section on how to teach your children to do things. Most people do learn to drive. If we apply the same principles that make a reasonably competent driver to other subjects, teaching will become a positive experience and learning will be fun.

To make this book complete there is also a section that explains a step by step method for you to teach your teen to drive. Simple exercises are included that allow your teen to practice working the gas and brake pedals while the car is sitting in the driveway. This will make him a much safer student driver for whoever teaches him to drive.

I hope you will enjoy this book. It is easy to read and really simple to use. It will bring you peace of mind when you apply it well and may prevent the young person you love from steering into disaster. In addition, some enjoyable special times will be shared by you and your children to later fondly remember.

An added feature is that your children's boredom in the car will be gone. This book will give you the tools you need to handle your children from being bored and distracting you as you drive. It's really very simple; if the kids have the job of helping you with your driving, they won't be continually distracting you by asking, "Are we there yet?" You will have taught them to figure this out for themselves.

They will learn to look for the next landmark or another point of interest on the journey, not just wait to get to the final destination. This book will show you how to make every family trip an adventure.

* * * * * * * *

Note: The glossary at the end of the book will help you, the reader, understand the terms used in the book and thus keep you reading.

INTRODUCTION

What this Book is About

This book covers not only teaching your child how to observe traffic from an early age but also how to teach your teen to drive. Let me explain why I have included two different age groups in the same book.

Science has discovered that when the brain is challenged to do something new it will set up systems to do that task. The surprising discovery was that if a task is no longer being performed, the brain will lose what it had earlier developed to handle that situation.

Based on miles driven, teenagers' involvement in fatal accidents is three times higher as compared to experienced drivers. Many experts believe that 16 year olds don't have an adequately developed brain to be safe drivers. They may be correct but raising the legal driving age is not the solution. If the brain has not been trained to respond to traffic, no new driver of any age will be safe until the brain has been exposed for some time to driving.

So here is the smart new idea this book explains. Why not build a driver's survival pattern into a child's brain long before he gets behind the wheel. Let the child learn what driving is all about, as a passenger, over an extended period of time. This will establish in the brain, safe driving patterns that will last a lifetime.

Just like a medical student watches an experienced surgeon at work, a child must watch how an experienced driver operates a car.

To be able to drive safely, as teenagers, the brain must be exposed over an extended period of time to traffic situations and road conditions that develop the skills needed to handle a car safely.

I was raised on a farm in New Zealand. As a child I walked a horse forward and backwards while a stacker lifted up hay to build a very old fashioned hay stack. I still remember the flies, the heat and dust.

I don't recall learning to drive a farm tractor. I must have been seven or eight years old because that is when tractors replaced horses. It must have been a very natural progression. One little step at a time without any stress or upset that I remember.

My kids were also raised in New Zealand. They learned to drive every time we visited their uncle's farm. It was something that I found enjoyable as a child and so I thought it would be fun for my kids too, but I put no importance on getting them driving.

I started to work on getting my kids reading the road as passengers while on a book promotion tour around New Zealand. My eldest child was almost old enough to get her driver's license and I was worried about her survival as a teen driver. Later, while teaching driver education I realized that student drivers, who had watched the road as passengers, were easier and safer to teach than those who hadn't developed this skill.

I didn't teach my kids from an early enough age but my daughter, who was very familiar with what I had written, started developing her kid's knowledge about cars while they were still strapped into a car seat.

My daughter raised her kids to drive. She bought them a Mattel electric car. (This is an amazing toy car; it never breaks down and will go anywhere.) As children, both Julie and Katie at first sometimes drove it into walls and ditches but after a couple of years they became skillful drivers.

My daughter has moved to her hotel in Costa Rica. Visit her web site at www.brasilito.com. As her car had no airbag it was safe to have her child sit on her knee and steer the car. From age six this is what Julie did while her mother drove on their own private road. Julie got lots of practice steering around the potholes in the unpaved road. Note: No child or baby should ever be on a driver's knee when the car has an airbag. It could explode out of the steering wheel and injure or kill the child.

I took a car equipped with airbags to Costa Rica so I didn't allow Julie to be on my knee to steer the car. One day while driving over a private road to the beach, Julie, who was almost ten years old, asked if she could drive. I stopped the car and told Julie to get behind the wheel. I explained about the airbag and said that she would have to work the pedals as well as the steering wheel. Julie jumped excitedly into the driver's seat and became a car driver.

Everyday as we went to the beach for a swim Julie drove the first three miles avoiding the potholes, horses and cattle. She learned to take the best path through a stream and gradually picked up speed as she drove the car out of the water and up the bank of the stream that we had just forded. Julie drove slowly but she handled the car beautifully.

I then thought I should drill her on how to hit the brakes with the car parked and the handbrake on. This technique is outlined later in this book. Julie protested this action as she was sure she knew it all. I realized that she was right; Julie had been taught to drive her Mattel car only with her right foot, moving it quickly to the brake before she hit a wall. Her brain was wired to hit the brake without having to think about it. Also the years of driving her Mattel car where she moved the car from forward to reverse every time she got stuck had already established a brain pattern for her to shift gears. All I needed to do was, with the car parked, have her practice revving up the engine. This would establish a brain pattern of how hard to push the gas pedal when driving a real car. She had not learned to do this because she drove her Mattel car with her foot hard down most of the time.

Learning to drive should be a natural progression over time. If you have already taught your child how to read the road and be responsible for the car's safety from an early age, a time and place may occur where there is some wide open space in which you can get your child behind the wheel without breaking the law.

Why is it so important to learn things from a young age? It has to do with neurons, the nerve cells in the brain. The spinal cord and nerves in the body also have neurons. Neurons conduct impulses. Modern scientific research has discovered that at birth the brain's neurons exist mostly apart from each other. A baby's brain needs to establish and reinforce connections with other neurons. These connections then form what is known as synapses. These synapses are created by experiences.

Between birth and age three, the brain creates more synapses than it needs. The synapses that get used a lot become established as a permanent part of the brain. Synapses that are not used are lost.

At the time of this writing, I got a report from Costa Rica that when Julie's mother comes home and stops the car to open the gate, Julie, by tradition jumps in and drives the car into the carport. One day the car was driven into the carport and then backed out and backed in again. Julie's mother found her other daughter Katie sitting on Julie's knee steering the car while Julie worked the clutch, brake and stick shift. Two young brains working together were building the needed synapses to drive a car.

It is interesting how ten-year-old Julie, after years of reading the road as a passenger and years of driving a toy car and then an actual car, is now teaching her six-year-old sister how to steer the family car.

When driving slowly over private roads Julie now likes driving her mother's stick shift more than my automatic. Julie says driving an automatic is boring and a stick shift is a lot more fun. She is getting practice working the pedals and steering away from traffic. This past summer she has been learning to read the road as a passenger on a 5,000-mile vacation to Yellowstone National Park.

Her brain had been building synapses about observing traffic from the time that she had been a toddler strapped into her car seat. After years of driving toy cars and now slowly driving real ones these synapses have become a permanent part of her brain. By age 16, she will have established a brain pattern that will make her a safe driver for the rest of her life.

I have been often told that my grandchildren are very responsible kids. On looking this over maybe there is another benefit to teaching your babies to drive. Not only will they be more responsible while in the car but also more responsible in every aspect of their lives.

Insurance companies charge more to insure drivers who have less than nine years of driving experience. Based on their records they know it takes nine years of driving experience to become a safe driver.

We know athletes can begin their athletic development from 18 months of age. Musical ability can be developed from an even earlier age by listening to music as a baby. We also know that the most vital teaching time for a child is between birth and ten years of age.

Max Planck, winner of the Nobel Prize in physics, wrote, "A new scientific truth does not triumph by convincing its opponents and making them see the light, but rather because its opponents eventually die, and a new generation grows up that is familiar with it."

You can be part of the new generation whose kids develop the needed synapses to survive as teenage drivers.

As traffic accidents are the largest cause of death among young people, parents and grandparents must realize that we should teach our babies to drive.

Section One

Teach Your Baby to Drive

Chapter 1

Our Children's Future

A Parents' Most Important Job

We agree as parents that our most important job is to keep our children from harm and to keep them alive so they can outlive us. We do this every time we strap a protesting toddler into a car seat. We react quickly when we think a toddler may run in front of a car. Every time we punish a child for playing with matches, we are doing this.

We teach a toddler that in order to be safe he must be strapped into a car seat. If a toddler is inclined to run out of control, we will put a harness on him to keep him under control. We explain, maybe over and over why we don't want him playing with matches. My then five-year-old granddaughter explained that she wasn't playing with matches, she was just lighting them and blowing them out. Her mother had to be firm and tell her no, you don't light them and blow them out. That is playing with matches.

The biggest killer of kids is not fire due to someone playing with matches. Its car crashes. Inexperienced teen drivers kill themselves and sadly, their passengers, who may happen to be their younger brothers and sisters. A compounded tragedy.

We need to spend considerably more effort educating our kids on the ways of other drivers and how a car works than we do on the danger of matches.

In fact, we must spend years educating them on how to be future safe drivers while we are still out in the car together. I believe this is one of the most important jobs a parent has because cars kill kids. It's your job as a parent to educate our future drivers. This book will show you how.

Why am I Publishing This Book?

It was Memorial Day, 1995. My wife and I were team-driving a Big-

Rig truck, moving computers from the northeastern U.S. to Atlanta. The computers had to be driven there nonstop, so that they could be up and running right after the long weekend.

After driving most of the night I was asleep in the truck's "sleeper" (right behind the driver's seat in the big, extended cab). My wife woke me and said she had seen a car in her left mirror that had veered across the road to the left and disappeared into some trees in the middle of the divided highway. She had stopped to help. By the time I dressed and ran back to where the car had disappeared, other stopped motorists told us the bad news. One young person was dead, and two were injured. It took a lifetime, or so it seemed, for the emergency medical teams to finally arrive.

My wife had been driving at the legal speed limit of 65 mph in the right lane when an old car passed her. The right front tire of the passing car blew out, and the car veered to the right, into our trailer, and then bounced off to the left, into the trees. As a result, a young person died.

My first concern was for the young people. My next concern was for my wife – I feared she would never want to drive a truck again. She was not at fault, but our truck and trailer had to be thoroughly inspected. My further concern was for the family of the young person who had just died. I could only imagine the heartbreak they would experience.

As truck drivers, we are taught that all accidents are preventable. I believe that if the young driver had taken the time to examine the car's tires before driving, the accident would have been prevented, and no one would have died as the tires obviously would have appeared to be unsafe. If the tires had been checked before the trip, that young person would not have been driving, or at least would have kept the speed down and wouldn't have been passing in the fast lane at 70 to 75 mph. Even if the tire had blown out, at a lower speed the accident may not have been fatal.

Commercial truck drivers must examine their vehicles, including tires, every single day. They're also trained to walk around and "eyeball" the tires every time they stop. If a parent had spent the time to show that young person what to look for, to make sure the tires were safe, then this death likely would not have marred that Memorial Day weekend.

On another occasion my wife was in the passenger seat and I was driving our Big-Rig. My wife told me to slow down; when I asked her for the reason why, she said she didn't know, but I slowed down anyway. She had never done this before, so I instantly paid more attention. The traffic was quite heavy, but I had plenty of room ahead. I could see there was nothing close to me in my lane, but there was a vehicle on my left. Within a moment, a car full of teenage girls suddenly jumped lanes and swung directly in front of me – traveling at only half the speed I was going.

They had come from another freeway that merged with the one I was on, and it had been obscured from my view. I hit the brakes and horn at the same time, and the car swerved back into its own lane just as I was about to hit it. Whatever it was that made my wife tell me to slow down had probably saved the lives of those teenage girls.

That's an example of a teenager being allowed behind the wheel just because she knew how the pedals and steering wheel worked – and that was about all. She had obviously never paid attention, as a passenger, to what was happening around her. If she had done so, she would have known not to jump lanes and cut right in front of a big truck that was traveling at twice her speed!

Many times, I have seen teenage drivers doing things that could result in accidents. I offer a very simple solution to this problem. As cars are now a way of life, we expect our children to drive them in the future. If we don't give our children any knowledge of cars or driving until they reach the legal driving age, expecting that they will suddenly magically acquire good driving skills, it's practically as if we are doing our best to kill them.

If a parent forbids a child to drive until they are eighteen, while it's legal to do so at a younger age, and that teenager learns to drive with only about ten hours of lessons behind the wheel, he or she is an accident waiting to happen. This is especially true if the new driver has been denied the full knowledge of how cars work, has been told repeatedly "don't touch the car," and has not been taught how to "read the road ahead" while being a passenger. Worse still, he will be that much more accident prone if he is driving (or, should I say, still learning how to drive) while also learning how to handle alcohol for the first time.

The younger a child is when he starts paying attention to the road ahead and other vehicles on it, and the more you teach him how to "read" and predict other drivers' intentions and actions, the better driver he will then be in the future.

Working the pedals and turning the wheel can be taught by any competent driving instructor in less than ten hours. But learning to read the road and predict other drivers are skills that take years of practice to develop. You need to be able to understand and predict what can happen in traffic – before it happens. If there is a potential danger ahead you must be able to recognize the problem and act quickly to avoid it.

Insurance companies charge higher rates for any driver with less than nine years experience – for good reason. So why not make sure your kids have had at least nine years of experience reading the road and other drivers, before they get their drivers license.

You have the kids in the car with you as passengers for many years. Use the time you have together in the car to develop their road "instincts" and judgment. You will be doing your job well if your ten-year-old tells you to slow down because he saw a dangerous situation before you saw it. But most importantly, they should survive their first few years of driving, the years when so many accidents happen, and so many young lives are needlessly lost.

Your State Driver Handbook

You'll need your state's driver handbook as you work with your child to get him or her familiar with the rules of the road. This book is meant to be used in conjunction with your state handbook. The two books have a different focus – but share a common purpose.

Children do well with structure and rules. Tell them in the simplest terms how the subject of driving has written, clearly defined laws that explain how you must go about doing things. This is necessary for safety.

The handbook gives the state's laws, written in a manner so as to be easily understood. The great majority of those laws were written and passed for the purpose of keeping traffic moving in an orderly, efficient and safe manner. It's your "bible" when it comes to knowing and understanding the laws of the road.

This book's purpose is to help you save lives by developing in your children, starting at a young age, the skills needed to drive a car safely. It's your "bible" when it comes to ensuring your children survive their first few dangerous years on the roads.

A safe driver needs to understand and follow the rules of the road as given in the state handbook, but he also needs to develop the skills of "reading the road" as described in this book. Keep a copy of both books in your glove box, and use them when in the car with your children.

Chapter 2

Making Confident Drivers

Confidence Comes from Doing

Most people end up as reasonably confident drivers. Why is it that even a nervous person can learn to drive a car, despite his having been injured as a child in a car accident?

A confident driver has very often practiced driving from a young age by playing with toy cars and trucks, and by doing simulated car driving in video games. By the time he is actually old enough to drive, he has practiced the actions needed, passed a test and gotten himself a driver's license.

Whatever you want your child to do well, you should start him doing the actions involved at a young age. Of course, if you played a sport like basketball or soccer in your youth, you will probably take your son out and play ball with him. My son can't dance, but he sure can throw, hit and kick a ball. Most boys practice their sport by the hour. The result is confidence.

Let's look at how we teach driving, and perhaps use the same approach to teach a child how to dance. When my daughters were small enough not to injure me, I would let them stand on my feet as I danced with them. This helped them develop their rhythm for dancing just like a child riding a bike gets the feel for how a driver steers. I did this long before they were self-conscious about boys, and the action of actually dancing with them built enough confidence in them to go to dancing classes as teenagers. My wife never danced with our son, and when we sent him to dance lessons he was too self-conscious to actually persist long enough to learn to dance.

From an early age, if you really make an effort to develop your children's sense of rhythm, it will get them dancing. This will give kids added confidence when they start socializing as teenagers. You may end up with safer drivers too, because they may go dancing instead of drinking.

Some boys think that having a few drinks is the solution to their confidence problem when they're out to meet girls. This will become an issue when that same teenager happens to be driving a car. A more sensible solution is to drill the teenager on manners and doing the things he needs to do in a social situation. When you go out to eat, help your child remain confident by letting him order for the whole family. Putting the kid in charge of ordering dinner is like you not grabbing the wheel, and not hitting the brake when you're teaching him to drive. You let him do the driving.

You feel confident only when you know that you can do something well, because you've practiced doing it and can achieve a result. Confidence does not come out of a bottle or from a pill – confidence is built by practice. Practicing the action gives confidence. It is only when you can do an action without thinking about what to do next that you feel confident in that area, subject, or skill. The reason champion gymnasts appear so confident is because of the many hours actually spent doing the actions in practice. The end result is a confident, smooth and stunning performance.

A pep talk will not build lasting confidence – it can only energize a person enough to get him moving. Doing the actions needed is what builds confidence, not a lecture.

The whole approach taken by this book is to build confidence in your child by practicing, at an early age, the skills necessary to drive – such as reading the road and understanding how cars work. As a result he will become a confident and safe driver in the future.

This same approach can be applied to the other things that your child will need or want to do in the future. The more confident you want a child to be, the more things you should teach him; have him actually practice doing the actions involved. The more he practices doing, the more confident he will be.

The Best Teacher

Sometimes the best teacher is a student who has just learned a new skill, and then uses his new found knowledge to teach another beginning student.

My younger brother Keith taught our mother to drive when he was only ten years old. How could he have taught her when the rest of us older experts had failed? My father, older brother and I had never managed to get Mom to feel confident enough in her ability to even attempt to drive.

Many years later when I asked our mother how Keith had succeeded whereas the rest of us had failed, she said simply that Keith was patient with her. Because he had trouble seeing over the steering wheel, it had been difficult for him to learn to drive. Driving for us older, larger guys just meant jumping in and driving. Keith, on the other hand, knew how difficult it was for a small-bodied person to push the clutch down and see over the wheel at the same time.

He'd figured out how to drive, overcoming problems similar to those Mom had. So he worked first to make our mother feel comfortable behind the wheel, before the driving began. Also, because of his smaller body and lesser strength, Keith understood our mother's needs, and so patiently worked with her until she got the feel of the car's controls. We bigger guys had no need to ensure the seat was positioned absolutely right, so we didn't understand and weren't patient enough to get Mom positioned correctly so that she could work the heavy clutch that cars had 60 years ago.

I've employed a truck driver, Ron, who had been offered the position of a trainer. Ron thought he was too inexperienced to take the responsibility of driving with a new driver fresh out of school, so he turned the job down. I then gave Ron a very inexperienced driver to run with and guess what – Ron straightened out the problem the driver had been having with shifting gears. My previous driver with many years of driving experience hadn't been able to help the new driver, but someone out of school for only one year still remembered how he was taught and therefore was able to help the inexperienced driver.

I'm giving these examples of how a person who's newly acquired a skill can be a good teacher, because how he learned it is still fresh in his mind. Someone with years of experience has usually long ago forgotten how he learned to do it, and he may not be able to teach the skill as well, unless he spends the time to understand what a new learner needs to do.

Anytime an opportunity arises for one of your children to teach another, let him as he will pass the skill on very easily to another. This will save you time – you just need to keep an eye on what's happening. Your "know-how" may be needed to handle a point the "new teacher" hasn't yet encountered. At times it is helpful to have someone who is experienced available to pass on the "tricks of the trade."

Teach to Learn More

There's an additional, very positive benefit gotten by you teaching a person how to do something – you yourself get an even better grasp of what it's all about.

As most people are not accustomed to teaching they don't realize that one of the best ways to improve a skill is to teach it to another person who is new at it. Because of this, you can become a far better driver yourself by teaching your child all about cars and driving.

How this works is really quite simple: You can't teach something and show or explain it clearly to another without having a pretty good understanding of it yourself. I myself became highly confident in doing many things only after I taught those things to my children.

For example, teach your child to check all the fluid levels in the car, and then supervise him as he trains another kid to do it. By doing both actions – learning it and then teaching another – your child will grasp what is needed very quickly and won't forget it. Of course, if he never grasped how to do it, this will quickly become obvious when he tries to teach another. Just knowing that he will need to show someone else how to do it should make him pay enough attention and ask enough questions to grasp what needs to be done.

Don't just have your children teach their siblings and friends things, but also have them teach your children things they know. Also make sure your children's friends have and use this book, so that they too will be safe drivers when they are old enough to drive your kids around.

Wise employers prefer to hire people who are unselfish and helpful team players. By teaching your children new skills, and having them teach other kids, you'll develop a team spirit in them, a quality that many employers think is the essential quality needed to do today's jobs.

We've all taken drivers' license tests and read the rules of the road, but how many of us actually apply all that we read? For example, the two-second rule is in the state handbook that you've read at some point. But if you're like me, you'll never apply it well (or possibly not at all!) until you start teaching that rule to your children.

You must set a good example if you want your child to drive safely. Don't drive aggressively! Obey traffic laws and be considerate to others on the road. Just by driving correctly your children will know what good driving is and be able to drive safely according to your example.

When you teach a subject or skill to another person, you gain a better understanding of it and become more skilled in it yourself. This book is based on this principle. My aim is not only to help your children be safe drivers, but also for you to become a better driver.

By the use of this principle, your children will be able to apply what they have learned, become helpful team players, and in many ways enhance their lives and those of others.

Chapter 3

Start Them Young and Make it Fun

Keep It Enjoyable

As you teach your children driving skills, keep it light and bright. It isn't do-or-die horribly serious all the time. In fact, it can and should be a great deal of fun much of the time. Just as no student learns well when upset, yelled at, or under pressure, neither can one learn driving skills well when it's made a deathly serious chore. A confident and light-hearted instructor gets much better results, much faster.

Over 40 years ago, I was fortunate to have my wife and two friends, Helen from America and John from Australia in the car while I drove in a very stressful situation. Let me explain. Almost all of my driving experience up to that point had been on quiet country roads in small New Zealand towns, on the left side of the road as is customary there and also in England.

In 1966 we took a car ferry from England across the English Channel to France, and I drove my car from there into Paris. I was driving a car with the steering wheel on the right side, as they're built for England and New Zealand. In France, driving on the right side of the road was the "wrong" side for me, and my steering wheel was also on the wrong side for the country I was in.

On top of that, I wasn't used to big cities, so the heavily congested streets of Paris with pedestrians darting between cars to cross the road was a huge culture shock for me, an experience I'll never forget. My nerves were quite on edge! It was very stressful for me as I drove on with deadly seriousness. Then I barely missed running down an elderly man and got really rattled!

Helen then imitated both my New Zealand accent and dry humor, saying to me: "Oh, Ed, what's all the bloody fuss? He's a very old man with one foot already in the grave – you'd get only one point for hitting him! If you really must run over pedestrians, to make it worthwhile, try to hit someone worth at least ten points, like a young pregnant woman pushing a baby carriage!"

Helen's imitation and joke of course broke my super-seriousness, and I busted up laughing! It was actually quite a relief, and I finally began to relax.

For the rest of our weekend in Paris, Helen and John turned driving into a fun experience for me. By adding their silliness, the seriousness of the situation was forgotten, and I enjoyed every moment of what would have been a very stressful few days. It was the highlight of my time in Europe, and I took great pleasure in driving around the beautiful city. The historic and magnificent Arc de Triomphe was truly awe inspiring to drive around from my relaxed perspective.

I still smile when I think of the French policeman who so very seriously approached the passenger side of my English car with a scowl – expecting to find the driver there – only to find the driver on the other side. Rather embarrassed, he then had to compose himself as he walked around to the other side. Then, whatever he was trying to tell us in French, we two New Zealanders, one Australian and one American had no idea of what he was talking about! It was altogether quite a pleasurable experience.

Years later, the first time I had a student driver almost hit a pedestrian, I explained to him that if he'd hit that pedestrian, it would have been worth only one point, and then I explained how the point system worked. Of course, the situation lost all its seriousness for him. That student was a very serious young man and up to this point, had been quite difficult to teach. By making a game of it, and refusing to be so serious, I not only made him into an excellent driver, I also taught him a valuable lesson in how to live life.

When close to death after being shot, former Republican President Reagan joked that he hoped the surgeons who were about to operate on him were all Republicans. A doctor responded by saying "Sir, we are all Republicans today." If he had the ability to take the gravity out of that truly serious situation, then we too can take the seriousness out of teaching our kids all about cars.

No matter what you're teaching, remember to keep it light and bright, and both you and your child will have many more wins, and make much better progress. I promise! So go to it, and have fun!

Ideal Driving Students

I once attempted to teach a lady to drive who had recently emigrated from Hong Kong, where she'd spent her whole life. She had absolutely none of the skills needed to drive. Having had a very different childhood – nothing to do with cars or vehicles – she was completely clueless. Let me explain why.

I asked her, "Did you ride a tricycle as a child and learn to steer?" She told me that in the small apartment where she was raised there was not enough space to ride a tricycle. When I asked her about riding a bicycle, she explained that most of the places she had to go had been within walking distance, or else public transportation had been available. She had not even been driven around in a car, since Hong Kong is very small and her family did not need or own a car.

She had never tried to "drive a car" in a video game. She had no teenage experience with driving go-carts, bumper-cars or similar vehicles at amusement parks. I was not beat yet. I asked her, "Have you ever used a sewing machine that had a foot pedal to control the speed of the machine?" I was hoping to find that she had used her foot to control something. Apparently, clothes are so inexpensive in Hong Kong that it doesn't pay to make or repair your own, so even this skill had not been learned.

I never did teach her to drive. She could afford only one lesson every two weeks, and she was not progressing fast enough to merit spending the little money she had. However, I learned a lot from her.

This experience made me look at all the things that children do which would help them to develop the skills needed for driving. Before school age, children ride toy cars, tricycles and other toys whereby they learn the basics of steering. Later on, they ride bicycles, requiring more skills. Some learn to use a sewing machine and develop eye-hand-foot coordination. Computer games develop hand-eye coordination. Amusement parks let kids actually drive vehicles, long before legal car driving age. Video games have them "driving" while using many of the skills needed to actually drive. Some teenagers also drive lawn mowers or farm tractors. Even skate boarding requires some observation of surfaces and surroundings, plus judgment of speed, distances, and timing.

Encourage all of the above. Prepare your children by letting them use all of the means available that will give them a "feel" of how it is to drive a car.

Musicians and Athletes Start Young

Recently, a young tennis player who had started playing seriously when she was only ten years old told me she was far too old when she got started. Many children are taught sports and music at a very young age, some even beginning as young as three. Tiger Woods began his golf lessons before he was two. If this is essential for athletes and musicians whose livelihood and success depend on mastering their chosen skills, then how much more important is it for young people to learn from an early age to watch the road while in a car. Not learning how to swing a golf club correctly is not fatal but failing to read the road and the conditions ahead correctly could cost the driver his life.

There will be other advantages to your child learning driving skills early. For example, a child trained to look ahead, to watch the road and surroundings, will be less likely to get carsick. With your children learning and practicing the basics of driving, they will also have something interesting to do (not just be bored), and can apply their knowledge in helping you, as well as taking some responsibility for everyone's safety. By understanding themselves how important it is for the driver to keep his attention on the road, your children will be less inclined to distract you as you drive.

When you are driving the car with your children, you can teach them to be "roadwise." You can use time that is not being otherwise utilized. It's not as if you have to find a special time. You don't have to find any equipment for the lessons. They're in the car with nothing else to do. All you need is right in front of you. When a traffic light changes, your child can learn to tell you to STOP or to GO.

The average 16-year-old soccer player has experienced 1,500 hours of coached soccer practice. Most states only require 50 hours driving experience to get a license. Why not plan on having your kids accumulate at least 1,500 hours of experience reading the road from the passenger's seat, coached by you while you spend time in the car together.

Regain a Lost Child

Don't lose your kids to the Internet. Bring them back to reality. There is a real world out there. All you have to do is to unclasp their fingers from the mouse or joystick and get them into the car with you, although in today's world you will have to limit the use of your car's DVD player to achieve this. It doesn't matter where you go. The fun is getting there and getting home again.

Show you care. Occasionally look beyond their physical needs and spend some time with them. Take your kids away with you for a weekend, or even better, a vacation.

Once on a trip with our 16-year-old son, my wife curled up for a nap and went to sleep. We had planned to stop at a motel when we got tired, but instead, my son and I shared the driving and continued on until dawn. We talked all night while driving, and caught up on what was happening in our lives. I know of no better way to get quality time with your children.

Years later, my son now runs a successful sales team where there are always demands on his time. Often, when his office calls him, I've heard him tell his secretary, "I'm having some father time." He still makes a point of getting together with me and his mom, so we can catch up on what's happening with one another.

Get your children off the Internet and onto the real highways of life. Get learner permits for your children the day they become legally old enough to drive, so they can get behind the wheel and have the hands-on experience of driving the car on family trips.

You'll be surprised just how much communication develops and how much honesty you can share. Later, if your children are like mine, they will remind you of the trip when you helped sort out their heads on certain problems. If it weren't for the real experience of going somewhere together in a car, you may not have realized there was a problem that needed to be resolved. Even if you were vaguely aware of a problem, if you were like me, you sometimes couldn't see any handling for it. It seems that just being in the small space of a car together, viewing the changing scenery, brings the family close enough to communicate exactly what needs to be said.

Extra Eyes Prevent Accidents

We have all experienced having a passenger warn us of an approaching danger that we didn't see, and thus avoided an accident. One day, after only six driving lessons, a young student of mine was being driven to school by his father. He yelled for his father to stop when the car in front of them suddenly stopped for no reason. Just as the car in front of them had begun to stop, his father had turned his head and begun looking at him while talking. With only six hours of driving, this student had gained the idea of looking ahead, rather than looking at his father while talking. He prevented an accident.

Having other people in the car can be a distraction to the driver who may pay less attention to the road when talking with passengers. It makes sense that if a passenger may distract the driver, then the passenger should know this (even if a child) and keep his eyes looking ahead to watch for any danger the driver might miss. It's simple. If you, as a passenger, distract the driver, you had better also start paying attention to the road ahead and share the responsibility.

My son reminds me that he once yelled when I was driving and prevented me from having an accident. If your child is experienced at looking ahead, it could very well be that the quickness of youth may warn you of approaching danger before you notice it. Teaching him this lifesaving skill at an early age could save your own life, as well as his.

Shared Moments you will Treasure

A great bonus to this learning strategy is the bond that is created or strengthened between you and your children. Today's large homes with YouTube, Myspace, Facebook, etc., can cause members of a family to almost lead separate lives. Sometimes the small space of a car gets the family talking together.

With my family, many important decisions have been reached during road trips. Goals have been set and plans have been made. It seems that getting together in a limited space watching the changing scene, without distractions, increases communication between people. Getting away from the problems of the moment can also give one a better viewpoint from which to work on them.

Your children will respond positively to being in the car with you when you're sharing a common purpose to develop new skills. While traveling, some special times will be shared that will be remembered for a lifetime. When you treat children as intelligent, able, and responsible individuals while working together to build up their skills, a great relationship can be established – or a good one can become even better.

Chapter 4

Roadwise

Reading the Road

"Roadwise" is a new word I use in this book. It describes a person who has learned to read the road ahead and has developed the skill to anticipate what other drivers will do. As a result, he or she will respond sensibly, and more quickly, to the changing traffic scene.

My first understanding of this was when, during the same time period, I taught two different women to drive. In New Zealand we have roundabouts also called "traffic circles". Drivers enter the roundabout by giving way to cars on their right. One older female driver drove through a roundabout for the first time very safely and confidently.

When I voiced my surprise that an inexperienced driver could handle traffic so well she explained that she had always watched for traffic and told her husband when it was safe to enter a roundabout. She was not inexperienced at reading the road at all. In a way she had been a back-seat driver for many years. She had been watching the road long enough to develop the necessary brain pattern to safely enter a roundabout.

The other student liked to talk to the driver and never watched what was going on outside the car. She would look at the driver while chatting away with them. As a result there was no brain pattern established on how to approach a roundabout.

I found this out when she attempted to drive into her first roundabout. My surprise turned to horror as she attempted to go around the roundabout in the wrong direction, heading straight towards a car coming towards us. There would have been a collision if I hadn't grabbed the steering wheel and jerked the car back to the correct side.

I still didn't grasp what was happening. I thought that one woman had common sense and the other was simply a scatterbrain. It was only later that

I realized one driver had developed the necessary brain pattern to drive safely and the other hadn't.

There's a tremendous difference between a learning driver who has never been taught to observe the road and traffic while riding as a passenger, and one who has been taught to do so. It has nothing to do with common sense or the lack of it, it has more to do with experience.

As a driving instructor, I had a student to whom I'd given only two lessons before the pressure of her overtime at work made further instruction impossible for a few months. She was very afraid of driving, and was so nervous that I took her on her first lesson to an empty parking lot to get away from all the traffic that terrified her.

At first, while I drove, I gave her my usual new student talk: "From now on, whenever you sit in the passenger seat of a car, or in the front of a bus, you must look ahead, focus your eyes on one object after another, keep your view and attention up ahead, and observe the road, back and forth." I explained that becoming roadwise was a skill she had to practice, as a passenger, while someone else was driving. She must stop looking at the driver while chatting with him and instead must start observing where the car was going.

After the second lesson she had to take a break due to her job, and I didn't see her again for four months. She hadn't driven since our last lesson, so I expected her to be the same nervous driver. I thought I'd have to start all over again from the very beginning, as she would have forgotten all I had taught her.

How wrong I was! I found instead a very able, roadwise driver. She was looking ahead, steering the car smoothly and confidently. Of course I asked her if she'd been practicing looking ahead, and she replied that yes, during the whole summer she'd been practicing driving while a passenger, just as I'd told her to. When I asked her to drive into a busy area, she handled it very well, and all her fear of traffic was gone.

That student was an artist who spent her day painting original designs on expensive fabrics. While doing that work, she always had her attention fixed very close to her. Also, because of her fear of traffic, she'd never looked out much as a passenger. Of course, it follows that if we are afraid of something, we will avoid doing it, and do our best to not have to face it. This girl had managed to avoid driving for years until her boss insisted that it was time she bought a car, so she would cease being late for work. Had it not been for her boss she wouldn't have tried to learn to drive.

Now if I were told to paint on expensive fabric like this girl did, I would have been afraid of causing damage, too. Hence, I would do my best to avoid such work, because I don't understand how to go about it. But if I watched how it was done, learned how long it takes the paint to dry, which thinners to use, how to clean the brushes, and all the rules of the job, then I could try to paint a design on an old t-shirt without any fear. Learning to drive a car is much the same. We must change our approach to teaching driving, and have the future driver learn how it is done – long before he or she gets behind the wheel.

Because of my student's four month "apprenticeship" of looking ahead while a passenger, she had gained experience similar to that of a medical student watching a qualified surgeon at work. What medical school would give a student a scalpel and let him practice for only ten hours with an instructor watching, before being permitted to operate on his own on a live patient? None! It's not done that way. The student has to learn all about the body, practice using a scalpel on dead tissue, and watch a great many operations before being allowed to assist a qualified surgeon.

My student had lost her fear of traffic by spending those months looking out as a passenger. She was then a lot calmer, safer, and much easier to teach because she had learned the skill of watching the road. The only thing she had left to learn was how to work the controls of the car, which actually takes less time to learn than the skill of reading the road ahead. It took only one summer for her to achieve that skill, once she knew she had to watch the road ahead while being a passenger.

Many of you will have closer to ten years to get your children roadwise, if you start teaching them at age four or five. Don't let these years go to waste.

What to Look For

Once you have the children looking out ahead, you must start teaching them to watch for road signs. Before this, all they've needed to watch for is probably a McDonald's when they're hungry.

Authorities know that if too many signs are put up, drivers will tend to ignore them, so signs are usually placed only where they're needed. When drivers are used to an area they tend to stop looking at the signs, so traffic authorities put up large signs to warn regular drivers when a traffic pattern has been changed.

As a new truck driver, I drove a Big-Rig from Las Vegas and across the Hoover Dam into Arizona. As the road winds down to the dam, different signs keep lowering the legal speed limit until it was down to only 15 mph. I was glad the signs were there to help control the traffic speed because the road was steep, narrow and winding. I moved over the dam and started climbing up the other side into Arizona. A large sign appeared up ahead, and I wondered what excitement awaited me. Was I going to get down to 15 mph again? To my surprise, the sign read "Drink, Don't Drive." It was at the top of the hill, and the road was flat from that point on, but it was still an unnecessary distraction for drivers who might think the road could hold more drama.

Road markings and road signs used to control traffic need to be understood by your children. Young children can learn the different shapes and colors of road signs and even start to read by looking at the letters.

Have your children start observing signs around your home. Most cities have constantly changing speed limits every few blocks, so children as passengers should learn to watch for the posted speed limit.

Once the kids get good at reading and understanding road signs and markings, teach them to look at the condition of the road. The state of repair and disrepair of roads needs to be known, so have your children get used to looking at the road and for any road repair work. They need to recognize when the road may be slippery from rain, and more so if you live in an area which has ice and snow. Good traction (tire grip on the road) is needed to drive safely.

Once they can understand traffic signs and can judge the condition of the road, get them observing the traffic – other cars and trucks. Have them notice those who are following too closely behind others. Let them see where other cars need to go to turn when they're in different lanes at intersections. To keep them safe on the road, predicting what other drivers are likely to do is one of the most important skills a driver can learn. Make sure your children get plenty of practice reading the road and "reading other drivers" before they're old enough to drive.

Teaching Babies to Drive – Say What You See

Teach babies to drive? Well, not quite babies, but children. You can start teaching the very young by telling them what you're looking at while you drive.

While driving, I talked to my children. I told them what I was looking at and where I moved my eyes to. For example: "I am looking way ahead – and I can see that green car. I'm now looking at the children up ahead on the left side, playing with a ball. This is dangerous since the ball can come onto the road with a kid chasing it. Therefore, I will keep those children in the corner of my eye and check my mirror to see what's behind, in case I have to stop quickly."

Long after those children with the ball were behind us, I told my children I'd looked to the sides to see if it was clear for me to swerve to miss a child, in case I'd needed to. I told them I'd also looked at the surface of the road to see if there were any oil patches or slick spots that would make me skid if I'd had to hit the brakes hard. (I was driving a car without anti-lock brakes.)

If we saw a school bus, it led to a discussion of children arriving home tired from school, seeing their mothers waiting for them on the other side of the road – and their running straight across the road to their mother without looking for traffic. I explained this is why there's a law that you must always stop whenever you see a stopped school bus with its lights flashing.

My children and I discussed why it was so important for me as a driver to keep my eyes moving and not fix on any one thing, and that they should do the same as they walk or ride their bikes to school. The children could use what they'd learned while we were driving and be safer on the road, even as pedestrians.

As we drove, I talked about what I saw, and very soon my kids were doing the same. The kids told me where they were looking and what they saw was a potential danger and what was not.

By having the kids tell me where they were looking, I could tell if they'd focused at the correct distance ahead. By listening to what they predicted might happen, I could tell whether they had learned to read the road correctly.

Advanced driving courses use this technique. It is called "commentary driving." The trainee is gotten to talk (give commentary) while driving, to tell the instructor what he sees and to constantly say where he is looking and what could happen up ahead. It's a very useful teaching tool because the instructor then knows what the driver is thinking and where he is actually looking. The instructor can tell when the driver is not reading the road correctly by listening to what he is saying and thus he can correct the driver.

By having your children tell you where they are looking, and what they think may happen ahead, you can acknowledge their good judgment and strengthen their weak points.

If your child is nervous about being driven, explain where you are looking and what is going to happen next. This will get his attention looking out and reduce the nervousness.

There are many games one can buy to keep the children occupied on long trips. However, the best games I know to play while driving are those which teach the kids what driving is all about. Having your kids practice commentary driving will make confident future drivers.

Predicting Others

You've taken the time to explain to your kids how strangers may approach them on the Internet. Without this knowledge, they could be victims of sex predators. You also need to give them the knowledge of other drivers and their likely and possible actions, so they won't become a traffic accident victim.

Before we can predict, we must observe. The observations we make will then take into account our past experience, and we are then able to predict what might happen in the immediate future.

To be able to predict another driver's actions requires good observation, a skill which can be developed to a remarkable degree. Some law-enforcement officers have the ability to "spot" (quickly recognize) a drunken driver just by noticing that a car is being driven slightly erratically.

Your children can learn to spot situations when care is needed. It takes practice and is something we keep learning as things change. We now have to look to see if a driver is being distracted while on his cell phone. It's more dangerous if it's a teenager talking on the phone. A teenager also usually makes fast motions and thus can do silly things quickly – for example, he can speed up and cut in front of you.

An elderly driver is treated differently, since he may hesitate and not move when he should. He may also drive too slowly, or may stop for no apparent reason. You don't have to be able to see the driver to determine his age since the make of a car can often give you an idea. If the car is a full-size American make like a Buick, especially with two people inside, it will probably be driven by an older retired couple. If it's Sunday, quite possibly they're going to church, and this is one of the few times each week that car is driven.

Two people talking in a car can do unpredictable things if the driver is being distracted by the passenger. Sometimes you notice the car in front of you swerves a bit for no apparent reason. That's when it pays to look inside the car to see what is happening. You may see a mother being distracted by a child, or an upset of some sort happening in the car. Either stay back, or get out and around that car as soon as conditions permit.

If there's a couple in front and you can see that their body language includes arms waving, realize they're having a fight. Again, either stay away or get past them quickly.

Before the invention of tinted glass for cars, a driver could always observe what was going on inside of other vehicles. Nowadays with tinted glass, that's sometimes not possible. However, the law still requires that the front windows allow visibility.

The different types of cars also give clues to drivers' actions and reactions. After all, we all know a minivan is often driven by a "soccer mom." Even if its tinted windows won't let you see inside, be aware that the driver could be distracted by kids.

A commercial van tells another story. Here is a driver used to being on the road many hours every day, and he's probably very familiar with the area. He's at work, so almost never has been drinking. You can treat him as a professional driver and trust his driving almost always. If it's a UPS or FedEx type of vehicle, know that the driver is very familiar with the area and expect him to do things quickly.

A rental van or truck is totally different, especially if it's a U-Haul type, driven by someone who's moving. Its driver won't be familiar with the vehicle which is probably bigger than what he's accustomed to driving. If he's in the area he's moving to, he may be lost. Additionally, moving is a very frustrating and stressful experience. In fact, moving companies' surveys have found it's the third most stressful action in life, after death and divorce. So if someone is driving a rented moving truck, realize he's likely under stress. The move may be the result of a divorce. He may have just loaded a truck full of furniture and thrown his back out, so he's also in pain. Put all those together – vehicle unfamiliarity, lost, stressed out and in pain – and the driver is liable to do almost anything, so beware!

Now, the professional moving truck driver who moves household furniture, such as one working for Mayflower or United Van Lines, is quite different. If it's an around-town truck, it's driven by a professional who knows where he is and what he's doing. A Big-Rig tractor-trailer moving truck with a large sleeper (an area for sleeping, behind the driver's and passenger's seats in the truck's extended cab), has usually arrived from out of town. It's a long distance move, and the driver may not know the area. Please give him room to maneuver.

Teach your children to recognize different kinds of cars. A sports car is often driven aggressively and possibly fast, so if one is coming up behind you, let it go past. Older cars need to be avoided, especially if they show a lack of maintenance such as dents and dings. Their turn signals or brake lights may be faulty. If it's a real clunker or battered wreck with worn tires, be prepared for the car to swerve if a tire fails or blows. Overloaded pickup trucks need to be kept at a distance since something could fall off and crash into your car.

If you have specialized types of transports that operate in your area, point them out to your children. Discuss the colors they are painted and tell the kids what they need to know to predict these transports' actions. This applies to light rail, trains you have to stop for or even horse-drawn carriages the Amish drive.

School buses usually have good drivers, but they need to be treated respectfully and cautiously. Buses contain young children who could possibly run out on the road without looking.

Garbage trucks and city buses stop often but not for long. You can expect that they might pull out into your lane quickly, with little warning. Occasionally, city bus drivers seem to be overly aggressive or inconsiderate of other drivers – especially after the last twenty-five cars have refused to let them into the lane they need. Realize a bus driver is sometimes under the stress of trying to stay on his route's schedule.

Watch out when a car moves away from the center of its lane – the driver is probably about to change lanes or turn, without using his turn signal. Drivers can show their intentions just by the way they have their vehicles positioned. It takes practice, but we can get a feel for what other drivers are about to do. This enables the good driver to keep out of the way of other drivers, and to leave enough space for the other driver to complete the action he intends to make.

If a driver in front puts on his turn signal, but then doesn't move in that direction, check ahead to see what he thought he had to move for. By the time you get there, you may have to move over, even if the car in front didn't.

When you see a car in front of you swerve, pay particular attention. The driver may have swerved to avoid something on the road that you may be able to avoid by changing lanes. If the driver ahead swerved for no reason, he may have nodded off and gone to sleep for a moment, or he may have been distracted by doing some other action such as placing a call on his cell phone.

Whatever is happening with a driver who swerves for no reason, it cannot be in your best interest. Be ready to blast your horn to wake him up, but most importantly, get away from him as soon as possible. Treat him as an accident waiting to happen, and make sure you are not involved in his accident.

When you're in busy parking lots, show your future drivers the things to look out for. A car showing white rear lights means the car is in reverse and about to back up. A parked car with its brake lights on means the car could start to move at any moment. Even if a car is in a parking space, if the brake lights are on, you know a driver is behind the wheel and has either just arrived or is planning to pull out soon.

Brake lights on an open road can mean different things. It could be the car has picked up speed going down a hill, and the driver is now slowing, possibly nervous about the speed. If this occurs below the speed limit, realize you're looking at a nervous driver in front and get away from him.

When brake lights appear for a moment and go off, look to see if there's something ahead which the driver in front is worried about. If on a freeway, look to see if the traffic is stopping because of an accident ahead. If all the cars are applying brakes, even if you can't see what's ahead, you need to also brake to tell the driver behind you that you're slowing and may be stopping soon.

Sometimes, inattentive drivers are misled by the actions of other drivers. It's like the football player who starts forward, before the ball is snapped, just because an opposing player moved slightly. We've all seen others start to move forward at a red light, just because another driver started to roll forward.

A friend of mine once stood on a corner at a red traffic light, waiting to cross, and observed a driver tragically misled. The driver of the stopped car closest to my friend was in a big hurry. That driver saw he just barely had room and time enough to make it across the intersection before cross-traffic arrived, so he hit the gas and ran the red light. Because of that, the driver immediately behind him assumed the light had turned green (it hadn't), so she followed the driver who'd run the still-red light – and she plowed right into a crossing car! The lesson here is: don't be misled by others' actions – be alert and decide for yourself.

Overall, it's simply foolish to assume other drivers will always do the right thing. Despite what others may do, you can still prevent most accidents. At all times when you drive, if you closely observe other vehicles and drivers, you can with practice, predict what can go wrong, prepare for it and avoid needless accidents. The knowledge and skills you gain by such attentive observation and practice are very valuable and should be passed on to your children.

You can have your kids make a game of observing stupid driving. One friend's favorite: a woman with a cigarette stuck in her mouth, a cell phone stuck in her ear, turning a corner while a little dog leaped on and off her lap. Maybe if the kids are lucky they can get some video to post on YouTube. Or maybe describe their worst driver on my Web site.

Roadwise Kids Need an Emergency Code Word

It's not just cars that kill kids; 17-year-old Lily Burk was abducted and killed after her killer made her try to withdraw money from her credit card at an ATM. Lily called both her mother and father to ask how she could withdraw the cash that the abductor demanded from her.

A spokesman for the family said that neither parent heard panic in her voice and never realized their daughter was in trouble. Next morning Lily Burk's body was discovered in her car.

Even though this type of abduction is very rare parents and children need to have an agreed upon code word to indicate something is terribly wrong. This code word can be slipped into a phone call without an abductor knowing that the child in trouble has alerted a parent.

This code word must be easy to remember because the child will be under stress if the code word is ever needed. My granddaughter's code word is simply to address their mom as Dad and their dad as Mom and they drilled this with their parents until they felt comfortable doing it. Walmart has a code word for when a child is lost that comes across the public address system to alert staff to cover the exits in case of a kidnapping in progress.

A code word needs to be established in case 911 needs to be called because a child is in the type of danger Lily Burk was in. Children's phones need to have a GPS feature so you can know their location should they call and use the code word.

Another code word needs to be established that shows the child needing the parents' assistance. For example, a child is at a party where things are getting out of hand and the child wishes to be picked up. No child will make a phone call and say in front of their friends that they need to be rescued by a parent. But if a code word was used, a parent could come to the child's rescue.

Maybe a Lily Burk phone feature or application could be developed for kids' safety. It could be programmed to dial all the numbers on speed dial and this could include 911 or college campus security. A prerecorded message would state that help was needed. This feature would ensure that someone was reached during an emergency and the phone GPS would give the location of the child in trouble.

A parent's most important job is to make sure their kids survive them. Unless we have personally lost a beautiful child like Lily Burk we can only imagine the heartbreak involved.

Chapter 5

Looking Ahead, Eyes Moving

Children Looking Ahead

Looking ahead is the most important skill that your children will ever learn about driving cars. It can be learned before starting to drive and should be taught to children before they reach driving age, just to make them safe on their bicycles.

A non-driver, especially a child, usually has no idea of what is involved in driving. We've all had a child ask a question about something they saw alongside the car as we drove, something we were no longer aware of because our attention was on the road ahead. They see what is in and just around the car close by, but usually not much more. Children have no natural inclination to look ahead and will not do so unless it's explained to them why it's important.

Modern cars can contribute to a child's habit of not looking ahead. For example, air bags make it impossible for a child to sit in the front seat. Front bucket seats give no room for a child to sit in the front between his parents. Years ago, roads were more twisting and uneven, and cars did not ride as smoothly as they now do, so a child often needed to sit in front and look out ahead to avoid getting carsick. Now with tinted glass, nice stereos, and DVD players, a child is encouraged to sit in the back and listen to music, watch videos, play games, or read books.

It's fine to have children entertain themselves in the back, but first spend some time on their "driving practice" by getting them to read the road ahead.

When my kids were young they would take turns sitting between my wife and myself while I explained how I was driving the car. If you intend to change vehicles, seriously look for a model that allows three people to sit across the front seat. Car manufacturers should be encouraged to make this an option on family sedans.

Never Taught It

A friend of mine had a girlfriend with whom he refused to ride. She had a very fast reaction time, but that was the only thing that kept her alive. As a driver she wouldn't look far enough ahead and so would get herself into all sorts of trouble. She'd be in the wrong lane for where she wanted to go and not having observed far enough ahead, she'd have to abruptly change lanes or go off in a direction she didn't want to go. She'd suddenly swerve her little car into any available small space between cars without signaling to get into the lane she needed. Scary!

She was "good" at this, though it was a very bad, unsafe habit. Her fast reaction time would get her out of the trouble she got into by not looking far enough ahead to begin with. Some drivers have never been taught to look ahead, and have never figured it out for themselves. Simply being told the concept of looking farther ahead, and putting it into practice, totally cures the bad driving habit of such drivers and makes them safer (and less nerve-racking) to ride with.

Focus Is Seeing Sharply and Clearly

I'm going to be using the word focus as I describe what you look at. A driver needs to look at and focus his eyes and attention on what he is seeing. A driver can look or glance yet not take in what he sees. This explains why a driver says after an accident, "I looked but I didn't see you."

A distracted driver looks but doesn't see, or if he sees, it doesn't register. Let me give you two different examples.

This is what happened to me. There was something unusual happening, a quarter of a mile away, that I had my eyes focused on. When I looked to see if the way was clear to turn, I looked, or should I say glanced quickly, but didn't focus my eyes on what I saw.

I turned in front of another vehicle without seeing it, resulting in a collision. I looked but didn't see the car. It was the same color as the trees in the background but I still should have seen it.

My focus was still a quarter of a mile ahead, not where it should have been. Hence there was a tearing of metal. This, I believe, is what happens when a driver "just didn't see" another vehicle. The driver looked but didn't see what was there, because he didn't focus his eyes on what he should have been looking at.

A friend described to me a different type of distraction. Her distraction was in her head, because she was composing a song in her mind as she drove; she looked and actually saw a pickup truck and drove into it. She looked, saw, but because she didn't focus sharply and clearly on the pickup, her brain didn't register what she saw.

You can walk and talk at the same time because two different sides of the brain are involved. If you are doing two things at once that involve the same part of the brain, the other thing becomes a distraction to your driving.

When I had my crash, I was turning into work and noticed some unusual vehicles. I was trying to figure out what was going on, and as a result I was too distracted to actually put my attention on looking for traffic before I turned. Sure I glanced, but I didn't really focus my eyes on where I needed to look.

My friend, when creating the song in her head, was using the same part of the brain needed to figure out what was going on with traffic. She actually saw the pickup truck but didn't put together what was happening, because the part of the brain needed to process the information was involved in creating a harmony.

Put simply, you must focus on what you see. Your attention must be on what your eyes are looking at, not something else in view or something going on in your head because you are deeply engrossed in thought. You can get involved in a cell phone conversation, composing a harmony, or even get involved in a song as you listen to the radio. Even a conversation on a radio talk show could get you so involved that the whole side of the brain you need to drive with is involved in what you are thinking about, and your driving is done automatically, not fully under your control.

Where to Look

Thirty percent of the human brain is devoted to vision, so you have a large portion of your brain available to help you drive. Ninety-five percent of the information needed to drive is visual, so it is very important to know where your eyes should be looking and where most of your attention should be concentrated.

When driving, focus on where you want to go. If you are playing soccer, you don't look at the goalie when you're trying to score a goal, you look at the empty part of the net you intend to kick the ball into. Football players look toward where they need to go. The guy with the ball doesn't concentrate on the tacklers approaching him; he looks for a "hole in the line" and goes for it.

The same idea applies to driving. You look ahead in the direction you want the car to go. You look ahead and keep your eyes up; you do not look down at the road only a few feet immediately in front of the car. For instance, if you're driving down a street approaching a parked car on the right, look ahead past the parked car, and you'll drive safely around it.

If you look at and concentrate mostly on the parked car, you'll find that you'll steer toward it. Looking at the parked car is like a soccer player with his eyes and attention concentrated on the goalie, instead of on where the ball needs to go, or a football player focusing on tacklers rather than on the space he's aiming to slip through.

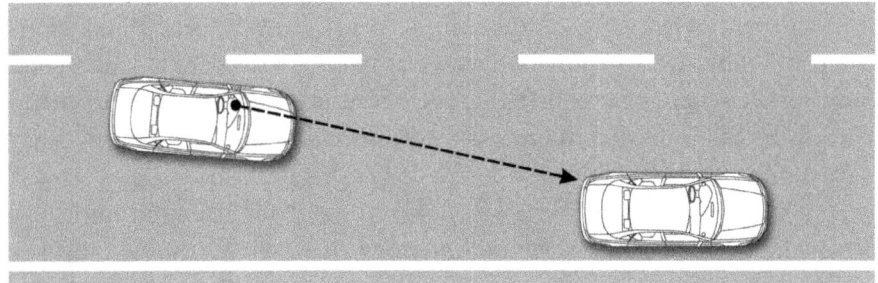

A driver is inclined to drive toward whatever he is looking at.

Demonstrate this idea to your young future drivers. When you come to the next parked car on your side of the road, be aware of it in the corner of your eye, but keep looking ahead – and you'll find that you will automatically steer around the car with no effort. If they follow your lead, as you explain this action, they'll learn an important skill which will make it easier and safer to ride their bikes, skateboards, etc.

When teaching their children to drive, some parents don't explain to them that they should be looking ahead instead of at the parked cars off to the side. Instead they become frustrated and tell their child not to drive so close to the parked cars. That doesn't help because the child then drives too far away from things and develops the bad habit of not staying as close to his side of the road as he should.

LOOKING AHEAD, EYES MOVING   43

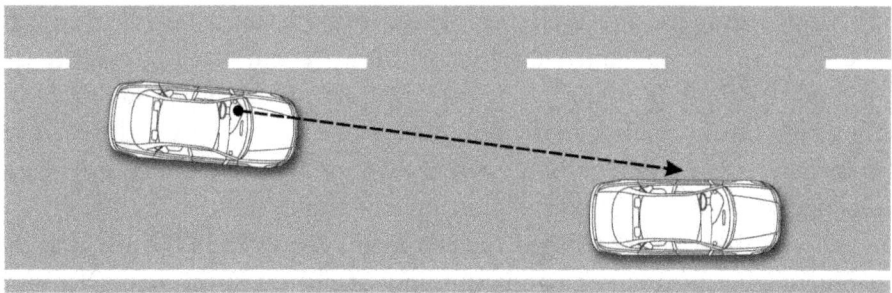

Incorrect

Correct

A new student driver's first lessons usually have to do with the brakes, transmission, signals, etc., and the student gets his attention fixed on the car, not on the road. Therefore it is of vital importance that the basic idea of looking up, outward, and ahead is learned at an early age while being a passenger, long before he or she is old enough to drive.

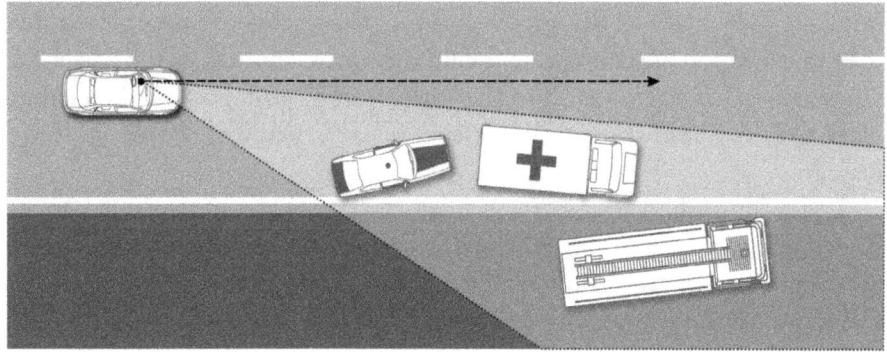

Driver views the parked emergency vehicles as one group
and doesn't get his attention stuck on any one vehicle.

Most beginners, and even experienced drivers, fail to look far enough ahead when they encounter the road width being narrowed by parked cars or road repairs. It is at this point that their attention can become fixed on the objects that are causing the road to become narrow. If the driver views these objects as a group of things, rather than individual items, he will be less inclined to get his attention stuck on any one thing.

Drivers must be encouraged to keep their eyes up and look ahead at the gap of space available to pass through, not at objects in the way. Of course they also can, and should, slow down to drive through a more narrow passage at a safe speed.

As one aims the car up the road ahead, it is like using the parked car and the center line as one would use the scope of a rifle to aim.

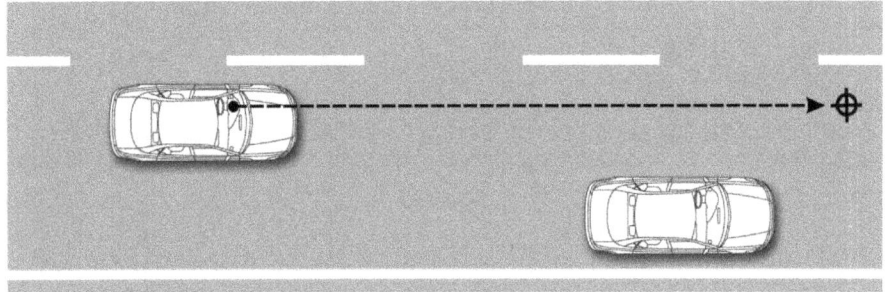

When a driver puts most of his attention on aiming ahead, through the gap, his attention isn't stuck on the car in the way.

Some children, as passengers, will just not look at "scary" situations. Students I've taught to drive have told me that as children they closed their eyes to avoid looking out, when being driven by another. If the driver had taken the child's attention off of the "threatening" obstacles and directed the child to look ahead through the open space, then driving would no longer be scary.

If a young child gets nervous in a fast moving car you need to get him looking ahead. When the road is scary, I get a game going with my grandchildren. I have them look ahead to see who can first spot the next car coming toward us. A nervous passenger turns into an excited game player.

Every time I've had a student who had earlier instruction (professional or not), and the student was having difficulties with driving, I have found that he was not looking far enough ahead. This problem is always handled by having the student look farther ahead, focusing his eyes and attention on objects ahead of him and keeping his eyes moving so he doesn't become fixed on any one point.

Looking Ahead: The Twelve-Second Rule

Once I have new drivers looking ahead, the brighter ones will ask how far ahead they need to look. So you had better teach them the "twelve-second rule" because your children will surely ask this question. This is how it's done.

While driving at an even speed, select any object ahead, such as a building or overpass, and start counting, "one thousand and one, one thousand and two, one thousand and three," etc., up to "one thousand and twelve." The time it normally takes you to say one thousand and one is one second. If you reach the selected object before twelve seconds have passed, then you need to try again, selecting an object even farther ahead.

By looking twelve seconds ahead, you'll see all the potential trouble spots ahead, such as disabled cars or road work. You'll then be looking far enough ahead to avoid being caught in the wrong lane or position; and you'll have plenty of time to adjust your speed or position and move away from, or go around, trouble spots.

Don't fix the eyes twelve seconds ahead. Look that far ahead and then also check what is happening closer to you. Check to see if there are cars approaching the upcoming intersection and look twelve seconds ahead again, or as far as you can see.

Explain the twelve-second rule to your children. Then have everyone in the car choose some point ahead they think is twelve seconds ahead. Count out loud "one thousand and one, one thousand and two," up to "one thousand and twelve," and see who has come closest to getting it right. This skill takes some practice to develop. Most people are surprised how far ahead twelve seconds is at freeway speed. Some drivers never seem to develop this skill and often miss getting into the correct lane soon enough, so they end up going the wrong way.

Why not teach the twelve-second rule and get your children's judgment of distance developed long before they get behind the wheel? Twelve seconds on streets around town is about a block ahead. At freeway speeds, twelve seconds is about a quarter of a mile ahead. On the highway, you should be able to see to the next hill or curve, and sometimes that is greater than twelve seconds so you may end up reading the road fifteen seconds or more ahead. You must "aim high" and look ahead to observe upcoming traffic conditions. That way, you obtain the needed information to make optimal driving decisions. Applying the twelve-second rule will help you do this.

Poor Vision

If your child just won't look far enough ahead despite your best efforts and explanations, get his long-distance vision checked. If his vision is fuzzy and blurry a quarter of a mile ahead, he will not look that far ahead.

For quite some time, my son wouldn't look far enough ahead. He had a business driving a truck slowly while looking for street numbers, and I always thought it was that training which kept him from looking far enough ahead. Also, a son doesn't always do what his father tells him so I had given up on trying to correct his driving.

It wasn't until he was 23, after driving seven years, that this issue was solved. He actually needed driving glasses due to his poor long-distance vision. Once he started wearing his glasses, he immediately began to look the correct distance ahead.

Even though his eyesight was within the legal limits for driving, his vision wasn't sharp enough to see things clearly a quarter of a mile ahead, where he needed to look when driving at 65 mph. As a result, he didn't look the correct distance ahead, and I couldn't get him to do so until his vision was corrected by driving glasses.

There's another aspect to poor eyesight. Even though my son's vision is legal for driving, he can't read road signs without his driving glasses. My wife wears her glasses for driving, because she has to by law, but she won't wear them as a passenger when I'm driving and I need help looking for highway or street signs. I believe this is a safety factor. To prevent sudden turns, it's best when street names can be read by both the driver and a passenger who's helping to navigate and who should also be wearing his or her driving glasses. I've seen a passenger in a large motor home looking for street signs – using a pair of binoculars!

Always get your kids involved when you are driving in a new area and need extra eyes to look for street names or numbers.

If anyone in your family has eyesight that doesn't quite measure up, get his eyes examined, get the glasses needed, and insist that they be worn when driving. He will drive better, and you both will feel a lot safer.

Slow Vehicles vs. Cars

There's another work-related experience which can make a bad driver – driving a slow-moving vehicle all day. In this situation, a person's attention at work is fixed ahead, but not far enough to make him a safe driver. I've noticed this problem with farm tractor and golf-cart drivers. They drive slow-moving vehicles and learn to handle them very skillfully but due to their low speed, the drivers' attention isn't focused very far ahead.

After spending many hours driving slow vehicles, they cannot handle a car well, unless they are taught to look farther ahead when driving faster. One of my friends had a husband who was a farm contractor and had driven a tractor for many years. She couldn't figure out why her children would get carsick on trips when her husband drove, but wouldn't get carsick when she drove the same trip at the same speed. She finally realized that her husband wasn't looking far enough ahead. This was because the car was going much faster than the farm tractor he was used to driving most of the time. The end result was that his steering was not as smooth as it could have been. He didn't change lanes or go around corners smoothly, and the extra motion made the children carsick. If he had been looking far enough ahead, as his wife did, then the children wouldn't have experienced motion sickness.

This driver had spent his whole working life handling his slow moving tractor in a very capable manner. However, when he drove the car his family felt a little unsafe and they preferred not to be driven by him.

If your kids don't like to be driven by someone check to see if that driver is looking far enough ahead. The solution is to give that driver the data on the twelve-second rule and have him practice looking twelve seconds ahead. By looking farther ahead than he has been, he will soon be driving the car at the same level of skill that he uses when driving his slower moving machinery.

Some retirement communities make it possible to run errands with slow moving golf carts. If you have parents in this situation, point out to them that when they are in a car they will need to look much farther ahead compared with driving a golf cart. If your kids drive lawn mowers, get them looking farther ahead when they are in a car. Of course, experienced cyclists must realize that driving a car is a whole new game, so they must start looking much farther ahead as well.

Keep Your Eyes Moving

While looking up ahead, the eyes and one's attention must be kept moving. If the eyes are not moved every two seconds, a fixed stare can develop. When you check your mirror, never fixate on the mirror because you could end up driving into something. If you don't see clearly what's in the mirror, look ahead again, then have a second look in the mirror and focus on what you see.

Always make sure you focus the eyes on the object, or group of objects, that you look at. Don't just scan without focusing. Remain aware of any activity on the side of the road and hold it in the corner of your eye, but have most of your attention out in front at all times. Use the "long-range, wide-angle lens" of your eyes so that you get to see the whole big picture. With experience, it won't be long before you are looking up ahead automatically and taking in the whole big scene.

How Pilots Focus

An air force pilot once explained to me how pilots are trained to look for other aircraft in the sky. The sky is mentally divided into sections, and the pilot is trained to focus his eyes on one section, and then to look at and focus his eyes on another section and so on. Each time the pilot checks for aircraft in a new sector, he must focus his eyes on the sector, not just scan the area.

Pilot focuses his eyes on one section of the sky at a time.

The Air Force found that when a pilot doesn't actually focus his eyes on something (even if only a piece of sky), then he will miss seeing other aircraft. Just scanning areas with the eyes, but not focusing on things, makes it possible to miss seeing other aircraft.

I imagine that this data is in the flight training manuals of most of the world's air forces. It is vitally important that this data be available to drivers because so often, "I just didn't see the other car" is the explanation following an accident. When air force pilots "just didn't see the other aircraft," the pilots were trained to stop merely scanning and drilled on how to focus their eyes.

While driving, your eyes should be focusing on an object or a group of objects if there are many things to view. When an air force pilot sees a group of three planes, he must focus on the group, not on each plane individually. A driver at the scene of an accident would then focus his eyes on a group of people, not each person individually. He would then focus on the emergency vehicles that were parked and view them as one group of vehicles.

The idea is not just to look ahead. It is to look ahead and focus your eyes on something or a group of things, and then move your eyes to another point of interest. The eyes and one's attention must be kept moving by looking and focusing on one thing after another. In other words, when looking ahead, look at something and when you see what it is, then look at something else. Simple, isn't it?

Once a driver has learned to constantly look for, focus, and refocus his eyes on things, he will not be inclined to fixate (get stuck) on things and miss seeing important objects and events that may require evasive action on his part.

Modern sports research has documented the importance of focusing the eyes on the target. Top basketball players, during experiments, wore measuring devices that recorded where their eyes were looking while aiming to shoot. It was discovered that the real professionals were looking at where they were going to shoot the basketball for at least a second before launching.

In contrast, players who were not as effective in throwing basketballs would only be looking at the hoop for a tiny fraction of time. When these players were then trained to focus for at least a second on the hoop, their score improved dramatically, over time.

The Whole Scene

Practice makes perfect, and a good driver will eventually learn to view the whole scene around him. To start with, a child or student driver needs to consciously keep his eyes moving from one object or group of objects to another, looking near and far. The learner must be encouraged to not stare or fixate on any one object or point of interest, but at the same time he should actually focus his eyes on what he sees.

However, if you constantly tell a new driver to look up, he may be inclined to fix his attention too far ahead. Staring ahead is not the answer. The student must view and really see the whole scene, not just stare into the distance.

Although one should still check the mirrors while driving down the open highway – one should develop the skill of looking and taking in the whole scene.

Of course, driving where there are traffic lights and pedestrians to watch for, still requires constantly moving your eyes, and at times moving your head to see all that's happening. Otherwise, you can't take in the whole scene and see the big picture. Keeping your eyes active is necessary to keeping up with changing traffic conditions.

I'm constantly amazed at how many drivers don't take in the whole scene. While driving, I saw ahead of me a stopped car, possibly disabled, in the lane I was in. So I changed lanes. To my surprise, another car changed lanes and headed straight for the stopped car! Even though this car was much closer to the stopped car than I was, he still hadn't noticed what was ahead! That driver didn't observe what was going on, and he sure wasn't taking in the whole scene.

Even an experienced driver needs to know the basics of how to read the road, because when he's tired or not fully alert, he'll be inclined to fix his attention and not take in the whole scene. Whenever I find myself fixating attention, I'll start looking around and focusing my eyes on different things both near and far. I will check the mirror, and then look ahead as far as I can see. Next I will glance at the gauges and check my speed and water temperature, then look ahead again. I do this until I'm alert again, or if I don't quickly become more alert, I'll pull over and take a break from driving. Usually just stretching my legs by taking a short walk and having a drink of water is all that's needed. If I'm fixating on things because I'm tired and need sleep, I'll stop and sleep.

Elderly drivers who don't drive every day stop taking in the whole scene. Quite often their solution for safety is to drive very slowly. That wouldn't be necessary if they'd take a short walk before driving and as they walked, practiced focusing on different things, both near and far. Once in the car, an infrequent driver should make an effort to keep his eyes moving without fixating on things. He should focus the eyes on different things, until he's once again taking in the whole scene.

Before your teen has his own car realize he will be an infrequent driver so make sure he gets his attention out before you let him drive your car.

I didn't realize how quickly the skill of taking in the whole scene could be lost, until I took some months off work writing "Driver Ed" books. During that time, I drove very little and I was amazed how my ability to see the whole scene was reduced – a result of having my attention fixed on things very close to me while writing. Hence, when I do drive, I make a conscious effort to get my attention much farther out again, looking near and far and focusing my eyes on what I see until I'm naturally taking in the whole scene.

Before a tennis match, players must get their eyes and attention adjusted by hitting a few balls. Likewise, a person who drives only occasionally must also "put his eyes back in," meaning get his attention farther out, before driving.

A tennis player needs to "put his eye in" to hit the ball. A driver must "put his eye in" to not hit anything!

Science to the Rescue

Scientific research related to studying the electrical activity of the brain explains why my technique of looking and focusing on things at different distances works.

This research discovered that the optic nerves directly link the eyes to the brain. Eye movement, such as, looking at things both near and far, can at once improve your alertness. If you feel stupid while staring at a computer screen look out and focus on an object about 20 feet away then focus your eyes on something closer. You need to do this a few times until you feel energized. Just like a driver getting drowsy behind the wheel, you need to do this exercise to reboot your brain.

To stay alert while driving I would make a point to check the mirrors, then look ahead, then glance at the truck's instruments to see if everything was in the normal range, and then quickly change my focus to something in the distance.

This exercises the muscles around the eyes and helps to combat any eyestrain involved with nighttime driving or continually looking at a computer monitor.

Had I known about this sooner, I could have applied what I had discovered about driving to my writing. Just looking around the room, focusing my eyes on different things would have regenerated me and restored my creativity.

This certainly would have taken a lot less time than taking the dogs out for a walk and I could have finished my book faster.

Looking at and focusing on different things works. Now we know why.

Don't Fixate

I have a story from my youth that demonstrates how a driver can fixate on something and get into trouble as a result.

A bunch of us teenage boys had acquired a life-sized cardboard picture of a pretty, smiling young lady, probably from a store toothpaste display ad.

While returning from a large sporting event, we learned how drivers can fixate their attention. My friend used his hand to make it look as if the life-size cardboard model was blowing kisses at a car full of young men behind us.

This caused great interest, and the boys in the car behind us started to wave and honk their horn. The driver of the car I was in turned to the right. The driver behind us turned right at the same time as we did – and ran off the road because his attention had been fixated on our cardboard model. No serious harm was done, and the other driver managed to get back on the road, more embarrassed than hurt.

Even though those were friendlier times and drivers weren't as aggressive as they are now, we got rid of the cardboard model. We didn't want the other car driver upset with us because he'd damaged his car. I'm telling you this story to show that fixating one's attention on an object can result in serious trouble.

No matter how interesting something looks, don't fixate on it when you're driving – if you have a passenger, ask him to tell you more about it while you keep your eyes on the road ahead. A passenger and this also applies to your kids, must realize that the driver may fixate on something which attracts his attention. When your kids think your attention has become fixated, they must tell you to pay attention to the road and they will explain more about the thing which appears to be so interesting.

Your kids will stop distracting you when you get them helping you to drive. Amazingly there is another added benefit. Your kids will be more responsible, not just while in the car but in most areas of their life.

Unfixate from Work or School

People's abilities and habits regarding looking ahead are related to their work. I once taught a young man to drive and found it very difficult to unfix his attention from right in front of him. He spent eight hours a day sharpening saws, with his eyes focused at a very close fixed distance. That is where he was trained to focus to do his job, so that's where he looked.

People who need to fix their attention at a certain close distance in front of them because of what they are doing (such as looking at a computer screen), must make a conscious effort to look farther ahead, to notice and focus on buildings and other scenery around them before they drive their car. This can be done as they walk toward their car. You could also do the following actions from a place that gives you a good view of things.

Look at other people and focus your eyes on them, and also look ahead and focus on buildings and trees. By keeping your eyes moving near and far, and refocusing them each time on a different object, you will become unfixed from your work. If there are many different things to look at, practice putting the different things into groups, and then practice focusing on different groups of objects.

This exercise also applies very much to children, especially those not involved in active sports and who are used to having their attention mostly on their books, computer screens, and TVs. They need to be coached on putting their attention farther out, even as pedestrians – otherwise, they'll put their attention no farther out than the distance between them and a TV.

You will notice that children get in the habit of always watching TV from the same distance, which is usually too close, even though they could watch it from any distance since they're sitting on the floor. Therefore, don't let children ride a bike with their attention still stuck at their TV watching distance. Tell them to go outside and look around, and focus their eyes on different things, both near and far, before they get on their bikes.

Golf is a sport which unfixes the attention. First, the golfer needs to look ahead for a long shot, and later needs to look only a few yards ahead for a putt. The golfer also has to focus his eyes on what he sees. Golfing enthusiasts look forward to the game and really enjoy it, possibly because it relaxes their attention from the fixed points and distances they use at work. You can get the same benefits from focusing your eyes on different things, both near and at greater distances. This can be done while walking, or if taking a walk or playing golf is not possible, just by looking near and far from a place where you can observe what is going on.

I won't give a driving lesson to a student whose attention is fixed close to him until after he's taken a walk, and while walking, has kept his eyes moving, looking and focusing on different things both near and much farther out.

I had one student driver who had no problem looking twelve seconds ahead. She explained to me that her interest was trees. As a passenger in a car or bus, she had always looked out and noticed the different trees as she was being driven around. Because of the remarkable difference this made in her driving ability, I would suggest that all children be encouraged to observe trees all year round, not just when their leaves change color in the fall.

We all fix our attention wherever our work demands it. If that is not the correct distance for driving, then a conscious effort has to be made to get one's attention to extend farther out by moving it from object to object before one gets behind the wheel. Doing this will greatly improve one's driving and bring comfort and safety to one's passengers.

Using Shopping Malls

As a driving instructor, I have students drive slowly around shopping mall parking lots – the busier the better. It teaches the student to keep his eyes moving and to not fixate on things.

Finding a parking space in a busy shopping area, with cars and pedestrians in great numbers, should be looked on as another opportunity to develop your children's skills, and to refocus their attention at the same time. This is not a time for you to get impatient; it's a time you can use to teach observation skills to your children.

By driving through the busy areas, your children will have to keep their eyes moving to notice all the pedestrians pushing shopping carts, or those in a hurry to get to the stores. Cars will be driven by mothers distracted by their children. Elderly drivers may pull out in front of you without noticing you are there, or they may stop suddenly and unexpectedly when there really is no need to do so. If it's raining, pedestrians will be hurrying with their heads down and may not be paying as much attention to the traffic as they should.

Drive around the busy areas for a few minutes before you park. Not only will you develop the skills your children need to survive on the road, but also you'll extrovert their attention and they'll become brighter and cheerful. What's more, they will participate by helping to find a parking space for you.

LOOKING AHEAD, EYES MOVING

Aim Up Ahead

You need to get your student looking twelve seconds ahead. Don't assume that he will always look that far ahead. Even experienced drivers don't always look far enough ahead. At certain times, they can fixate their attention on something close to the car. Most noticeable are times when road repair or construction work reduces the width of the lane the vehicle needs to travel in.

The worst situation occurs when there's a long stretch of road under construction, and you're facing oncoming vehicles at night. Because of approaching vehicles, you must have your lights on low beam and therefore you can't see far enough ahead. At these times, we usually look ahead only as far as the headlights show the road in front of the car. If traffic is moving fast, this means that the eyes are not looking twelve seconds ahead. You must look near and far, at the scene the headlights show, and then farther ahead, aiming the car into the night darkness, looking for a taillight ahead. This will keep you from fixating on the road barrels or whatever is separating you from the oncoming traffic. By doing this, you will not feel the space is too tight to drive in, and you can travel the narrower than usual lane with confidence.

Even an experienced driver will sometimes fixate his attention on the barrels, unless he aims his car through the open gap up ahead.

Realize that when emergency vehicles reduce the width of the road, drivers easily fixate on any unusual, threatening or interesting things close at hand. This is called "rubber necking" and it's a known fact that if there is something out of the ordinary to attract drivers' attention, then drivers will fixate on it and slow the flow of traffic. This is true even when the things they're looking at do not block the flow of traffic.

At night, children will not want to look into the lights of oncoming cars because, of course, it hurts their eyes or is uncomfortable. You need to explain to your children that doing this strains your eyes too. Show them where you look at night instead of straight at approaching lights. Have them look a little to the right toward the curb, with quick glances more straight ahead to see approaching cars better.

Visualize the Path

Before you jump in your car, you've decided to go somewhere. You not only have a place to go to, but also have in mind how you're going to get there – the route you'll take. So it's not just a matter of looking ahead, it's also looking ahead to where you want the car to go, the path you want the car to take.

On curves and turning corners, the driver must visualize the path his car will take. If he keeps looking straight ahead when the road curves, he will be inclined to drive off the road. When this happens, the driver has fixed his attention on some point or direction. Attention must remain fluid, not fixed. He needs to look around the corner in the direction of where the car will go.

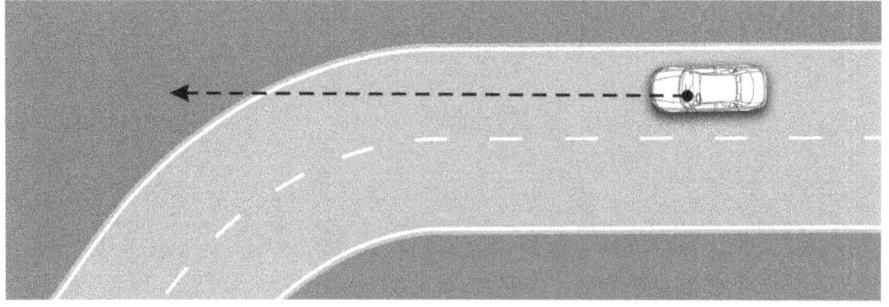

Incorrect: Driver is looking straight ahead instead of around the corner.

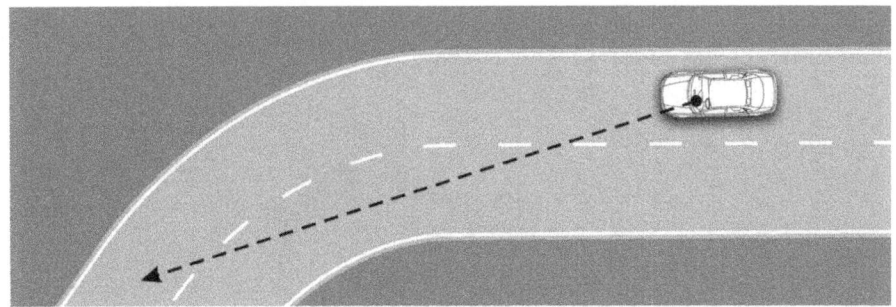

Correct: Driver looks around the corner to where he wants the car to go.

A driver needs to visualize an "imaginary" path which follows his lane and the road, the path where he wants the car to travel. My wife not only creates an imaginary path where she will steer our big truck, she also mutters to herself, "Don't even think about it," when she sees some other driver who appears ready to pull his car out into the path where she intends to go.

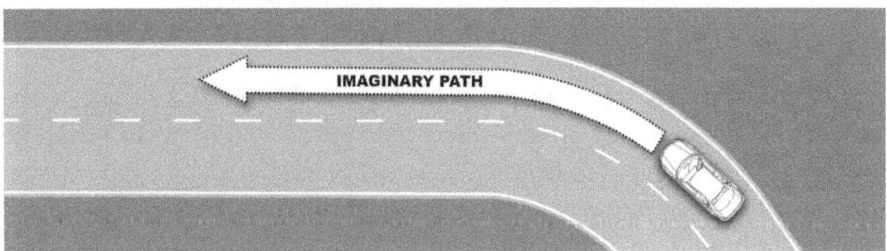

A driver must visualize an imaginary path for the car to follow.

You can show your children how this works by looking down right in front of the car as you drive and letting the children see how you have to keep correcting the steering wheel as you go around corners and curves. (Don't attempt this on a busy or narrow street – do this only on a wide and very quiet, deserted street!)

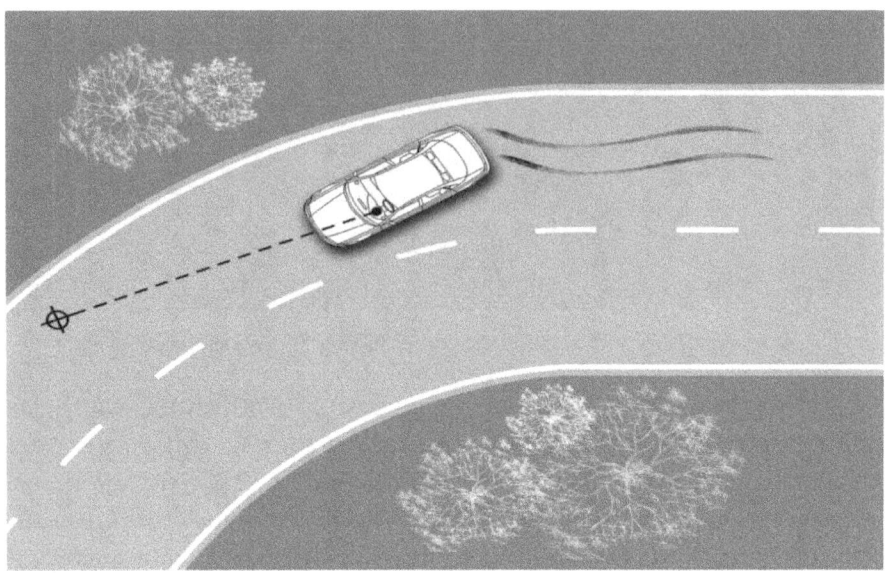

When the driver doesn't look far enough ahead the
car tends to wobble and jerk when going around corners

When a driver is not looking at points far enough ahead, he won't be able to steer his car smoothly around the corner and he will keep correcting the steering wheel to keep it in his lane. This sort of jerky steering happens when the car needs to be guided around a curve on the road, but the wheels have been turned too far. The steering wheel then has to be turned back again, the other way, to correct the error. This is called over-correction and it occurs when the driver is looking only a short distance ahead, a distance that is too close to the car.

A driver needs to visualize an imaginary path, steer along it, and continue to look well ahead. It works like magic. The car almost seems to steer itself and will go around the curve almost as if it were on train rails.

When You Can't See Around a Corner

When going into a "blind corner" (one you can't see around) and the view is partly blocked, don't just look down in front of your car at the point where the visible road ends. Still keep your vision up. The height of where an approaching bus or truck driver sits is a good height to aim your eyes. Look where the road should be, if all of it were visible, then look ahead again at what you can see.

LOOKING AHEAD, EYES MOVING

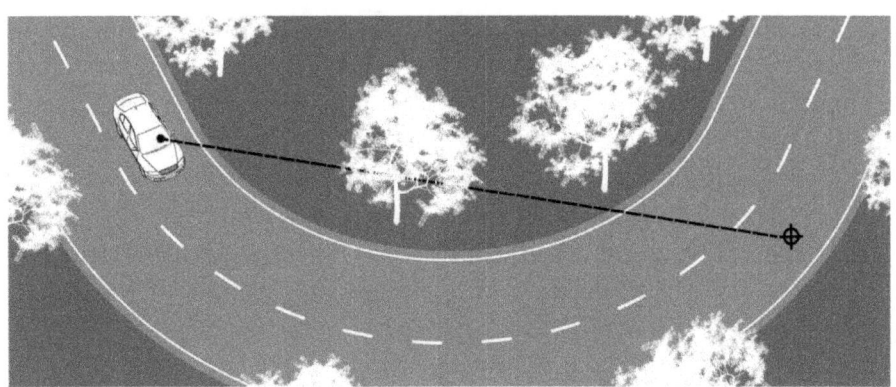

Driver looking to where the car should go, even when an object blocks part of the view.

Quite often, a new student will start steering a little jerkily just before a blind corner. I tell him to look up and put his attention around the corner, and to watch for a bus or truck that might appear. This corrects the natural inclination of the student to look at the road just before the point where the rest of the road ahead is hidden from view. That point is too close to the car to steer it correctly and smoothly and the eyes have to be raised to look higher as well as around the corner in the direction the car needs to travel. Telling him to watch for an approaching bus or truck will get him to do this.

Looking into a row of trees as you drive around a corner may not make sense, unless you understand the reasoning behind it. A soccer player doesn't look down near his feet just because he can't see the goal clearly. When a player aims for the goal, he will look toward the goal, even when his view of it is obscured by other players.

A soccer player aims at the goal, even when his view of it is blocked by other players.

The same applies to a driver. When the "goal" is obstructed from view, the driver should still look to where the car needs to go, the road ahead which he can't yet see clearly. Dropping his eyes down onto the road just in front of the car is like a soccer player looking down near his feet. If a player makes a shot for the goal without looking at the goal, he'll likely miss it.

The driver who doesn't keep his eyes and attention on the goal – the road ahead where the car should go – will not have his car going smoothly around the corner, and it may not travel on a safe course.

Keeping the Car Centered in the Lane

To keep your car in the center of a marked lane, aim the car down the middle of it. Use the lane marks on each side, like a rifle sight, and aim between them, with your eyes raised and looking ahead. Glance down again to see if the car is still in the center of the lane, then again focus up ahead. Keep looking near and far, and you will have no trouble staying in the center of the lane.

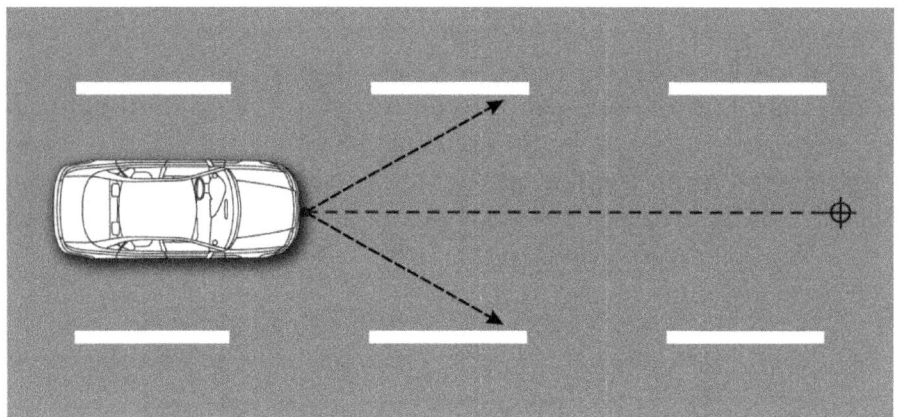

Driver aims up, glances down at lane markings to center the car, and then aims up ahead.

Even an experienced driver may need to use this technique if the white lines are hard to see. Look down at the lines close to the car to see if you are between them, and then look up ahead.

To see if you are in the center of the lane, you can also look in your rear-view mirrors and observe the lane markings to check your position and then again look up ahead.

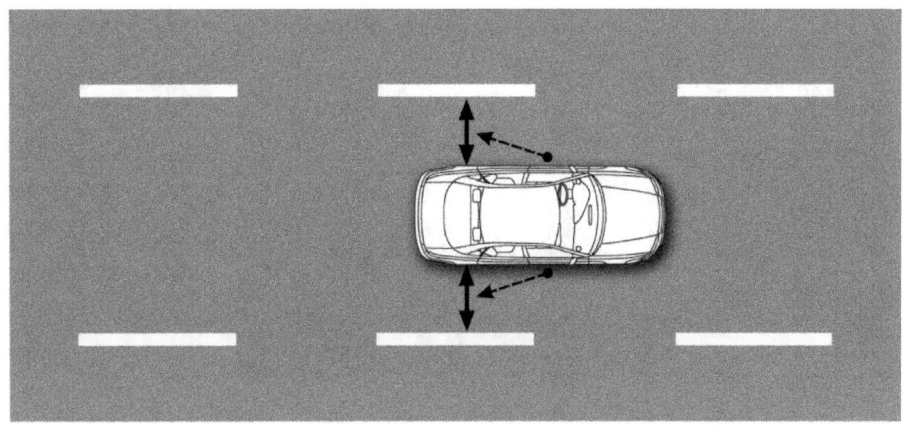

Driver uses mirrors to center the car in the lane, then aims up ahead again.

Long Curves

To drive around long, sweeping curves (not sharp curves) I teach a slightly different technique. Look at the road in front of the car, positioning it between the white lines, then look up and follow your visualized path, looking way ahead around the curve to see where the car needs to go. By practicing "looking near and far, near and far", you'll go around the curve centered in your lane as smoothly as if the car were on rails.

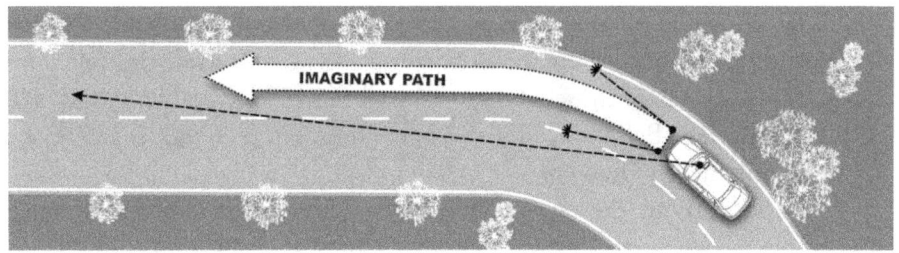

The driver is looking near and far as he follows his visualized path ahead.

By using another vehicle far enough ahead, you can do it the lazy way, by pretending that it is "towing" your car around the curve. Keep looking near and far as you follow your chosen path, then look at this vehicle in front of you. You'll find that by putting your eyes on this vehicle in front of you, it will seem to tow you around the curve, and you'll stay in your lane very easily, without overcorrecting.

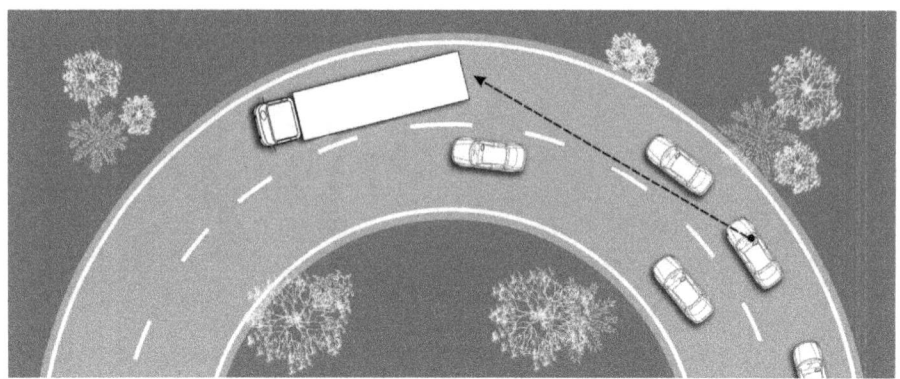

The driver is using a truck to "tow" his car around a long curve, preventing overcorrecting.

If travelling on a high overpass upsets a child because of their fear of heights, encourage him to look at another car ahead or focus on the lane your car is in. This should handle his fear of travelling on high overpasses. This also applies when travelling on mountain roads with a steep drop off. Get the child looking ahead, not at the scary drop off.

Required Skills

A computer test was devised to determine how quickly and accurately a person takes in a scene. This test can identify elderly drivers who are likely to get into an accident. Work done with this test at the University of Alabama studied 300 drivers between the ages of 66 to 90, and found that 74% of those who scored poorly on the test had an accident within the following three years, whereas of those who scored well only 3% had an accident. The researcher, Karlene Ball, said, "That's a better accident predictor than age, eye health or any medical diagnosis."

Perhaps if kids are taught well enough at a young age to accurately take in a whole scene, to see all that is going on around them, they will be safer drivers over their whole lifetime.

Chapter 6

Following Distances

Following Distance – Cars the "Two-Second Rule"

There's a game you can play with your children while driving which helps to teach them the "two-second rule", a rule that creates a safe following distance. The rule is very simple and answers the question of how closely you can follow a vehicle safely, regardless of the speed.

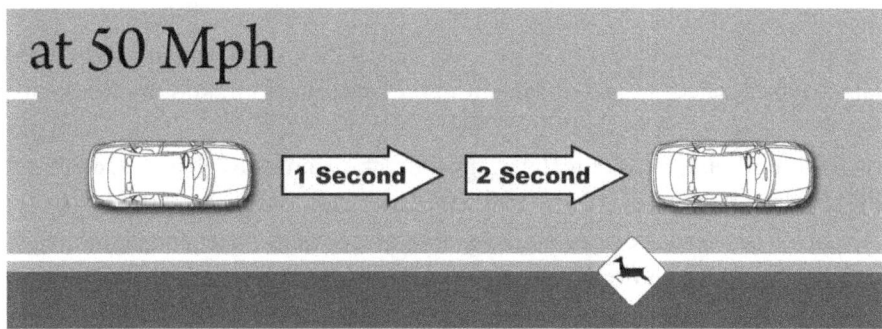

Two seconds ahead – the distance at 50 mph

Here's how it is done: As you observe the vehicle just ahead of yours, look farther ahead of it and select any fixed object, such as road marker, sign, pole or even a shadow coming up. At the exact moment the vehicle in front reaches this selected object, start counting out loud, "one thousand and one, one thousand and two." If you reach this same object before you have finished counting, you're following too close!

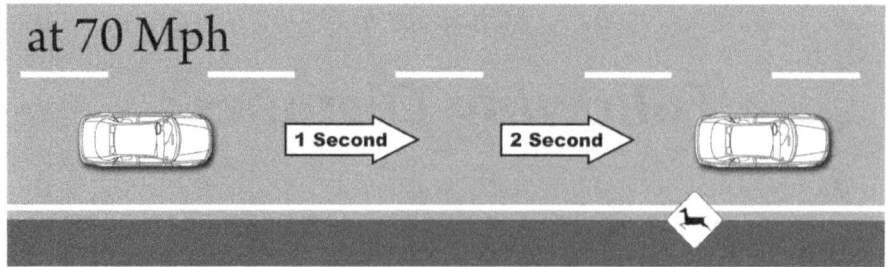

Two seconds ahead results in a greater distance at 70 mph

By using time to measure the distance between two vehicles, you have one stable and accurate rule to apply, one which safety engineers have taught for decades. The two-second rule works for any speed, whether it is 20 mph or 75 mph. The distance between two cars will increase as their speed increases. This is because they will travel a greater distance at higher speeds during two seconds as compared with the distance they will travel during two seconds at slower speeds.

The game to play with your children is to have them tell you whether or not you are following at a safe distance. When they think you are at a correct safe distance, select a fixed object ahead of the car in front, and the moment it reaches the object start counting, "one thousand and one, one thousand and two," to find out if you're really at the correct distance. Repeat this, changing the distance between your car and the one ahead, until it takes two seconds for you to travel to the selected fixed object after the vehicle ahead has passed it. This needs to be done many times, until the children learn to judge it correctly every time.

Also do this at different speeds, so that the children will learn to see and judge the correct distance, one that gives a driver enough time and space to react and safely brake should something happen ahead.

By not following too closely behind the vehicle in front of you, you leave a "cushion of space" in front of your vehicle which gives you a margin of error, in case your attention is distracted or your reaction time is a little slower. With more space in front of you, you'll also have a more open view farther ahead, and that will also give you more assurance that you can stop in time, if the vehicle in front suddenly stops.

When someone is following you too closely, i.e. "tailgating," apply a four-second following distance between you and the car ahead by counting up to one thousand and four. This greater time/distance will allow you to slow down or stop without the car behind rear-ending your car.

FOLLOWING DISTANCES

When you notice you're being followed too closely, suggest playing the "two-second game" to your children to see if they realize you should be applying the four-second rule instead.

My daughter was riding with a friend who was getting very upset because of an aggressive tailgater. My daughter told her friend to keep her foot on the gas and at the same time lightly touch the brake pedal. Doing this activates the brake lights. It worked, the tailgater backed off.

Note that two seconds is the minimum safe following distance on good roads, with good visibility and in good weather. Three seconds is even safer. When roads are wet and conditions poor, you should use a four-second rule. Also use four seconds when you're towing a trailer, to give you twice the distance to stop, because you really have two vehicles to stop. When following a motorcycle, it pays to stay farther behind, especially if it looks like the bike rider is inexperienced.

Even after more than fifty years of driving, I still count, "one thousand and one, one thousand and two," to ensure I'm at least at the minimum safe distance behind the vehicle ahead. This is especially true if I haven't driven for a while, such as after spending some weeks at home writing. I check my distance mainly at freeway speeds because, even though I've driven the car for errands around town, it may have been weeks since I drove on the freeway.

At one time my wife and I were driving on Interstate 70 in freezing weather. It was the first time I'd driven an eighteen-wheel Big-Rig in ice and snow. We passed six other Big-Rigs lying on their sides in the snow after sliding off the icy road. The road conditions couldn't have been worse.

We had to sit, stopped in traffic for one and a half hours because a seventh overturned Big-Rig was blocking the freeway ahead. When we finally got moving again, I mentioned to my wife that I may have been following too closely and should put more space in front of me.

Moments later, a sport-utility vehicle started to spin in front of me for no apparent reason. Of course I hit the brakes and my long trailer started to jackknife. I could see the trailer coming up sideways toward me in my left mirror. I got a clear picture of the eighth Big-Rig lying on its side in the snow – it was going to be my crashed rig. I started to do the right things. I ceased braking, and steered the truck ahead, having now moved from the slow lane to the fast lane by the action of jackknifing. Luckily there was no car alongside of me, I had enough space in front, and everything miraculously turned out alright.

The sport-utility vehicle continued to spin on the ice like a toy top, and

I watched my mirrors as the traffic behind avoided hitting it. Most likely my 53-foot trailer going sideways down the road alerted others to the danger ahead. What had caused the SUV to lose traction (tire grip on the road) was the absence of fresh gravel on the ice to give it more traction. The gravel truck had been blocked by the seventh Big-Rig. I think I'll always remember the sight of my long trailer coming toward me in my left mirror. If I ever forget to stay far enough behind a vehicle ahead, I'll always have that picture to remind me.

That day I learned a lot more about following distances especially when the road is slippery – stay way back!

Three-Second Rule?

A safe following distance is important because when another driver makes a mistake you need time to react to it. A safety cushion of space is a must for all sides of your car. If you have the correct space cushion, you'll have room to maneuver or brake if necessary.

From the minimum two-second rule, the "four-second rule" evolved. While driving on slippery roads, or when following a large truck that blocks your vision, or under other adverse conditions, you should increase the following distance to four seconds.

The California Driver Handbook recommends a three-second following rule for a safe following distance in good conditions, although I found that some other states have stuck with two seconds. The Massachusetts Driver Handbook sums it up pretty well: "The two-second rule is a minimum safe distance when road conditions are clear and dry, and traffic is moderate but moving. Count three or four seconds for added safety, allowing more distance when traffic allows."

A safe following distance gives you the visibility needed to see the big picture and allows you enough time to determine what is going on around your car. Don't ever tailgate other vehicles.

Following Distance – Trucks

In the Following Distance – Cars section, I gave the "two-second rule." That rule applies to cars, not trucks. You're not driving trucks, but you need to know this: Trucks use a four-second rule at speeds under 40 mph. Over 40 mph, the truck rule is one second for every ten feet the truck is long. So a

60-foot-long truck and trailer should be six seconds behind the car in front. That's three times the distance a car needs. A safe truck driver always follows with at least twice the distance a car needs, or three times more at speeds over 40 mph.

Most car drivers don't realize this, so they often pass a truck and then pull into the lane right in front of the truck, the space that the truck driver had allowed for safety. This can force the trucker to quickly hit his brakes in order to get back to a safe following distance again. The car driver himself is being put at risk when he does this. If he and the trucker both hit their brakes at the same time, it's very likely the truck would rear-end the car, due to the greater stopping distances a truck requires, as detailed in a later section of this book. An 80,000-pound truck rear-ending a 4,000-pound car is not in the best interests of the car, nor any people in it.

Now that you know more about this, you can explain to your children why you shouldn't pull in front of a truck too soon. The truck driver deliberately left a bigger space in front of him for safety, and the last thing he wants to do is have to slow down to put more space between you and him. This is especially true when the trucker is using cruise control. After he's been forced to brake and slow down because a car cut too close in front of him, it's a pain in the neck to re-set his cruise control after he slowly returns to normal speed. So please, let the trucker have his four to six seconds of space in front of him. It's for your safety, as well as his!

Fast Moving Trucks Can Deceive

Large trucks with big trailers can appear to be not moving or moving very slowly, when in fact they are moving very fast. Occasionally when you look at a truck coming from the right or left, all you see is the truck. No background scenery can be seen, since the truck is taking up the whole view. As a result, there is no sense of motion and the truck then appears to be not moving or moving much slower than it actually is.

Driver looks and only sees Mayflower. No background is visible – hence no sense of motion is established. Driver thinks it is stationary when it could be moving fast.

Inexperienced drivers have been known to pull out in front of big-rig trucks which appeared to be stopped or moving slowly, with fatal results. Work with your children and show them how a large truck, which takes up the whole field of vision, can make it harder to judge speed.

Chapter 7

Small Things Seem Farther Away

Children Are Closer

Small children appear to be farther away than they actually are. We're used to seeing a person ahead and recognizing that he is a certain distance away. The image we normally use as reference for this is a fully grown adult, and if we see a child half that size, we still think of him in reference to an adult, when in fact the child is closer to us than we realize due to his smaller size. In fact, he's much closer – only half the distance away as an adult would be who's twice as tall.

There is a basic rule you need to apply: A child is always closer to you than you think he is. So when you see children up ahead, slow down, because they are closer than you expect. Also slow down because of the very nature of children – they may suddenly do something unpredictable.

There is an experiment you can do with your children in the car which will prove this point. Have your children spot an adult ahead, and then have them spot a child ahead at what they think is the same distance – and show them how much faster the car arrives at the spot where the child is compared to the longer time it takes to get to where the adult is.

For their survival as pedestrians and bicyclists, children need to know that smaller things appear farther away than they actually are. Teach the kids this data when they are small, because that's when it applies to them.

Motorcycles Near You

The same circumstance of children and small things appearing to be farther away than they actually are also applies to motorcycles. Over half of all motorcycle collisions are the fault of the driver who looks, sees a motorcycle, thinks it is farther away than it really is (because of its much smaller size, compared to cars and trucks) and pulls out or turns in front of it.

When you see a motorcycle in your mirror, if it's moving fast, realize because of its small size it will be alongside you before you expect it.

Because a motorcycle can appear to be farther away than it really is, one is also likely to follow it more closely. Additionally, motorcycles weigh less and can stop faster than cars – so allow yourself more space to stop; don't follow closely behind one. If you see a bike rider wobble, or jerking as he starts to go, realize that the rider is probably inexperienced, so stay back an even greater distance. If the road is slippery, stay even farther back.

As an inexperienced rider, my son fell on wet pavement when riding his motorcycle. The car behind him stopped quickly enough, and my son wasn't hurt – but that car got rear-ended, and the third car behind rear-ended the second one. The lesson here is that a motorcyclist can fall because of a wet road or oil slick, and you should always allow for this to happen by staying at least five seconds back. Also, if there's a motorcyclist in front of the car just ahead of yours, stay farther back just in case the car ahead has to stop quickly to avoid hitting a fallen biker.

A friend of mine was once driving a fire truck to a fire in heavy rain, when a biker ahead fell off his motorcycle. Visibility was so bad that my friend had trouble differentiating between the bike and the rider on the road. When he stopped, he found the biker – unhurt, lying between the wheels of his fire engine! He was really shaken by this incident. Never before had he come so close to killing someone.

In conclusion, to safely drive behind a motorcycle maintain a following distance of minimally five seconds. This also applies when you are behind a car that is directly behind a motorcycle. If the rider appears to be inexperienced, then stay back even farther.

Bicycles Aren't Toys

Bicycle riders have the same rights – and duties – as other vehicle drivers on the road. Children need to understand that, when riding their bike, they are not "just a kid on a bike." They are a fully responsible "driver" of their vehicle, which happens to be their bike.

All of the common sense stuff applies such as wearing a helmet. Just as car drivers shouldn't drive while carrying things in their hands, teach your child not to carry things in his hands while riding his bike. Have him put it in his backpack or in his bike basket.

Following are some things a bike rider should know and do. When riding a bike make your intentions known to others on the road by using hand signals to point in the direction you intend to turn. Look back to see if the way is clear before you change lanes. If a rider finds it difficult to hold a straight line while turning his head to check for traffic then consider purchasing a rear view mirror to attach to the helmet.

Read the road ahead. Keep your eyes moving near and far, first by looking closer for potholes and other obstacles immediately in front of you, then focusing on cars and pedestrians farther away from you. Look near again for things like gutter storm drains and car doors that may suddenly open, and then shoot your attention out ahead of you, looking at the big scene.

At an intersection, look far enough ahead to notice any vehicle that may turn across the path in front of you. Also, at every intersection and whenever leaving a driveway always look to the left first (the closest possible cross-traffic to your path), then look right and to the left again.

Take care of your bike and keep it in good working condition. You don't want the chain coming off, or the brakes not fully working right. Have someone show you how to keep the brakes adjusted correctly and how to fix a flat tire.

Above all, make sure you are seen by other vehicle drivers! Compared to a car, a bike is very small, so it's much harder for drivers to see, and children who aren't fully grown appear to be farther away than they really are. Most drivers haven't been taught that small things appear to be farther away than they actually are. Since bikes are not a threat for serious car damage, many drivers think, "it's just a kid on a bike," and don't regard them as vehicles. A driver will put his attention on the other cars and trucks around him, because he knows they will cause damage to his vehicle if they come into contact.

You can always improve your visibility by wearing brightly colored clothes, such as yellow, during the day. A bright fluorescent colored mesh helmet can make your presence known to a motorist, even one deep into a phone conversation. At night, wearing white or light colors and reflective bands helps. Also make sure your front- and back- lights as well as your reflectors are clean, working and turned on.

Anything you do to make yourself or your bike look bigger helps your safety. A pennant flag, flying high, can get a driver's attention. Wearing bulky clothes that make you look bigger and more of a "danger," especially to that absent-minded driver who, safe in his car, may otherwise miss seeing you.

Riding a bicycle safely is a lot like driving a car safely. Long before you teach your child to ride a bike, you should be teaching him how to read the road and traffic ahead. There's more to safely riding a bike than staying balanced as you push the pedals, brake and steer. Teach them all you can while they're still in the car as your passengers.

Many people decide they'll never ride a bike again once they get their driver's license. I know I did, after living on a farm and having to ride a bike six miles to school and back for four years! Maybe when your kids start to ride a bike, you can get a bike of your own and ride with them for family enjoyment, and to show them exactly where they should be looking to keep themselves safe.

Traffic Wise Cyclists and Cyclist Wise Drivers

It's more than just kids these days on bikes. Some commuters are leaving their cars and becoming pedal power commuters. Car drivers need to understand the rights of cyclists. In America, cyclists are inclined to keep to the right and not take up the full lane, yet legally they are entitled to occupy the whole lane because they have the same rights as a motorist.

When a cyclist stays over to the right, he tends to blend into the background and becomes less obvious to a car driver. The cyclist also subjects himself to the risk of being hit by a suddenly opened door of a parked car. Additionally, a driver might try to squeeze into the available space between the cyclist and his car, thus pushing the cyclist even farther to the right into the debris in the gutter.

If a cyclist stays too far to the right at an intersection a driver may assume the cyclist is planning to turn right (when the cyclist actually intends to go straight ahead.) This can become problematical especially when the car driver intends to turn to the right. The car driver will pass the cyclist then make a right turn, cutting across the path of the cyclist. To avoid this situation, a cyclist needs to stay in the middle of the lane to ensure a driver does not try go around him and then cut him off.

An experienced cyclist will make eye contact with a driver. A wise driver will nod or use some other movement to tell the cyclist that he has been seen and will remember he is there. A safe driver needs to catch the cyclist's eye and by pointing find out where the cyclist wants to go.

Evidence suggests that cycling becomes safer when there are more cyclists on the road so that they become a normal part of traffic and drivers get used to looking out for them and sharing the road with them. Your kids as well as commuter cyclists must be extra alert when they ride their bikes especially when they do not form a normal part of traffic. And drivers not used to seeing cyclists must realize that when one does appear it will be closer than expected because of its small size.

Bicycles in traffic can move surprisingly quickly. Drivers don't realize this and pass them and then may cut them off because they underestimated the speed of the bicycle. Also the size of the bicycle makes it look further away than what a driver is used to when compared to cars. Misjudging a cyclist's speed and size can lead to trouble especially if a driver is not used to sharing the road with bicycles.

While your kids are being driven around in the car they need to understand the things that car drivers do wrong when dealing with cyclists. This will be invaluable to them whenever they have to ride a bike in traffic.

Bike Riders Looking Ahead

I once taught a messenger bicycle rider to drive a car. He had spent a couple of years pedaling his bicycle in downtown traffic, delivering documents and small packages. He was a real biking enthusiast, and on his days off he would go for long bike rides in the country. I really admired him for managing to survive in the dangerous confusion of downtown traffic – not a place I would want to ride a bike. I assumed he would be traffic-wise, and thus easy to teach car driving to. How wrong I was! I couldn't get him to get his attention off the road directly in front of him. He was constantly looking close by around him to make sure nothing was about to knock him off his bicycle. It seemed impossible to get him to look a whole block ahead.

He saw – and concentrated on – the close-by oil slicks, water puddles, potholes and litter that I never even noticed. I discovered that he was doing this when he asked me about something that was directly in front of the car. This was something I hadn't noticed. On questioning him about it, I found out it was a small object only about twelve feet out.

Show your kids that when driving a car, how much farther ahead they must look as compared to when riding their bike. At 60 mph, twelve seconds ahead is a quarter of a mile. A bike's speed of 10 mph is one-sixth of 60 mph, so one-sixth of a quarter mile is about 70 yards (more than half the length of a football field). This is how far ahead a cyclist should look. Most bike riders keep their eyes on the road only a few feet in front of them so as to make sure they don't hit a bump, hole or run through a puddle.

Teach your kids to learn how far 70 yards is, so that when they are riding their bikes they will know how far to look ahead. At the 70-yard distance, they should be looking ahead to see the big picture. Then looking directly in front of the bike keeping an eye out for the pot holes and bumps before returning to look 70 yards ahead (a twelve second distance.) By keeping their eyes moving they will not only avoid the potholes, but more importantly they'll also avoid the cars whose drivers should have seen them, but didn't.

Once while teaching a motorcycle rider to drive a car, I had the same trouble I had with a cyclist of getting him to look far enough ahead. As his motorcycle travelled the same speed as a car, I assumed he would look ahead the distance needed to drive a car safely but this motorcycle rider knew he had to look out for those oil slicks that were sitting right in front of his front wheel. Then to my surprise, when I told him to look farther ahead, I found he was only looking 100 yards ahead instead of his usual 50 yards. Even though he had doubled the distance, it was still far short of what was needed to safely drive a car (or to safely ride a motorcycle, for that matter). The twelve-second rule was a total revelation for this motorcycle rider who was still trying to avoid oil slicks while driving a car. When he finally got the idea, he became a better driver and rider.

Chapter 8

Knowing the Machine

"Carwise"

"Carwise" is another new word I use in this book. A person who is carwise is one who knows how a car works.

The more you understand how a piece of machinery works, the better you'll be able to control it. A race car driver understands exactly how his engine works and how many revolutions per minute he can push the engine to. He knows all the steering characteristics of that car so well that he doesn't have to think about how to steer it, he just knows. He has not only learned how to drive a car, but he's also a specialist in the way a car functions and handles.

To be a good driver you should have some idea how a car works. This data should be taught in schools to both children and adults. The driver education class should have "cutaway" working models or at least all the parts of engines, brakes and clutch, so that student drivers can see what they look like. Working models could be built by car enthusiasts and given or loaned to schools to teach students about how cars work. Another way students can see the parts is visiting technical schools where auto mechanics are taught.

As cars become more and more sophisticated, the day of the home mechanic is fast vanishing, and unless there is an attempt by car manufacturers to create educational programs about how cars work, these expensive and brilliantly designed cars will be driven by drivers who have inadequate or no understanding of how they work. This lack of understanding will result in a lessening of the drivers' ability to control these fast cars, especially in emergencies.

Most schools these days don't have working or even plastic models of car engines, brakes, etc. Moreover, car manufacturers haven't given schools "carwise" videos that teach how to be a safer driver by understanding how cars function. So how can you teach your children this knowledge? It can be done. While your child is in the car, show how all the controls work.

You can point to pictures in the car owner's manual while your child is in the car. The illustrations will give a child the ability to relate pictures and diagrams to the real thing. You can start with simple things such as where the controls are for the heater, air conditioner, lights, turn signals, windshield wipers, and windshield defoggers, explaining how they work. Your ten-year-old needs to be able to do this just as well as he can program your cell phone.

Next, take a trip to your local library and borrow books and videos about cars. Try to find simply written books full of pictures. Then go to the car with books in hand and with the pictures, help your child recognize the different parts under the hood. Learning is not just sitting down and studying books: it's a matter of seeing and touching and finding out what the books are talking about as it relates to your actual car. It will sometimes require getting your hands a little dirty while showing the relationship between what's in the book and the car itself.

Look at the tires and observe how little of the rubber actually touches the road. This will help make your child see the importance of slowing down on a wet pavement. On wet roads, worn tires will float on a thin film of water like water skis do, technically called "hydroplaning." In heavy rain at high speeds, even good tires with little wear have less grip on the road. With the tires not fully grabbing the road, one can lose control and skid.

When a book shows a picture of disc brakes, it's a good idea to jack up a car, remove one wheel, and let a child have a good look at the disc brake to see how it works. Another thing that can be checked is how far the brake pads have worn down and also observe how small the pads are – only that small area touches the disc. If not on your car, you can demonstrate this at a car shop, at a technical school or in a junkyard.

When applying the brakes, the pads are forced against the disc. The friction resulting from this is what slows and stops the car. This generates heat as well as wearing down the pads. When going down a very steep hill or mountain road it is wise to use the engine to slow the car down by shifting down to a lower gear. In an automatic this is done by shifting down to D3 or D2.

It would be a good learning experience for you and your children, after having gone down a steep hill, to pull off the road and stop the car (where it's safe to do so), and let them inspect the brakes. This will demonstrate to you how much heat can build up. Be careful as the brake discs can be very hot and burn your fingers! If an inexperienced Big-Rig truck driver overuses his brakes going down a mountain, smoke will be coming from the brakes. In the dark the brake drums can glow red-hot!

Show your child where the car's fuse box is and where the replacement fuses are should a fuse blow and need replacing. A child should also know how to disable a car to prevent a drunk or an abductor from driving – one easy way is to remove the fuse. Show him how to replace a fuse. Also show him where the fuse boxes are on different cars, so he has an idea where to look for them. This will be a good learning experience as most parents – like most people – are never taught this. Find the fuse box using the car owner's manual.

While the car is turned off, pull off just one spark plug lead (insulated wire), then start the car to show the child how the motor then runs roughly. (Don't pull the lead off while the car is running as you may get an unpleasant shock. Likewise, after this demonstration, turn the car off and reconnect the lead.) Show how to check to see if all the spark plugs leads are connected correctly. Removing the spark plug leads is another way to disable a car.

The movie The Sound of Music would have had a different ending had the nuns not known how to disable a car. The nuns removed the spark plug leads (and other parts), so the car that would have chased them wouldn't start. Your children should have this knowledge too.

Another good way to get children to understand how cars work – and see the actual parts – is to take them to a wrecking yard or junkyard, usually listed in your yellow pages under Auto Parts – Used or Auto Salvage. At a junkyard, you can show your children what the parts of a car look like when removed. Look for whole engines that are sitting around. Not only can they see different car parts, they can also see what happens to cars in accidents. If your teenagers don't have enough respect for the potential dangers of cars, a walk through in a junkyard, looking at the damaged vehicles, will make it very real to them that accidents do happen and how deadly they can be. If hard steel can be so easily bent and broken, how about soft bodies?

By showing them junkyard cars, they'll get a greater understanding of how cars are built. Show them a door that has side impact beams (reinforced walls), and help them realize that even this additional protection won't stop a Mack truck. This will remind them to always look both ways when helping you to pull out into traffic.

Show how a car is designed to crumple on impact, in the front and rear, in order to protect the passengers from the full force of a crash. Show them the "crumple lines" built into the underside of your own car's hood. In the junkyard, let them point out cars damaged in the front and rear, and see how they crumpled as they were meant to. Show them how cars are designed so engines on high impact go under the car instead of coming into the driver's and passenger's seat area. Show them a car with its air bag inflated from an accident, to get an idea of how air bags work.

Many junkyards are self-serve, where customers walk through and remove the parts they need. It's an ideal place to explore and learn about cars, but you'll need to wear suitable shoes or boots to protect your feet from sharp objects and to meet the junkyard's insurance requirements. One hour in a junkyard can help you teach your child more about cars than twelve hours of reading books.

It is only by understanding how cars work that a driver will know what a car is capable of. Good weather driving at low speeds takes no extra skill. It is when weather conditions are bad, or another driver is out of control, that a complete understanding of how a car works can help to save lives. Those are the times that both carwise and traffic-wise drivers may be able to avoid or prevent an accident. A carwise driver will better understand how a car handles on wet surfaces and can better predict and maneuver around another driver who has lost control and is skidding across his path.

Teach your children to be traffic-wise, and then work with them on becoming carwise. If you start at an early age, you can continue to develop those skills over the years. By the time the law allows them to drive, they will already have completed huge steps in their complete driver training program.

Let's be like professional sports coaches. Start them on driver education while young; train them well so as to develop roadwise and carwise drivers who understand the road and the car. In this way, they can drive safely without accidents.

Car Care

Long before they reach driving age, you should teach your children how to take good care of a car. Have them not only fill the gas tank, but also show them how to check the oil and all other fluids (battery, brakes, power steering, radiator, automatic transmission, windshield washer).

Show them the different colors of the fluids, so if there is any leaking they'll know where it comes from. Green is the color of coolant that may be leaking from the radiator or its hoses. Red fluid can be from the power steering or automatic transmission. Brown or black oil comes from the engine. Clear water condenses from air conditioners. Light golden-brown is the color of brake fluid – and if there isn't any, you won't have any brakes! All of this data is in the owner's manual.

Let them study the car's washing instructions and then wash the car, doing what is recommended in the owner's manual. If you're mechanically inclined and do minor maintenance on the car, have your kids help you - for example when you change the oil. Keeping the oil full, and the oil and its filter changed often enough, is vital for good gas mileage and for protecting the life of your engine. My son was too busy kicking, hitting or catching a ball but my eldest daughter helped me maintain the car. As a result men now stare in wonder as she handles minor mechanical problems be it with the car or even plumbing or electrical repairs in her home or hotel.

Once, when shopping for a used car, I checked the oil and found no oil on the dipstick. Talking with the young owner of the car, I found she did not even know how to check the oil. She said she had the oil changed every 3,000 miles, but never checked after the work was done to see if the correct amount of oil had been added. As a truck driver, I've often had to sign a form stating that I personally saw the drain plug was correctly tightened and the oil filled to the correct level. A large truck driven without any oil could cost over $20,000 in engine repairs! Also teach your kids how to check the car oil themselves at least once a month. This is in case their car develops a leak or starts burning oil. It isn't hard to learn or do and could save them costly repairs. In the future, your kids may drive older cars that leak and need to have oil added.

Have your children check the headlights to see if they are working correctly. Put your foot on the brake and let them see if the brake lights are working, and similarly check each of the turn signals, plus the four-way emergency flasher. If a turn signal flashes faster than usual, it can mean a bulb is burned out. Teach the children how to change burned out bulbs.

Burned out signals or brake lights mean you're no longer telling other drivers what you intend to do. Dirty headlights can reduce your night vision by half! So make a point of washing the road film off the headlights regularly. The best time to do this is when you wash your windshield as you gas up the car.

When teaching a student, I've occasionally found the inside of their car's windshield to be dirty. One girl, who was using her family car, was unable to see ahead while driving the day before. The sun caused glare on the windshield. I pointed out to her that the inside of the windshield was very dirty, and that was why she had trouble seeing ahead toward the sun.

The insides of all windows should be cleaned at least once a month, more often in cars used by smokers. Chemicals in car upholstery and plastics vaporize in the sun's heat and collect on the inside of the windows. Air pollution and dust also stick to inside glass. When the weather is rainy, cold, or very humid, water will fog up on the windows much more heavily and quickly when the inside glass is dirty. Reversely, windows fog up less and more slowly and are easier to defog faster when the inside glass is kept clean.

The outsides of windows need to be cleaned often. All glass can be cleaned with plain water and paper towels and then gone over a final time with dry or damp paper. Don't use store bought window cleaner unless it's wax free. Wax is put in some window cleaners to make the glass shine, and that's the last thing you want when you're looking toward the sun – it increases glare. Simple water and paper towels or newspaper clean windows beautifully and leave no wax buildup.

Gas stations sell windshield washer fluid or you can add a small amount of mild dishwashing detergent in the windshield washer bottle located under the hood, to cut the "road film" on the windshield. Road film is unburned fuel (especially diesel), exhaust fumes, bits of motor oil, and tiny bits of tire rubber in the air. When it starts to rain, it's a good time to use the windshield washer to cut the road film. For safe driving, you must be able to see clearly and well.

Make sure your children know how to keep all windows clean, inside and out, and know what to do if they fog up. It could save their lives once they're driving.

Worn Tires Kill

Worn tires are not only dangerous because of the possibility of blowouts but they also make a vehicle hard to handle and control. Tires must be in balance for a car to drive well. A tire is balanced by attaching small weights to the rim of the wheel so that it will spin smoothly without any wobbles. When a tire isn't balanced, it also wears unevenly.

Tire "tread" is the grooved outer layer of rubber that rolls on the road. To be legal car tires must have at least 2/32 of an inch of tread. You can see if this point has been reached by observing a series of molded bars that run across the tire at the bottom of the groove. When these molded bars reach the surface of the tire it shows that the minimum tread of 2/32 of an inch has been reached and that it is time for the tire to be replaced.

If you live in the U.S. there is a very simple way to measure tire tread depth. Grab a penny and hold it by placing your fingers over President Lincoln's body and insert his head into the tread. If any part of his head is covered your tire tread is legal.

A tire might look safe when its tread, at a quick glance, appears to be all right. It's only when you examine all of the tread around the tire that you can find flat spots and places where there's not enough tread left for it to be safe.

Teach your children to get down on their hands and knees to look at as much of the tire as possible. You can also roll the car, stop it, and have them check again to see all of it. If they find something unusual, you need to check it out.

If you don't already have one, buy a tire pressure gauge and have your kids check the tires when they're cold, not after being driven a while and becoming hot. Correctly inflated tires reduce tire wear and improve gas mileage. Show them where the spare tire and jack are kept and how to change a tire using the owner's manual, and let them practice doing it. This should be mastered before they ever need to change a flat tire in the dark. A friend of mine who was 19 and on a "first date" had to change a guy's flat tire as her date had never learned to do so.

Fifty years ago when I first learned to drive, tires were not as safe as they are now. I learned to drive with the constant thought that a front tire could blow and the car could then go out of control. I've actually had a front tire blow out and experienced how difficult it is to keep the vehicle on the road.

Tires are not as expensive today as they were forty years ago. There's no good reason not to replace all four tires before they show a lot of wear.

If a tire does blow out, don't stomp hard on the brakes. Instead, first concentrate on steering, holding the wheel tightly so you don't lose control of the car. Then slow down gradually, braking gently once the car is back under control.

The driver is responsible for a worn tire blowing out. If this happens, the driver was never trained to examine the tires before driving, or never applied common sense to maintaining his car. Point out to your children worn tires on a car whenever you notice them in a parking lot.

Your kids may end up being passengers in friends' older cars, especially when away at college where a new car is beyond the budget of a student. They need to know enough about older car types and tire conditions to not ride in an unsafe car.

Seat Belts

Seat belts are the best safety device in a vehicle. Studies show a belted passenger is more likely to survive a crash, with or without an air bag. And an unbelted passenger is more likely to be hurt by an air bag when it inflates.

My granddaughter at age three was very independent and had quite a mind of her own. Getting her buckled up safely in her car seat was at times difficult, to say the least. Her mother finally found something that worked. She told her: "Julie, your job, after you're buckled in, is to make sure that all the rest of us put our seat belts on too."

When Julie was in the car with me, I was surprised at how quickly she had settled into her car seat – and then insisted that I buckle up! My daughter later told me the reasoning behind her plan. Most of us like to be in control of things rather than being controlled by others. By letting Julie be responsible for the adults putting on their seat belts, she had to willing to be buckled in herself.

Julie knows that everyone needs to be buckled up in case there's an accident. She's doing a good job of reminding us to keep safe. After all, we need to be there for our kids and grandkids.

Let Youngsters See Out

A child can be taught to look out of the car, even when he's in a child's car seat (safety seat). His or her car seat should put the child up high enough to see out. If safety laws allow it, put the child's seat in the center of the car's back seat, so the child can look forward through the open space between the front seats. Otherwise, put it on the side opposite the driver's side, in the back seat, where you can also see him in your rearview mirror.

When traveling, don't block the child's view by stacking things on the side. If your windows are not tinted, a baby equipment shop can sell you tinted material or car window see-through blinds to protect the baby from the sun and still let him see out. By having him in a car safety seat, you know where he is; and you, as a driver, can have your attention on driving and not be distracted by the baby's movements.

Because of the installation of air bags in cars, never let a child or baby sit on your knee as you drive. An air bag could explode out of the steering wheel and hurt them because of sitting too close to it.

Chapter 9

Developing Senses & Judgment

Sense of Distance

Learning to judge distance is important, because every driver needs to know the distances required to stop a car. Even if you've never learned to judge distances, don't give up on this – let an older child figure it out, or get grandpa or another person to help with this.

The different stopping distances are often shown in your state's driver handbook. A modern mid-sized car with anti-lock brakes takes about 140 feet to come to a stop from 60 mph. Allowing for the average reaction time, that car will also travel an initial 66 feet at 60 mph before the driver even hits the brakes; so at 60 mph it takes about 200 feet to stop a car. Now, if exact distances aren't real to a person, these facts are meaningless.

So how can a person develop a sense of distance? Well, the length of a football field is 100 yards or 300 feet. The distance once around a high school sports field track is 440 yards or 1,320 feet, which is the same as a quarter of a mile. Freeway signs show distances to approaching exits in quarter, half, three-quarters and full miles. Help your kids learn to recognize and judge how far those distances are.

Show your children how far a landmark is from your house – perhaps simply the top of a road or a hill. Pick a point about 100 yards from home and show them how far that is. You can roughly measure this with normal walking – about one yard per stride. Using your car's odometer, show them something a half-mile from home. Find and show them something a mile from home. Measure the distance between home and your children's school. Use this to let them judge that particular distance. While going to high school I had to ride a bike three miles to catch a bus and as a result I'm an excellent judge of how far three miles is.

Measure the distances to all of the familiar places you go to regularly -

such as grandma's house, the church, shopping center, etc., and let your kids use these measurements to judge distances.

They can then use those distances for comparisons and be able to tell people, for example, that the next gas station is about one mile away. When you ask most people how far the nearest gas station is, they say it's "a long way" or "close" – they can't give you a measurement distance, and if they do it's usually inaccurate. No one took the time to teach them this skill.

Do this with the kids: Stop the car and set the trip odometer to 000.0. (If your speedometer doesn't have a separate trip odometer you can reset to zero, just let the speedometer add tenths to whatever number it's on when you start.) Then drive along the road and when 0.5 comes up on the odometer, tell the children you've traveled half-a-mile. (The last numbers at the far right are each one-tenth of a mile, and five-tenths, 0.5, is the same as half-a-mile.) Then set the trip odometer to 0 again, and have each child select a point half-a-mile ahead, and go. When the odometer reaches 0.5, see how accurate they were. Once they can judge half-a-mile, play the same game using the distance of one mile, shown on the odometer as 1.0.

This is a worthwhile exercise. You don't need any special equipment to help your children develop a good sense of distance. They'll be able to tell you, for example, that their friend's house is half a mile past the church, and you'll be able to get them to the party on time.

As a truck driver, I often had to get directions from a customer before delivering a load. I know that even successful, well-educated businessmen don't necessarily have the ability to judge distances. "Two miles" down a road can actually be six miles. "A mile" can really be only 300 yards, less than a quarter mile.

If your children can't tell you in yards or miles how far down a street their friends live, then they can't judge nor communicate distances to others in measurements. Why not spend a little time to give them this skill while out in the car together?

Instead of leaving their "Are we there yet?" questions unanswered, you can teach them how to figure it out. Show them how easy it is to convert miles to hours. For example, if the car averages 60 mph, and there are 60 minutes in each hour, then the car is traveling one mile each minute – so it will take 50 minutes to go 50 miles. At 30 mph, a car travels one mile every two minutes – at half the speed, it takes twice the time.

A great way to work on their math is to have them figure out the distances traveled. This also helps them understand actual distances. If you've gone 29 miles from home, and pass a sign which says the next town is 11 miles ahead, let them figure out that the town is 40 miles from home. Help them learn to do simple addition in their heads, so they aren't so dependent on a calculator by developing the skills of adding and subtracting without one.

Sense of Time

A sense of time can also be developed. To teach your children to judge how long fifteen minutes takes to go by, you can explain that it's about half the length of TV situation comedies (usually 30 minute shows), or some other usual period of time they're familiar with.

As with developing a sense of distances to all of the familiar places you go to regularly, you should also educate your kids on how much time it takes to get to these familiar places.

Let them learn to judge distance in relationship to time. For example, they need to know that grandma's house is 30 miles away and it takes about 45 minutes to get there.

On longer trips, have them look at the route ahead on a map to see how many miles to the next stopping point and let them estimate the time that it will take to get there. When you've just passed a sign stating how far the next town is, let your kids figure out how much time it will take to get there. Doing these things will overcome the constant questions of, "When are we going to get there?" and "Are we there yet?"

Whenever you take them on a trip, set the trip odometer (or note the mileage) and also note the time as you leave. Upon arrival, note how far you traveled and how long it took. If your children are old enough, have them figure out the average speed, and discuss why it may have been different than usual. This will lead to safer drivers in the future, because they will be able to correctly estimate the time it takes to get somewhere without speeding to get there on time.

If you have developed their sense of time, you can tell the kids to be back in 45 minutes, and they will have a good idea of how long that is. They might even think to look at their watches, so they will make it back on time.

Sense of Speed

An important reason for children to be able to judge speed correctly is that they'll need this skill when they learn to actually drive a car. If a student driver has already been taught to judge speed before he first gets behind the wheel, then he'll be able to keep the car at correct speeds without having to constantly look at the speedometer. A new driver needs to be looking ahead, without the distraction of taking his eyes off the road often to check the speedometer.

Their sense and judgment of speed can be developed but, like anything else, they need experience which they will only get with practice.

People normally judge the speed of a car by the noise level, the motion of the car, and what they see. Of course the speedometer is the main reference, but a driver who rarely checks it can think he's driving at a different speed than he really is. Speed can be a remarkably deceptive thing.

After many hours of traveling on freeways, getting back down to lower street speeds can seem like crawling awfully slowly. Conversely, if you haven't driven at highway speed for some time, then the speed of the freeway seems fast and unless you make a conscious effort to speed up, you'll slow down the drivers in your lane.

Some car clubs have events in which the drivers have to drive at a set speed with their speedometers covered so they're not visible. The remarkable thing about this is that many drivers can get extremely close to the desired speed.

By starting early, you can develop your children's judgment of speed. Cover up the speedometer, drive at an even speed, and let the children guess the speed. After you've been playing this game for a while, if they don't get extremely close to the exact actual speed, find out why they're getting it wrong. Most people observe speed by how quickly fixed objects approach. So suggest that they look at a fixed object ahead and by seeing how quickly it approaches, judge the speed of the car.

If the speed is being judged by the noise level of the car, some road surfaces make more noise than others, and your children need to recognize and take this into account. Some people have a "sixth sense" for judging speed. They don't know how they do it, they just can. So realize that this can happen.

Teach Your Child Left and Right

A car is ideal for teaching children left and right because the steering wheel is on the left and you drive on the right-hand side of the road. I didn't spend time drilling left and right with my daughter. She had a freckle on her right hand and used this to tell left and right. The freckle faded, and by the time she went to get her driver's license she had trouble knowing left from right.

DEVELOPING SENSES & JUDGMENT

I had earlier taught her north and south and she had a perfect sense of direction, but even with a watch on her left wrist and knowing she was right-handed, she could not "think with" right and left.

If I had to do it again, I would have taught her left and right at about two or three years old. I would have put an ink spot or other mark on her left hand because that is the hand most people wear a watch on. Then I would have had her look ahead while we were driving, and every time the car turned a corner I'd have her tell me if it was to the left or to the right. At a later time, I would not have put a dot on her hand, but would have expected her to know left and right. I would have had her practice this until it was something she would just know.

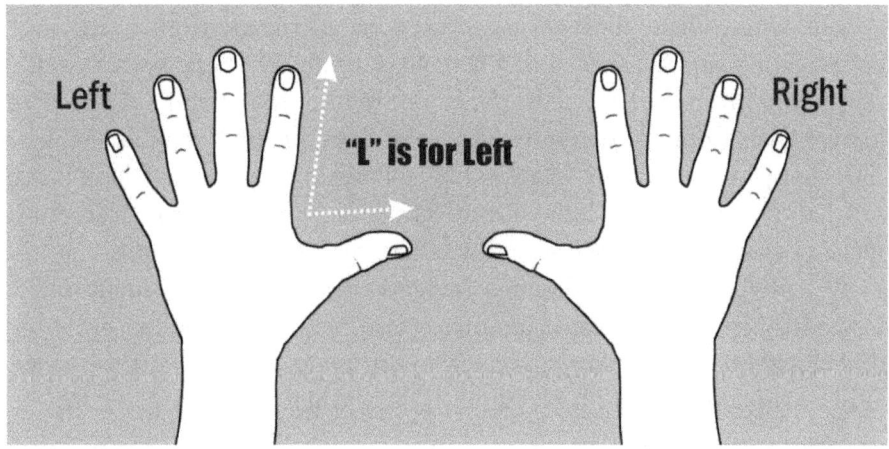

If a child already knows the alphabet and still doesn't know left and right there is a way to demonstrate where left is. Have your child put her hands out, fingers up, as if to push on something. If the thumb is pulled away from the fingers it forms the letter L on the left hand. But knowing this is not enough; left and right have to be drilled until they become an automatic response.

Knowing left and right is important because, later in life, if someone suddenly said "Go right!" to avoid an accident, I wouldn't want them to have to think about which way right is. They need to just know it.

Rule for Crossing – Left, Right, Left

This rule for crossing a street applies very much to driving a car, and if it's not learned well as a child, it will need to be learned and developed as a basic habit or "training pattern" before a driver can be considered safe.

When cars travel on the right-hand side of the road, we need to look first to the left, before we step off a sidewalk onto the road, because cars coming at us from our left will be on the side of the road nearest to us. The rule, therefore, is first look to the left to see if it's clear, and then look to the right. If no vehicles are coming from the right, then check again to the left to see if it's still clear– and only then is it safe to cross. Of course, don't just glance to the left and right – you must look and focus on what you see.

The same rule applies when driving a car or bicycle from a side street onto a busy road. A driver should first check to the left, because cars coming toward him from the left will be the closest to him. If a person has a problem knowing left from right, another way to explain this is: Always look first on the side where the steering wheel is – as you pull out, you have to look first to see that no cars will run into your driver's door. This works for a car, but to make your kids safe on a bike they will have to learn left and right.

As a driving instructor, I've had students who'd never been taught to look to the left first. On coming to an intersection, they would look in the wrong direction first. I once had a student who had no training to look to the left. When I discussed this with her family, I found they didn't like her riding her bicycle, because she'd been knocked off it several times after failing to look to the left.

Too many accidents happen at intersections. If the rule, "Look left, then right, then left again," were drilled (taught and practiced) from an early age, many such accidents would not occur. Even when a driver has looked, he still may not have seen another vehicle – if he hasn't also focused his eyes on what he looked at. This explains what happened when someone says, "I looked but just didn't see you."

This rule must be taught to very young children when they first start school so they can safely cross the street but it should also be taught again later. This is not only a rule which applies to getting to school safely, it will also make a child safer on a bike and later make him a safer driver. Parents must develop this habit, or custom, in their children from an early age. Most skills we learn have to be drilled (practiced), and the only way to develop the ability to look left every time is to drill it in over the years. Then, when they start to drive, they will look to the left in plenty of time and won't need to have an accident at an intersection to realize that they must always first look to the left.

Landmarks

Landmarks are important for getting a sense of direction and distance. When I first visited a city that was flat with no visible landmarks and spent a week getting lost, I realized how we depend on landmarks to establish our sense of direction and location.

When you're out with your children, point out the landmarks you use to gain your sense of direction. This applies to times you're driving and when you're walking around, such as at the zoo or the shopping mall. Point out how you use landmarks to find where you parked your car.

Some stores (like Home Depot) have an exit that is away from the point of entry. This can be disorientating when leaving unless you look for your car in reference to the entrance rather than the exit.

By developing a sense of direction early in life, and by teaching them to look for landmarks, your children will not get lost so easily at large events such as a wedding or reunion. Point out "landmarks" the kids need to use to find their way around when attending events. For example: "There's the kitchen, the bathroom, the back patio door. Even explain to young children that if they get lost they need to "look for Mommy in the red dress." Then they can go off by themselves and not hang on to you – and everyone can enjoy the occasion more freely.

On a long trip, when you're familiar with the route, tell your children what the next landmark is so that they can keep a look out for it.

If you're going to a place you've never been before, as soon as the children are old enough, have them study the map and points of interest, and let them think about and determine which landmarks they will need to look for.

To make any job seem shorter, it is only necessary to break down each part of the job into separate actions. It's far more enjoyable to do six small jobs and achieve six good results, than to work for a long time and get only one thing done. The time you spend will be the same, but you'll feel you have achieved more when you break the job down into smaller individual actions each of which you complete separately.

For me, as a very young child on the way to the beach, the greatest point of excitement was when we could first see the ocean. Of course, this was a point very close to our final destination, and my parents were then pestered about when we were going to get there.

If all the previous landmarks had been looked for on the way to the beach – such as the mountain, the river, the town with the large soda bottle in the main street, the winding gorge with the train tunnel, the town with the palm trees – then interest in the trip would have been kept high along the way and a sense of location would have been established for us kids. Here's a contest for you: Name the towns we drove through that had the above landmarks. (Hint: you will need to take a trip to New Zealand to find them.)

It's the same thing when driving with young children in the car. Driving for twenty minutes and finding a mountain in view achieves something. And then, the next landmark is looked for. This will help keep boredom away, because the children will feel they've achieved something each time a landmark is reached.

By doing this as you drive, your children will be happier. They will be developing a sense of direction, while gaining the all-important skills of looking ahead and keeping their eyes moving while traveling. They will also be learning about their own country, which will help them in school.

North, South, East and West

If you yourself have little or no sense of compass direction, then have grandpa, or someone who does understand it, help to teach your children this. Grandma could be even better at this because she may have navigated for grandpa and might be better at reading maps. They should be taught north and south, east and west. It's important that your children gain a sense of direction at a very young age.

Sailors develop a natural awareness of where the points of the compass are. There is no reason why a sense of direction can't be developed in your children, both at home and when you're out traveling in the car with them.

Get a simple compass and show the children its four points N/S/E/W, and how a compass with a needle always points to the north. If they don't know, teach them that the sun always rises in the east and sets in the west. They also need to know that when facing north, east is always to their right and west is to their left.

Next, help them grasp where north is in relation to where you live. Show them where you live on a big map of the whole country. It will be easy to show them that north is at the top of the map. Next, show them your local

DEVELOPING SENSES & JUDGMENT

area on a map big enough to show landmarks, such as a sea, river, lakes or mountains. Or, if there are none of those, the map should show the freeways and major points of interest.

Show the children where home is on a map. Ideally, mark exactly where you live on it, even showing which side of the street you live on. To find your home you can use a street guide and find the page in the guide which shows where you live. You can also use free Internet map sites, such as MapQuest or Google Earth (at http://www.MapQuest.com and http://Earth.Google.com). It is fun to use Google Earth, put in your address, look at your home, and get the kids to locate it from the satellite photos.

From this, you can show your child which way north is in relation to home. It may be that the front of your home faces north, or their favorite room faces north, but whatever the case, find something about their home that can give them a stable orientation point to recognize where north is.

Next, establish the position of their home in relationship to a freeway or major road. Show them that they live east or north of the highway, or whichever direction it is. Then show your children where their school is on the map and point out where north is in relation to their school, the supermarket, grandma, your church, and other major points. You need to orient the children to where north and the other compass points are in relation to all of the places they often go to.

If you're lucky enough to have a landmark in view from any of those locations, orient the children to the compass direction of the landmark in relation to where they are. For example, "The water tower is north of the school, and the tower is west of the supermarket."

Compass direction can be taught in the car. In fact, it is a perfect place to learn, because one can see where the sun is in the sky. You can get a small compass which can be mounted on the dashboard.

With a compass in the car, you can make a game out of which direction the car travels. On a long straight road, cover up the compass and ask the children which direction they're now traveling. Let them determine the direction by first looking to see where the sun is in the sky, relative to the time of day.

When you stop and get out of the car, if there is a wind, ask which direction the wind is coming from, and then have them check the compass to see if they are correct.

When it's dark, teach the children about the night sky. Major newspapers usually have articles on the positions of the stars. National Geographic magazine and NASA's Web site on the Internet are other resources. From this data, one can use a compass to point one in the right direction to find planets and stars which are visible. Vice versa, one can use the stars and planets to determine compass direction, just like sailors do. I did this for my daughter, and now she's taught it to my granddaughter. Last Christmas, the gift my granddaughter wanted was a telescope to observe the night skies.

After turning at an intersection, tell your children the new direction the car is now traveling. Another example: "We've been traveling west, but when we get on the freeway we'll start going north." This is especially important when one gets on a freeway because, driving around a long, curving, freeway on-ramp, one can lose sense of direction and "get turned around."

Point out major landmarks and their compass direction as you drive. For instance, "Look to the west and you'll see the park we go to." By doing this, you'll develop in your children a sense of direction which will serve them well throughout their lives. Children can always learn this subject even better when they're a bit older, and they can read this book and study maps. Perhaps they can teach you, if it's something you never learned. But don't wait until then to start teaching them this valuable skill. Get another person to help, if needed.

Location – Where Am I?

If you move to a new home when your children are young, get them quickly oriented to the new place. Spend time with them. When we first arrive in a new area, we will naturally be confused unless we have a stable reference point, such as a landmark, to operate from. This is extremely important because the kids will be unsettled, due to the change in location. Find one major road that the children can relate to their new home. Continue to use that major road until the kids really know where they are, and only then is it wise to find a shorter, more direct route.

This is especially important if you have a good sense of direction. The better your sense of direction, the more inclined you will be to take a shorter, quicker route. But do this only when the kids can direct you the easier way.

You can use your previous home to give your children a better grasp of their new location, especially if they spent a long time at your previous residence. For example: "Before we moved, when we went to church it was very close to home and near your school. Now, the church we will be going to is farther away from our new home on the other side of the freeway."

Clear up any confusion your kids have with the location of their new home. They may confuse some things about the new place with the last place you lived. Find out, for example, if a gas station or store near the new home reminds them of a gas station or store which was near their old home.

Travel Routes

A sense of direction and familiarity with travel routes, even giving directions to others, can be developed at a very early age. I have a friend whose three-year-old daughter could direct her mother to places she'd been driven to only once before. The mother had not made any special effort to show the child the way. Her daughter had learned to do it without any encouragement.

This then leads to the possibility that, if a three year old can develop this ability, then most children could similarly learn how to get to places if they're assisted and encouraged to do so.

To teach your child how to direct you to go to places in your local area from a very early age, turn it into a game. Give the child the job of "navigator," and tell him, on this outing, he is going to give all the directions to get you to the destination. (Explain what "navigator" means, and what an important job it is.) When I visit my grandkids, I say I am not sure of the way to go and insist they give me directions when I am driving them around the areas that they should know.

If you give him this job, the child will pay attention to the road ahead and be on the lookout for signs. While a passenger, he'll learn valuable skills needed for his later driving and develop a sense of direction that will be invaluable in the years ahead.

Make an effort to explain the route you take when you drive with the children. Have them look ahead for the turnoff you are looking for. Tell them, for example, "We'll turn off this road soon to get to Grandpa's – do you remember how far and where the turn is? You watch and tell me when to turn."

Teach the children how to give others directions to their home. They've probably traveled the route often, but a school teacher won't necessarily have taught them this, so if you don't teach them, no one will. Show them how to give full directions to their home.

Example: "We live north of the city. Going north on I-45, get off at Brand Avenue, turn right and go east on Brand for five miles, another ten minutes drive. At the fifth traffic light, turn right on Cherry Avenue. It's a white house and our number 4762 is above the garage door." If your state has freeway exit numbers, the directions can include, "Get off on Brand, Exit 141." They can also say the name of the next major road before your street, e.g., "Brand is just after Colfax."

Don't Be Distracted By Carsick Kids

As a child, I was the kid in the family who got carsick. I thought I was the exception, but up to fifty percent of all children between the ages of two and twelve get carsick. So you need to know about carsickness because you don't need the distraction of a child vomiting in the back of the car as you drive.

The main prevention is to have a child who is prone to motion sickness keep his eyes on the horizon. Position any child who gets carsick so he can see out. The middle seat in the back lets them look forward to the horizon. If it's a real problem, buy a vehicle that can seat three across the front and let a motion sensitive child sit between his parents. No reading, watching videos, or playing computer games as you drive. Even now I get nauseous as a passenger when I spend too long studying a map.

Sing, talk and play games to get the kids looking out toward the horizon. If you have a motion sensitive child then make sure that you as a driver have your attention out far enough to view the horizon so that you can eliminate any unnecessary vehicle motion.

Stop often and let the kids stretch their legs. A breeze seems to help, so open a window. Before you encounter winding roads get the kids looking out. Observe your children for the typical motion sickness symptoms which include paleness, cold sweats, nausea and vomiting.

If your child goes pale or complains of feeling cold, realize it may be the first signs of carsickness. Take a brief driving break and once you are back on the road get them looking out.

If carsickness is a real problem, don't let it stop you from traveling. I have been told that homeopathic motion sickness tablets can work wonders especially if you don't want to use Dramamine.

Chapter 10

Braking

Young Children May Need to Use the Brakes

Teach your child what the dashboard instruments tell you. Show him which light comes on when the hand-pulled parking brake is on. The parking brake is also known as the "emergency brake" for good reason. On a very gentle slope, if your hand brake is between the seats, let the car roll forward and let him learn to use the hand brake to stop the car. This exercise needs to be done long before driving age. Knowing this, if he ever gets left in a parked car alone without a driver, he'll be able to stop the car if it starts to roll.

Make sure your child also knows which pedal is the foot brake. I have been near a car when it started to run down a hill by itself. The driver had left the car without putting on the parking brake, and I managed to run after the car, open the door and use the brakes. If this happened to your 13-year-old walking home from school would he know how to apply the brakes?

I once saw a TV news clip showing a school bus being stopped by a student passenger. The student used the brakes when the bus driver passed out. That demonstrates the need for our children to know how to use the brakes and to stop an out-of-control vehicle.

How Cars Stop

Many cars have computer-controlled anti-lock brake systems which prevent wheels from locking up, no matter how hard one pushes the brake pedal.

For cars without anti-lock brakes, explain to your children that if the wheels lock up when braking, you actually lose stopping power – because the wheels are no longer gripping the road but are now skidding (sliding) out of control. If this happens, you must ease off the brakes until the wheels have stopped skidding and push the brakes again.

A driver needs to know if the car he's driving has anti-lock brakes, because if it does, he needs to just hit the brakes hard and let the computer do the work of preventing wheel lock-up. Cars with anti-lock brakes usually give a pulsating feel to the pedal, and if this is not known and not expected, a driver may let off the brakes when he shouldn't.

If you drive a car with anti-lock brakes, you should apply the brakes hard in a practice situation, to get the "feel" of how they work and the pulsating sensation under your foot. Get the car up to 30 mph on a quiet street and apply the brake as hard as you can.

These are two totally different approaches to braking. You can ease off the brakes, if the car starts to skid, when you don't have anti-lock brakes. But if you do have anti-lock brakes, you slam on the brakes as hard as you can and let the car do the work. Keep in mind that anti-lock brakes don't work as well on snow or gravel, and it will take you longer to stop.

With anti-lock brakes, a car can be steered out of danger while you're braking hard. **Stomp, steer, stop!** Without anti-lock brakes, if the wheels lock up you won't be able to steer yourself out of trouble unless you quickly ease off and regain control.

When a car goes into a skid, the back end can try to catch up to the front of the car, and you can end up going down the road sideways or even facing the wrong way. This can happen when braking on a road wet with water or an oil slick, or on snow or ice. To correct this, simply steer in the direction the car should go.

During dry weather, roads get covered with a fine layer of oil that has dripped from vehicles. After a long period without rain, the road becomes extremely dangerous when a light rain first falls – it creates a very slippery surface of oil and water. After more rain the oil gets washed off the road.

I was once in Los Angeles when a light rain ended a year-long drought. My wife was out on an errand in the car, and I'd stayed home with our first child who was being breast fed at the time. With the onset of light rain, the freeways got extremely slippery, and there were so many accidents that traffic came to a standstill for several hours. My wife returned five hours later than expected and found me frantically trying to satisfy the baby's hunger by putting honey on a pacifier. (Giving honey to a baby is not recommended nowadays.)

Of course, any road surface that's wet requires driving with extra caution and reduced speed to be safe. But when there's a light rain on a previously long-dry road, it needs to be thought of as practically an ice-skating rink!

Brake Harder

Studies have shown that some drivers don't step on the brake hard enough in emergency situations. If you have anti-lock brakes, in an emergency they need to be applied with all the force you can muster. It is stomp, steer and stop because you can steer the car out of trouble while braking. You must have your car seat adjusted so that you can reach the brake pedal well enough to put maximum pressure on it with your right foot. That's your foot – not just the toes. If you can only touch the brake with your toes, you need to move the seat forward or get and fasten a "pedal extender" onto the brake pedal (available at dealers and auto supply stores).

A short teenager may have additional problems. You may need to adjust the height of the seat on vehicles which have that feature. He needs a good view of the road, as well as ability to reach the brakes. His shoulder needs to be at the same height as, or slightly above, the steering wheel. If needed, use a cushion to raise his height. If an outside mirror blocks his view of traffic, again use a seat cushion to put him higher.

He should also sit at least ten inches away from the air bag stored in the center of the steering wheel, to prevent injury from the bag if it inflates. When seated correctly, the center of the steering wheel should be pointed at the chest. If an air bag inflates, it's safer to hit the chest than the head.

Sometimes, pedal extenders are the only way to keep a short driver far enough away from the air bag, high enough for a good view and still reach the brake pedal. Some newer cars and pickups have adjustable pedals thus eliminating the need for pedal extenders. You should consider this when you're buying a new car that will be driven by a short driver now, or in the future.

Newer cars also come with height-adjustable shoulder belts. If a teenager or other person driving your car can't get comfortable with the seat belt, then look for this feature in your next car.

Prepare to Stop

If you read the road ahead, you hardly have to use your brakes. If you're looking far enough ahead, you'll see the traffic light change and can start slowing down before touching the brakes.

Once while riding with a friend I finally saw why he often had to have brake work done on his car. Even after seeing the light ahead was red, he would keep on driving at full speed until he was forced to apply his brakes hard to come to a sudden stop! That unnecessarily wears out the brakes quickly.

When I first learned to drive, we didn't depend on our brakes – they weren't always reliable. One 1934 sports car I owned had only "rod brakes." Steel rods running under the car, between the brake pedal and wheels, were used to apply the brakes. A 1936 car had cables running to the brakes on all four wheels, similar to those on today's emergency/parking brakes, or the cables to brakes on mountain bikes.

"Hydraulic" means "pushed or worked by the force of a moving liquid." Today's hydraulic brakes use a fluid to push the brakes on. The brake fluid travels in long, but narrow pipes called "brake lines." When you push the brake pedal, pressure is forced down the brake lines to the brakes on the wheels.

Fifty years ago, cars and trucks with early hydraulic brakes sometimes had to have the pedal pumped a few times before the brakes started to work. The pedal would go all the way to the floor (it would seem to have almost no resistance), but rapidly pumping the pedal several times would get the brakes working.

In today's cars, the brakes are worked by two separate systems. The right front and left rear wheels work together on one system, and the other two wheels work on a separate, second system. If one system fails, you still have brakes.

If you want to save money on brake jobs and be a safer driver, read the road ahead. Let the car slow down, foot off the gas, braking without having to apply the brakes hard. You should alert the cars behind that you will be slowing by touching the brake lightly to activate the brake light.

Just because you have brakes that work every time, explain to the kids how they don't need to be over-used. For this, slowing is better than stopping. If you can vary your speed to suit the circumstances and don't have to apply the brakes hard to stop you've saved your brakes unnecessary extra wear and also saved gas. If the light up ahead has been red for a long time, ease off the speed a little. You may get there just as it turns green – and really avoid having to apply the brakes at all.

An educational game to play with your kids is to pretend you have no brakes. Let the speed be reduced by taking your foot off the gas pedal. Have the kids tell you when to take your foot off the gas so you can stop at the red light ahead without having to touch the brakes. (You'll still have to brake a little to finally stop.)

When you read the road ahead, you may notice a slow-moving truck in your lane with traffic starting to build up behind it. If you have room to move over into the other lane and you do so, you won't have to use your brakes. By getting your children to read the road ahead, they can tell you when to ease off the gas and when to shift lanes. Have them get the feel of how to do this, long before they get behind the wheel.

When the freeway jams up, you often expect to see a disabled vehicle up ahead, but then you find no reason for the traffic to be stopped. Engineers have discovered new data about traffic jams that you need to know. It's quite simple: the solution is to keep rolling.

Braking hard on the freeway and coming to a stop can bring all the traffic behind you to a stop. When you see traffic slowing ahead try not to stop. Slow down but try to keep moving. The wrong thing to do is to brake hard, come to a complete stop, then race ahead only to stop again. If you can keep moving at a slower speed, it prevents cars behind you from having to stop – therefore the cars behind don't back up and cause another slowdown.

Gas to Brakes Instantly

Before reaching driving age a child should be taught how to stop the car with the brake pedal. If you teach your child to drive, you don't want to yell "stop!" and have the child miss the brake pedal or hit the gas! Hitting the wrong pedal can add a bit too much excitement to your day! It's easy to teach him braking, because you can have your child drill (practice) braking when the car is parked in your driveway.

He should be approaching driving age, because he needs to be big enough to fit comfortably behind the wheel and reach the brakes. Get him behind the wheel and adjust the seat. Use an extra cushion if necessary. With the car in the driveway and the engine off, have him practice working the gas and brake pedals. Have him move his foot quickly from the gas to the brake. He can either brake hard or barely touch it; both should be practiced.

Drill them by saying, "Touch the brake – speed up – hit the brake hard – ease off the brake – speed up," etc., until the child has good control over the leg movement needed to hit the brake pedal. Once your child can do this correctly, let him sit in the car and practice moving his leg back and forth from the gas to the brake without your supervision.

Next, you drive the car with your child in the front passenger seat, and have him move his right foot from an imaginary gas pedal to an imaginary brake pedal, as if he were actually driving. When you slow down for a traffic light, tell your child if you had to use the brakes hard, or only very lightly. This will give your child an idea of how much braking it takes to stop a car, and he can see if he was judging it correctly when he applied his imaginary brake.

As a driving instructor, the first thing I would do is have the student sit in a parked car and practice quickly hitting the brake. Between lessons, while he was a passenger in a car or bus, I would also tell him to imagine he was driving and move his foot to the imaginary brake from the imaginary gas pedal.

If he still didn't have it, I would insist that he practice moving his foot from an imaginary gas to imaginary brake pedal while sitting in school or watching TV or whatever. I wanted to be totally certain that the new driver knew how to stop the car without having to think about moving his foot.

As an experienced driver, if you're a passenger in an emergency situation, you'll find yourself trying to hit the brake as you sit in the passenger seat. You can develop this as an automatic response in your child – to stop the car without thinking about what to do, before he even starts to drive. By doing just this you will make him a lot safer for you or another person to teach when he actually learns how to drive.

This is a good drill to teach to a nervous passenger because it increases their understanding of how a car is driven and practicing applying a pretend brake will give him something to do besides worrying about something he does not understand.

Shifting Sticks Can Begin at an Early Age

I have a friend, Chris, whose mother drove a stick shift when he was a child. Starting at age nine, while sitting in the front passenger's seat, Chris shifted the gear stick into the next gear as his mother worked the clutch.

When I discussed this with Chris he realized that he had also learned to observe the road and traffic, as well as shift the gear stick. He had done this for seven years before he actually drove a car at age 16. Chris realized that this early learning experience was the reason he had never had an accident.

If it is possible, have a stick shift as one of your cars so your children will be able to observe how you shift gears. I have two friends who successfully drove a stick at their first attempt because they had carefully observed how it was done. Also if a child passenger manipulates the gear stick, the action will develop driving skills and coordination to shift gears.

Later in the "Teach Your Teen to Drive" section you will find a simple way of teaching stick shifts. See Chapter 22.

Chapter 11

Defensive Driving

Preventing Accidents

Your children must understand that we've been using the word "accident" when we should have used the word "collision" or "crash". An accident is something that happens by chance, with an unknown or unpreventable cause. When dealing with horses in the early days of transportation, accidents happened over which the drivers had no control. Horses sometimes got spooked and bolted (made sudden, mad dashes ahead). With the introduction of motor vehicles, accidents could happen because of a lack of engineering know-how. A new tire could fail, or a wheel could fall off while in motion due to a faulty design, resulting in an accident beyond the driver's control.

These days, car manufacturers get hit with massive lawsuit awards against them if the accidents that caused injury or death were due to design faults or equipment failure. Most accidents due to equipment failure are the result of the driver not replacing worn-out tires or other car parts.

Road engineers have designed roads to be safe. When something about a road is causing collisions, the way the road is constructed is then changed.

A real accident happens when an earthquake destroys a bridge, for example, and a car runs off the end of it. It would have been unavoidable. Have your child figure out what kinds of accidents are unavoidable. Then have him figure out which "accidents" are preventable. He will realize that most car collisions are preventable. One or more of the drivers involved is wholly or partly responsible. Whenever you come across an accident, see if the kids can "work out" who caused it.

"Defensive driving" means recognizing that collisions can be prevented, and doing everything possible to prevent them. The airline industry follows this sensible approach. When an airplane falls out of the sky, sometimes the whole airline or, more often, all planes of that same model are grounded –

because it was not "an act of God," but rather a preventable "accident." In the case of the 1996 Value Jet crash in Florida, the crash was caused by things just not being done right and training was not at the level necessary for the airline employees to act responsibly. The plane was carrying explosive material that should never have been on the plane.

In 2007 only 965 people worldwide died in accidents involving planes big enough to carry at least six passengers plus crew. Compare this to the 1.2 million people killed each year in car crashes worldwide.

It's easy to see that car driver training today is not nearly as good as most airline training, because if as many people died in airline accidents in America as in car accidents, a jumbo jet would have to crash every other day!

Part of defensive driving is to "leave yourself an out," meaning a way out to prevent an accident. For example, position your car so that you have open spaces on at least one side in case you may need to suddenly change lanes to prevent a collision. Don't simply drive alongside another vehicle if it is at all possible to avoid doing so. If there's no choice but to drive beside a large truck for a time, don't get involved with other distractions while in that dangerous position – be extra alert for that period of time. (I've seen drivers dial numbers on their cell phones while running alongside my big-rig truck.) Move over, behind, or ahead as soon as you can. Always try to keep as big a "space cushion" as possible around your car. The bigger the space and the more visibility you have, the better your chances are of getting out of dangerous situations.

Even though you have a green light, still look left and right, with the knowledge that drivers waiting at a red light, or approaching a red light, will sometimes jump ahead just before the light changes. Especially watch for this when you're approaching a light that has been green for a long time and is about to turn yellow, or has already turned yellow.

Defensive driving is about communicating with other drivers and letting them know what you intend to do. You can communicate with your turn signals, horn, and lights and when possible establish eye contact with other drivers or pedestrians to become reasonably sure of their intentions. Teach your children the importance of using all signals for safety. There is another very important signal that some drivers don't use – the brake lights. Your brake lights are your most important way to communicate to a driver behind you and they must be used when slowing down, especially on a fast-moving freeway when traffic is heavy.

As a truck driver, I find the biggest menaces on the road are drivers who decide to reduce speed but don't signal with their brake lights that they intend to slow down. When you "cover the brakes," you move your right foot off the gas pedal and lightly touch or tap the brake pedal – just enough to make the brake lights go on. Don't push down hard enough to apply the brakes (unless of course you need to). By putting your foot lightly on and off the brake pedal, you attract the attention of vehicles behind you.

Drivers depend on the brake lights of cars in front of them. The moment a brake light shows on a car ahead, a driver will automatically "cover" or use his own brakes, in case there's a situation where he has to slow down or stop. A safe driver warns the drivers behind him that he may need to quickly stop, and in so doing he prevents himself from being rear-ended if he does have to stop quickly.

When going uphill, a car can slow down quite rapidly after the foot is taken off the gas pedal. If the brake pedal is not "covered" and the brake lights activated, then the driver behind doesn't get the message that the car ahead is slowing down. This then puts the driver behind in a dangerous position, because he now forced to slow down quickly, having had no advance warning that he needed to do so from the driver ahead.

In a sudden downpour of rain, all too often drivers will suddenly slow down without covering their brakes and activating the brake lights. With visibility already reduced by the heavy rain, the drivers behind now face the menace of some nervous driver in front slowing down without telling them what they are doing. If weather conditions make you want to drive slower, "cover" your brakes before you start to slow down.

Some states require that headlights be turned on anytime the windshield wipers are turned on, even if it's mid-day. Even if there is no such law in your state, this is a good defensive driving action. When rain causes poor visibility, it makes perfect sense to turn your lights on – so you can be seen better by others.

Your four-way hazard lights are also a good tool to communicate that something up ahead is not right. If you see the traffic ahead is stopped, you can put on your hazard lights to warn those behind you of the problem ahead. But please turn them off once the driver behind you has stopped, because it can be irritating to be sitting in traffic with flashing lights in one's eyes.

A defensive driver learns to "give" a little to prevent crashes – meaning he'll allow for others to be distracted or make mistakes. It also means he changes his driving to take into account weather conditions. He even recognizes how he feels, and if he knows he's not as alert as usual, he won't drive as fast. If he has just had a personal upset, he'll take a walk to "get his head together" and become calmer before he gets behind the wheel.

He will take everything into account: The way he feels, the weather, road conditions, the number of other vehicles and pedestrians around him and even the time of day. Are other drivers alert or could they be not fully awake yet if it's early morning? At night could they be tired or drunk if it's closing time for bars? What's the mood of other drivers? Are they busy getting to work and know what needs to be done or are they on a "Sunday drive" (more sightseeing than paying attention to traffic) where they could do unpredictable things? Maybe a collision has delayed traffic and other drivers will now be bad tempered and in a hurry because they're behind schedule.

Defensive driving is also knowing the condition of your own vehicle and recognizing the condition of other vehicles around you. If a car is old and not maintained on the outside (you can see dents and dings), then its brakes, tires, and steering are likely to be in a similar poor condition.

Defensive driving includes being aware of how you feel, the conditions of your vehicle and other cars, the road surface, traffic, weather, time of day, mood and alertness of other drivers. With all of the above taken into consideration, you must then teach your children to adapt their driving habits according to the existing conditions.

I did not drum this into my daughter's head well enough. She had a cute little 20-year-old car that she knew could go around a certain tight corner at 40 mph. One day a light drizzle made the road dangerous and she slid her little car into the guard rail and put a big dent in the fender. That corner was just two miles from home and she probably drove around it almost every day, always at the same fast speed. By not taking the weather into account and not "giving" a little, she damaged the car she loved.

Whenever you notice conditions have changed, you must be prepared to "give" a little on one's usual habits. Also point this out to your children, ensure they well understand and practice this, and you will do a better job than I did.

When Traffic Lights Change

When approaching a green light that may turn yellow or to handle any confusion and uncertainty about when to stop and when you should keep on going, you need to determine a safe "point of no return." That means you decide on a point ahead at which (a) you'll begin to stop if the light has already turned yellow, or (b) you'll keep on driving through the intersection if the light is still green.

If the light turns red for any length of time before you've passed all the way through the intersection then you've misjudged your point of no return. The point of no return needs to be moved farther away from the intersection.

The "Walk/Don't Walk" signs are a clue as to how much time you have on a green light. This especially applies if the sign is counting down the number of seconds left for the pedestrians to cross.

Some traffic lights have a longer yellow phase than others. The higher the speed limit, the longer the light stays yellow so as to give the faster moving cars more time to stop. By choosing a point of no return, you'll avoid dangerous sudden stops and not have to make a last-second decision: "Should I stop or speed up?"

Once you start doing this you'll learn to judge it well, and worrying about a light changing won't be a problem anymore. You can establish points of no return for lights you cross often. In areas where you don't usually drive, if the light ahead has been green for some time, determine a point of no return as you approach it.

Teach this to your children. Let them work out their own points of no return as you drive through traffic lights. Let them look to see if the light stayed yellow as you drove through it. By learning how to choose decision points which become points of no return, your children will later have no fear of traffic lights changing. They will no longer have to suddenly stop because a light changed. There will no longer be a need to speed up to avoid running a red light. With this ability, your children will gain another way to make driving less scary.

Swerving

You should swerve for deer or elk because when hit they've been known to go straight through the windshield and kill all the people inside the vehicle. An animal never backs up so, if it's moving, expect it to keep coming towards you. Try to swerve behind the animal if you can.

However, it's not wise to swerve to avoid a small animal such as a cat or dog. My own children needed a lot of convincing about this, thinking that a child's pet needed to be looked after. I had to explain that I will brake for a cat, but if I were to swerve to avoid one – and run off the road, hurting or killing a passenger – it would be a lot worse than running over a cat. I explained that even if one doesn't swerve for the animal, there's still a good chance it won't get hit; after all if you do swerve, the animal may swerve too and run into your new path. I once explained this to a student driver, and he said, "Yes, I know one shouldn't swerve – my father swerved for a dog on this road we're now on, and he skidded off the road and wrecked his car."

I explain that the time one should swerve to avoid something is when a car is coming straight toward you – then do all you can to avoid a head-on collision, because those are the accidents which often kill people. It's better to hit a fixed object than an on-coming vehicle. When a head-on collision occurs, both cars come to a sudden halt. So it is the combined speed of both cars that creates so much damage. It is much better to run off the road into vegetation than to stay on the road and have a head-on collision. When avoiding a collision, you'll be in better control and safer if you aim for something soft, not something hard. Every race car driver knows this one. If you lose control, look at something which won't hurt you if you hit it. If you fixate on a solid object, you will hit it.

A glancing blow, not hitting head-on, will increase your chance of survival if you do have to hit an on-coming vehicle or a fixed object. Your hitting of a vehicle which is moving in the same direction as you are, or even hitting a stationary vehicle, will give you a better chance of survival than hitting an on-coming vehicle head-on.

Sometimes it may look like the correct way to swerve to avoid a head-on collision is to swerve to the left and go onto the wrong side of the road. However, should a car be coming straight at you, and there is room for you to go over to your left to avoid him – don't! Forget movie stunts. He can (and often does) suddenly pull to your left – at the last split second! So instead, you should stay to the right and swerve or move to the right to avoid a car coming toward you. Just keep moving your steering wheel to the right, away from the other car.

I had a friend who found herself in this position once. She told me her strongest instinct was to pull her car to the left to avoid the car coming toward her. But she knew she shouldn't, because the approaching driver, at any instant, could realize that he was on the wrong side of the road and suddenly pull his car correctly to her left. That's exactly what the on-coming driver did. So, by her steering the correct way, to her right, there was no collision. Had she had steered to the left – which at first looked like the way out – there would have been a head-on collision.

No matter how tempting it may appear to go around an approaching car the wrong side, don't. Steer hard to your right, blasting your horn as you do so to attract the attention of the on-coming car. Turning on your headlights or flashing the high beams also helps get his attention (an action often used by experienced motorcyclists). The moment he sees you, he will pull back to his correct side of the road, and all should be well.

Blind Spots and Mirrors

Teach your children about "blind spots." Blind spots are any areas a driver can't easily see, not even with correctly adjusted mirrors. These are mainly areas unseen in the limited view which mirrors show. The most important blind spot areas are to the left and to the right of the driver. See the illustration below.

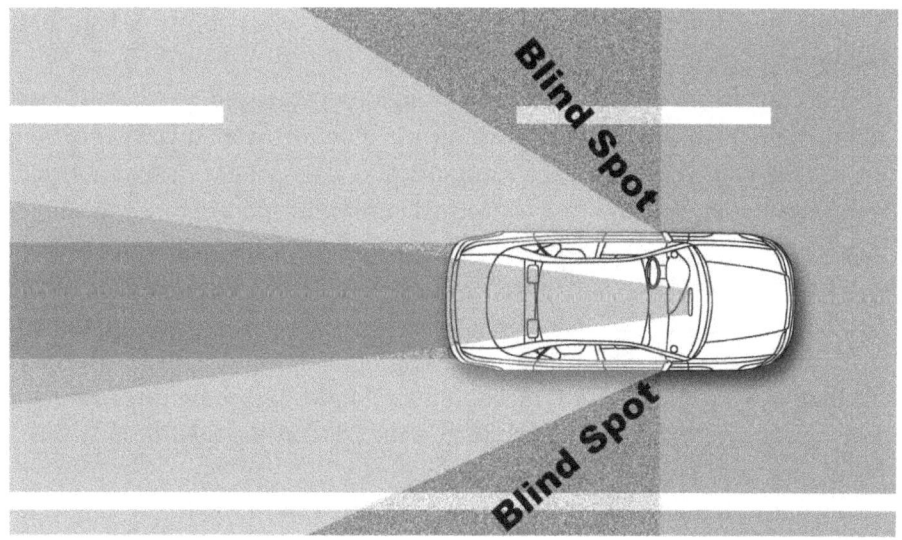

The driver must turn his head to view the blind spot to his left or right.

Blind spots that can't be seen in the mirrors to the left or right must be checked by turning your head to see if anything is there. It's important to turn your head and look first before moving or turning the car (especially to the right). Small objects, such as a motorcycle, bicycle or pedestrian, can be hidden in the blind spot where your mirrors don't show them.

Today, traffic congestion in many cities makes mirrors one of the most important tools a driver has. Anytime you switch from driving one car to another, always take a moment to check and adjust the mirrors. Properly adjusted mirrors don't eliminate blind spots, but they do reduce the size of them. Modern cars have power adjustment controls inside which are easy to use, so you should always take a moment to check and adjust them correctly as needed – every time you get in a car. Teaching your children this could save their lives and the lives of others.

When checking your mirrors, it's very important that you focus your eyes on what you see. If you just scan what the mirror shows, but don't focus on what's reflected, you will miss seeing something that's there. If needed, take a second look if you didn't see all you wanted to on the first glance.

When you turn or move your head to check the blind spots, move your head, but not your hands. There's a natural tendency for the hands to follow in the same direction as the eyes. Some drivers will start to steer the car over in the direction they're looking at as they check their blind spots. So practice keeping your hands steady on the steering wheel when you turn your head to look.

Cars accelerate much faster today than a few years ago, so you also need to be aware of that and check your mirrors more often for a fast car coming up behind you. It could be up alongside you a lot sooner than you expect, so always signal, and check your mirrors and blind spots before you start to change lanes.

Show your children the blind spots. While driving and about to change lanes, tell them and ask: "I am going to move to the right; is there anything in my right blind spot?" This will do two things: It will help you make sure there's nothing in your blind spot (you should also look), but more importantly, it will educate your children on the importance of turning their head to check blind spots and reinforce left/right awareness.

By understanding blind spots at an early age, a child will know to not ride a bike in a vehicle's blind spot and risk being killed when the vehicle turns.

The easiest way to teach a child where the blind spots are is for you to sit in the driver's seat while parked, and have the child slowly move around outside the car, and you tell him when he's in view of the mirrors and when he's not. Also, when a child is tall enough, have him sit in the driver's seat (or kneel, depending on how big his body is), and then you move around the outside, in and out of the blind spots, and have him tell you when he can't see you in the mirrors. Sometimes I find this is the only way to get students to learn what blind spots are.

A passenger can sometimes use a mirror on his sun visor to see what is happening to the rear. Unfortunately, there are no outside mirrors a passenger can watch to see what a driver sees, so using outside mirrors is one thing which can't be taught from a passenger's viewpoint. This may change when there are TV monitors that replace mirrors.

Two last points: It's important not to place your car in another vehicle's blind spot – especially that of a large truck. Change your position by speeding up or slowing down, and get out of danger. Likewise, if a car is in your blind spot, change your speed to get away from such an ignorant or inexperienced driver. When your children understand the dangers of blind spots they can warn you when a vehicle is running beside you in a position that you are not able to see.

Left Turns

When you drive with kids in the car, it's a lot less stressful if you avoid making left turns. Look over your regular routes of travel and see if you could make your drive less stressful. Left hand turns should be avoided whenever possible. Left turns result in much more damaging crashes than right turns because left ones often involve head-on collisions. When you turn right, you have to watch for a break in traffic coming from only one direction. Plan your trips to avoid dangerous left turns onto busy streets where there is no traffic light.

I once lived on a residential street that intersected with a nearby busy street, and for most of my trips around town I needed to turn left onto it. Since there were no lights to control the traffic, I started going the other way from home, driving around the block to a street which did have traffic lights. I drove only a little farther, but was saved the hassle of turning left into a busy street, and as a result I avoided long waits for a break in traffic.

UPS has programmed their delivery vans and trucks so that they make only right-hand turns, and they report that this has resulted in a substantial savings in gas and time.

Your kids should be taught the danger of making left turns so that when they do ride their bikes, they can do so more safely by only making right turns when the traffic is heavy.

Pedestrians at Lights

You need to teach your children what traffic to watch for when they cross a street at a pedestrian cross walk where a traffic light controls cars and pedestrians. Even though they will have a white "walk" signal, permitting them to cross the street, they need to know where to look for cars that may have run a red light. They also need to know where to look for cars that are turning and by law, should yield to pedestrians, but don't because the driver is being inattentive. These inattentive drivers may have more attention on a phone conversation than actually looking out for pedestrians.

Pedestrian survival can be taught as you wait at traffic lights in your car. Show your children the directions from which vehicles may approach pedestrians crossing the street. This will teach them the directions to look, to make sure they don't get hit by a car running a red light, or by a car turning at a cross walk without noticing and waiting for pedestrians.

When in the car waiting at traffic lights, make good use of the time you spend waiting by showing your children how cars must yield to pedestrians.

If your children have to walk to school and use crosswalks controlled by traffic lights, walk with them and show them the directions from which the cars approach. Make it very real to them that, if they cross the street from the opposite side, they have to watch for inattentive drivers approaching them from a different direction.

Sounds of the Road

The wail of an approaching emergency vehicle's siren means action will be required by the driver. Your children should know that cars are required by law to pull over to let emergency vehicles with flashing red lights pass through. Let them tell you what to do. Later on, as a new driver, when this unexpectedly happens to them (as it always will), their "built-in" response of what to do will take over.

Other sounds that your kids should know about are noises coming from the car telling them that something may be wrong. If the fan belt slips and squeals, point it out to the children before you have it fixed. If the brakes squeal, it may be because a stone has become stuck between the brake lining and the metal brake drum. It may be more serious than that and it may mean the brake linings or pads need to be replaced because metal is now touching metal. If this happens, explain it to the children so they can recognize the noise should they hear it sometime in the future.

A thump-thump noise means that it is tire trouble and that you either have a flat tire or part of your tire tread has come off.

Kids have more sensitive hearing than adults so teach them that hearing loss can result from playing an iPod too loudly.

When you hear tires screeching, have the kids figure out why some driver had to come to a screeching stop and who was in the wrong, or help explain it to them.

Also teach them that hearing loss can result from playing a stereo too loudly. Standing too close to big stage speakers at a rock concert can also damage hearing. Teach them that to be a good driver, one must be able to hear well, in addition to seeing what is going on around the vehicle.

Report Even Minor Accidents

A car was behind Clarence as he waited on his bicycle for the light to change. Clarence was on his way to work so he was on familiar ground, and he felt safe until the driver behind him pulled up on his left side and turned right. Clarence was not turning right, he was going straight ahead and he ended up being knocked to the ground. The driver apparently failed to see Clarence, even though he was a big man of dominating stature.

I met Clarence at work an hour later, and he was still mad as he showed me his grazed arm. It turned out that this was the second time he'd been knocked off his bike by a driver simply not seeing him there. Both times, Clarence got mad, dusted himself off, and made no attempt to get any information about the driver who'd hit him.

I pointed out to Clarence that when a car rear-ends me, even if it looked like my car wasn't damaged, I always got the license plate number, car model, driver's name, address, and phone number – just in case later, on closer inspection, I found that some hidden damage had been done. Clarence had exactly that happen to him, on another occasion when his car was rear-ended no rear-end damage was visible. When he later thoroughly checked his car for damage, he found the car's frame had been bent in the accident and consequently a back door wouldn't open. Clarence realized that when he was knocked off his bike, he may have received a bodily injury which could need medical care in the future, even though no symptoms were immediately apparent. So he decided that if he ever got knocked off his bike again, he wouldn't get so mad, but would start writing and get the license plate number and car model, plus driver's name and address, if possible.

He also realized that he should have gotten the police involved. If that driver hadn't seen Clarence's big body, then he was even more likely to not see, and maybe even kill, a small child on a bike. So the next time, should Clarence get knocked over by an absent-minded driver, he's going to ask another driver with a cell phone to call the police. He now believes the police should investigate and handle the matter to see if the driver is drunk or on drugs.

Another friend, Bill, was also hit by a car as a pedestrian. The driver stopped and asked, "Are you all right?" Having a positive outlook, Bill replied, "I think so," and so the driver left. Bill wasn't okay. He needed immediate surgery to pin a broken bone!

You should likewise make your children familiar with what they should do if they are knocked off their bikes or hit as pedestrians. At least get the car's license plate number, so you can report the driver to the police.

Backing Skills and Toys

Toys can be used to teach things like steering and backing. Unlike sitting in a car, the child can see the wheels actually turn, and learn how the steering mechanism works. Learning to drive can start at an early age, by playing with toys.

I once had a student who had taught himself the basic skills of how to back up a car, by backing up his bicycle. From that, he learned which way to turn when going backwards.

My young brother spent many hours playing with a toy tractor and trailer as a child. The tractor could be steered by using the steering wheel. He learned to back not only a car, but also an attached trailer, long before he was big enough to see over the dashboard of a real vehicle.

Large play mats can be purchased that have roads, traffic lights, and driving situations for toy cars. Children should be encouraged to play with these and can be taught when to stop and when to go to avoid accidents. Toy tractors that can be steered can be bought with fittings to tow trailers, so very young children can also be taught the skill necessary to back a trailer.

Take the children to a boat launching ramp, and show them that by practicing backing a toy trailer, they will develop a skill they can use later in life to back a boat on a trailer down a steep and narrow boat launch ramp.

I use a toy to demonstrate how to back a large truck and trailer when I'm teaching someone to drive a Big-Rig. It lets them see the mechanics (physical motions) involved in what actually happens – and see it from a viewpoint not available without having a small toy which can be seen from above.

Your Strength is to Know your Weaknesses

I am not a perfect driver. I have my weaknesses, but I know what they are and drive accordingly. Most drivers consider that they are good drivers and have no idea what their weaknesses are. Your strength is to know your weaknesses. I know what will distract me. As I'm a car nut, I will fixate on some unusual car that I don't instantly recognize. Since I'm aware of this, I force myself not to fixate but to take a second look.

With age, night vision can deteriorate. An average 60-year old perceives light about one-third as well as a 20-year old. I can have trouble seeing ahead when other trucks are going 15 mph faster than I am, and they seem able to see the road just fine.

If your night vision is not as good as that of a young person, have one of the children look ahead for the turnoff. Also, by telling your kids or grandkids, "Your eyesight is better than mine," they'll stop fighting and help you look for what you need.

I can also be an impatient driver and follow the car in front of me too closely, as I try to hurry to get somewhere. If you are like me and expect things to happen more quickly around you, realize this is a driving weakness and make a deliberate effort to have at least two seconds distance between you and the car in front.

The accident rate in the U.S. was declining for many years, but since about the late 1990s that trend stopped and more accidents have been occurring. Some experts think that drivers are becoming more aggressive and won't give a little to prevent an accident. If you are an aggressive type, realize this is a weakness as far as driving is concerned. Make sure you're not following too closely. Before you change lanes be certain that its all clear. Realize that you save very little time by being aggressive so go with the flow of traffic and relax and enjoy the drive.

You may not be aggressive enough. You may wait too long before pulling out into traffic, causing vehicles to stack up behind you. It's been my observation that waiting too long most often happens when a driver doesn't notice there's an empty lane for him to pull into.

If you don't know your driving weaknesses, ask your family. The kids will probably be dead right about what they observe. Let your children know your weak points as a driver, so they don't pick up your bad habits. If the children know your weak points, they may even be able to assist you on those things.

Fear Makes Poor Drivers

There is a lot of fear-instilling and false information given to children by adults on the subject of driving. Some examples are: You must always drive slowly, you have to drive very carefully, other drivers are always in the wrong, speed kills, don't drive as fast as your father, etc. (When I heard that last one about a father I found out that the mother drove much too slowly and interfered with normal traffic flow while the father actually drove at the correct speed.)

I once rescued a student from another driving instructor who, for four lessons, had the student do nothing but creep around a quiet area, only in first gear, and without once putting his foot on the gas pedal. My first lesson consisted of explaining the facts of speed to this firm believer in "speed kills." I told him it's often the slow drivers who hug the center line and won't keep to the right who cause accidents. By driving slower than the normal traffic flow, other drivers behind them get impatient and try to pass. Because of their pent-up frustration after being held up for a long time, perhaps not wanting to be late for an appointment, they will pass at an incorrect time and have an accident. Such an accident wouldn't happen if there wasn't a slow driver ahead.

So then I would ask a "must drive slow" learner: "Do you want someone to get hurt because of your slowness?" When he says no, I then would tell him, "If that's the case, you must forget what you've been told about driving slowly, because it's a lie."

Children must learn that it's not necessary to always drive "slowly" and "carefully," but rather to drive confidently, sensibly and to keep up with the normal traffic flow.

Children, especially nervous ones, should not be continually told that driving is dangerous, and shouldn't be told that they must not drive fast. It's much more productive to give them positive, helpful data, than to fill them with fears by always bringing up the negative or bad aspects of things. Life is to be lived confidently, not fearfully. Driving is part of most people's lives so let's raise our children to look forward to the time when they can drive, with a high expectation of the enjoyment they will get from being behind the wheel.

Chapter 12

Set a Good Example

Multitasking While Driving

As congestion increases and people are increasingly stuck in traffic, there is an effort to utilize the time that many consider wasted. Hence, drivers multitask and do other things while they drive. If the multitasking driver gets distracted and hits something, it is usually not fatal at slow speeds. Being rear-ended by a driver sending a text message at 20 mph may ruin your day, but no one dies.

When multitasking becomes an established pattern, and it's not just being done while sitting in traffic but is done when traffic is moving fast, death can result. Law enforcement agencies now check cell phone records to see if a driver was being distracted by talking or texting on his cell at the time of a bad accident.

When traffic is stop and go, moving slowly, there are many first person stories about fender benders when a driver was distracted by multitasking. I cannot give you first person examples of accidents caused by attempting to multitask at high speeds. All I can do is refer you to the funeral notices one all too often sees for inexperienced teenage drivers and their friends or young family members.

When Multitasking Makes Sense

New research from England shows that some people who were listening while doodling (drawing random things on a piece of paper) could recall what they were listening to better than those who were not doodling.

This research found that someone doing a boring task may have their mind wander and start to daydream. Daydreaming may distract them from the task at hand. As a result they will not handle a task as well or drive as safely as they should.

This explained a lot to me. While driving in light traffic I can listen to instructional type lectures and have no trouble understanding and remembering the new concepts that I am taught. I can keep my attention on what the speaker is saying without daydreaming. When I have the mindless task of driving the open freeway, it's a lot like the doodling example. I drive and listen just like listening on the phone while doodling increases one's concentration.

I have also found that I cannot listen to instructional lectures at home when all I do is sit and listen. My mind starts to wander and I daydream.

How does all this apply to driving? I have had drivers who can only concentrate on driving, without even a radio playing. I am like this. When traffic is heavy I turn the radio off and do nothing that may interfere with my concentration on driving.

I once turned the radio off when I thought an inexperienced female truck driver needed to concentrate on traffic and find the exit we were looking for. This action of mine upset her. I thought that she was a very irresponsible driver that was trying to do too many things at once. This recent research suggests that she was not being irresponsible as she was able to concentrate better with background music.

Music and singing throughout history have been a part of mindless work. Slaves sang while picking cotton and almost all cultures have had singing as part of their work. Even soldiers have sung while marching.

I did further research and found that women seem to have a better ability to multitask than men. This makes sense if we look back to living in caves when we were hunters and gatherers. The men were the hunters who needed, without any other distractions, to concentrate on the kill. The women did the gathering of seeds and edible plants as well as cooking while always having their attention split between their work and what the children were doing. After all she couldn't let a child fall into the fire or be eaten by a wild animal as she did her work.

As time evolved women would knit or create handcrafts or even iron as they talked or helped with the children's homework. With the advent of the Internet and e-mail, those who like to multitask will check their in-box or play solitaire on the computer as they chat on the phone.

Older brothers and fathers who have spent time looking after young children will be more inclined to multitask, as they have learned to do things while keeping an eye on the kids. My son tells me that if he wants to have a serious conversation with his sister he has found that it is best to talk to her as she works in the kitchen. He has found he can hold her attention better if she is doing something with her hands while she listens.

I have learned not to cause an upset by turning the TV off so my granddaughter can concentrate solely on her homework. It seems she does her homework better when she is watching a mindless TV show.

For a long time, I considered that just being in a car together increases conversation. Now it seems that it is not just being in a small space together. Rather, it is also viewing the changing scenery that creates the mindless doodling-type distraction that increases concentration for the important conversation that can take place in a car.

How does this apply to driving safety? I now realize we operate in two different modes, and I think of them as the "hunter mode" and the "gatherer mode."

When I am driving and need to concentrate, I am in the hunter mode. I need to turn the radio off or stop talking on the phone or to a passenger. In the same way as a hunter goes for a kill, I concentrate my attention on exactly what I am doing so I don't get killed.

When there is little traffic and the road is long and straight, driving can become a mindless job. When I find my attention wandering, I realize that I need to operate in a gatherer mode so I split my attention between the road and some other task. This is when I will try to find something of interest on the radio or control my daydreaming by deliberately thinking through some idea while I drive.

One of my truck drivers will chat to his wife on the phone to stop daydreaming and nodding off and going to sleep, when not much is happening on the road to keep his attention occupied.

I should have let my kids doodle when I was trying to explain things. They would have better recalled my words of wisdom and I may even have produced an artist to illustrate my writings.

So, explain to your kids when one should drive in the hunter mode and when one should operate in the gatherer mode. Your kids will then not interrupt you when they see you need to keep your attention on traffic but will understand why you can play games and chat when traffic is light.

Multitasking and Cell Phones

Multitasking is seen as a good thing, but further research points out its weaknesses. You can't do two things at once if those things involve the same part of the brain. You can walk and talk at the same time, but this does not apply to driving and talking on a cell phone. Talking on a cell phone, and driving, uses the same part of the brain. When driving you need to read the road ahead and envision where to go. You also use the same part of the brain to imagine what the caller is talking about as you get in deep conversation on a cell phone. This becomes a distraction.

A simple call like, "what time will you be home Dear?", is not going to distract you because you are already observing the traffic conditions as a driver and you can quickly say "traffic is good, I will be home in 20 minutes." Calls that get you to envision what is occurring somewhere else or is going to happen in the future distract you from envisioning and predicting what is happening while you drive. This is when accidents happen.

You can use a cell phone wisely as you drive providing you understand when cell phone use becomes a distraction. You will need to get this across to your kids before they get behind the wheel.

Cell Phones

Cell phones – dialing for disaster? A British study found that drivers using cell phones have slower reaction times than drunk drivers! It's not just the distraction while dialing, though hands-free features do help. Such features won't help if you become involved in a conversation and lose your concentration on the road and traffic. It's been found that drivers tend to stare straight ahead when on a cell phone. If you start to envision what the caller is talking about in your head instead of seeing all that is going on around the car, this is when you are being distracted by the phone call.

Experts suggest that you should pull over before you make a call, and right after taking one. Here's just one of the good reasons why: You wouldn't let yourself be distracted by another person in the office when you're on the phone. Why would you give someone you're negotiating with an advantage because you're distracted by traffic?

When you need your attention on the road let a passenger answer the phone. When the kids are old enough to do so, let them handle your phone as you drive. Not only will you be setting a good example, you can help develop your kids' telephone handling skills. I find I have better conversations with my granddaughter when she answers the phone while her mother is driving. At home she is too busy to talk to me but it seems that as she watches the passing scenery as a passenger from a moving car she can develop the skill of chatting on the phone.

For incoming calls while in heavy traffic, let the phone ring. You won't miss the call, since all phones now have voice mail and will record the caller's message. Of course, this isn't necessary when traffic conditions are good, but if you need to pay attention to traffic, be willing either to not answer or if you already have, be willing to tell your caller, "Traffic is bad – let me call you back," and end the call.

When you're calling someone who's driving, don't distract him any more than necessary. You wouldn't let anyone drive drunk, so why distract someone by talking about problems which could give that person a slower reaction time than a drunk driver? Let the problems wait until you have the person's full attention.

Problems with cell phones and driving have often been in the news. One law firm is being sued because one of their lawyers had a fatal accident while on the phone. Personally, I think a lawyer's client should also sue, if the lawyer is billing him for hours spent talking while driving. The lawyer should have his attention either fully on driving when in traffic or fully on the client if dealing with complex legal matters – one or the other. When you pay lawyers the high hourly rate they charge, you don't want them trying to avoid a collision while they try to solve your legal problems.

You may well ask, "What's the difference between talking with my passengers, and talking on the phone while I'm driving?" Let me explain. Most passengers are experienced drivers who don't make conversational demands on a driver when they know he needs his full attention on driving – especially when the passenger can see a traffic situation. A caller can't see it. Also, a passenger will be watching the road and may notice something the driver missed seeing and tell him, if the driver is distracted by the conversation.

Someone talking to a driver on a cell phone doesn't see and doesn't know what the traffic situation is unless he's told. Many times we don't even know we're talking business to someone being distracted by traffic. Before you get involved in a long or attention-demanding conversation ask, "Are you driving?" If the person is driving, play it safe and call him back later.

Cell phones have even turned parking lots into dangerous places. It seems that some drivers feel they must get on the phone as soon as they get behind the wheel. My daughter has seen two cars bumping into each other outside her coffee shop – when both drivers were on their phones. Both were also young drivers. I've seen a young driver come out of a parking lot onto a very busy street while on the phone. Since then, traffic lights have been installed at that location because there have been so many collisions.

I currently employ a Big-Rig truck driver with over 20-years of experience. He will use his hands-free cell phone only when he's on the freeway and traffic is light. The moment he needs his attention for the road, he tells his caller, "Traffic is heavy, I can't talk now." and quickly ends the call.

Hand-held cell phone use while driving has been outlawed in some states and their use may be outlawed altogether if they are not used more responsibly. Young, less experienced drivers must realize that they need to have their attention on driving and not a phone conversation. When I was a teenager, my generation had to drive with only the distraction of a radio playing. If today's teens insist on driving while talking on the phone, this will likely be outlawed for all of us.

Another solution is education in cell phone use. Cell phone companies need to spend some of the billions they spend on marketing to teach sensible cell phone use – and keep their customers alive.

Drivers should be told that getting into a deep conversation and envisioning what's going on somewhere else while on the phone is dangerous. It's distracting, unlike a call where you state where you are and then end the conversation.

Technology is available today that lets the phone's GPS recognize when a car is moving and it won't allow any calls while the car is being driven. There is another system that allows you to dictate text messages as you drive. To keep your teen drivers safe find out what the latest device is that will stop them texting or talking while driving.

Some states are making it illegal to talk on a hand-held phone while driving. This still does not handle the problem of getting involved in a conversation and being distracted from your driving job. A hands-free phone gives a false sense of security and will encourage drivers, especially teenagers, to talk longer and more often. This will increase the chance of an accident as drivers get involved in longer conversations.

We survive a flight in an airplane where cell phones are banned because of the remote chance that the phone signal may interfere with the electronic systems of the plane. We know that cell phone use distracts drivers so we need to learn to survive a trip without using a phone when traffic is heavy and we need to pay very close attention to the road.

Texters 23 Times More Likely to Crash

A study involving 100 truck drivers who drove for 18 months and covered three million miles, used video cameras to record when the drivers took their eyes off the road.

These cameras showed that before a crash or a near crash the drivers took their attention off the road and looked at their texting devices for five seconds. At highway speed the driver had his attention off the road for the length of a football field. This new study found that those drivers talking on a cell phone were four times more likely to crash than drivers who were not distracted. But when drivers texted, their collision risk was 23 times greater than when not texting.

Americans drive the safest cars in the world designed to crumple on impact. Airbags, active head restraints and seat belts that tighten up when needed all help drivers to survive a crash.

Modern technology has made cars safer while other miracle technologies – cell phones and texting – have made drivers more dangerous. Most young people are addicted to this new technology and feel they must respond to all messages instantly. Texting turns their car into an unguided missile when their attention is on the message they are sending rather than on the road. Cars have gotten safer and smarter but texting drivers can turn these cars into computerized death machines.

Sending text messages doesn't work too well even for train engineers. A 2008 Metrolink train accident in Los Angeles may have been caused by the engineer being distracted by his sending a text message. The resulting head-on crash resulted in 25 deaths.

You need to set a good example for your kids and never text while driving. Smart cars do not need dumb drivers!

Sun in Your Eyes

Try not to drive into the sun. Have your children look for a good place to get off the road until the sun is no longer a problem.

No matter what techniques you use, realize that you temporarily can be completely blinded by the sun and unable to see ahead. This is how I handle it.

First I slow down and I'm prepared to stop if needed. I then pull down the sun visor. If that doesn't do the job I put on a baseball cap that I keep handy. (Once when no cap was handy my wife made me a cap out of a burger box.) The next step is wearing sunglasses which I keep in a case that is clipped onto the visor.

If the sun is directly in my eyes I sometimes use a fighter pilot technique of putting my thumb out in front of me. A thumb manages to cover the sun – a finger being too small. When I'm turning and the sun will only be in my eyes for a short time the thumb trick works well.

If I'm going to be driving directly into the sun for any length of time and the sun visor is not low enough to do the job I extend the visor, making it lower, by sticking a Post-It note on it. I keep a Post-It note pad handy to write messages on. By sticking a Post-It note on the bottom of the visor and moving it as necessary I can avoid looking directly into the sun.

The best solution is not to drive for the next 20 to 40 minutes while the sun is right in your eyes. It takes this amount of time for the sun to rise or set enough so that it's no longer a problem.

Knobs and Buttons

Handling your radio or CD knobs or buttons while driving, besides decreasing your safety, can also result in a traffic ticket. I've been issued a ticket because I didn't notice a reduced speed zone and this happened because I was searching the radio for a new station. We think of changing the radio station as routine, since we've always listened to music as we drive. It's an even bigger distraction when we insert a tape or look for a CD. At 65 mph, if you look down for only two seconds to change a CD, you've traveled half the length of a football field!

When turning your head toward the radio or CD player you are also liable to unintentionally swerve the car a little because the hands tend to follow the eyes. This might attract the attention of a law enforcement officer, the one that you didn't observe because you were too distracted to notice. He would now look for some additional reason to pull you over thinking that you might be drunk. Being distracted by knobs and buttons can get police interested and at worst cause accidents. So don't fixate your attention on adjusting knobs.

Better yet, take advantage of normal stops to adjust controls, and if you listen to CDs or tapes, position them close at hand before you start to drive.

Child Distractions

Being distracted by a child while you are driving can be disastrous. The way to handle this is to be prepared to handle the needs and problems of a child. Always have extra diapers and snack food in the car. If your child becomes upset, pull over as soon as you can and find out what is going on and then handle it. Change their diapers or give him a snack – or if that doesn't help, try to find out what else could be upsetting him. It might be as simple as the car seat hurting him, or he's sitting on a toy. Once stopped, use your usual technique(s) for calming him down. If you're out of diapers, and that's the problem, find a store to buy some, and then change your child's diapers in the store's restroom.

If you need to continue driving because there's no place to stop, or if your child is going to stay upset until you get home, realize you are going to be distracted by him. To stay safe you'll need to take control of your driving. As you look at things, deliberately focus your eyes on what you see. Don't let the crying baby make you miss this step, because if you only scan your eyes without focusing them, you may miss seeing things.

While driving, if you notice a parent with an upset child, realize that he or she is distracted and may make a mistake. Stay back and don't crowd, no matter how pressed you are for time – give the other driver plenty of space and keep out of the way.

From an early age, children need to be taught that a driver must pay attention to the road. The easiest way to teach them to know this is to have them participate in and help you with your driving. This is how it worked best with my granddaughter, Julie, when she was three years old.

For example, I'd say, "Julie, I need your help. Your eyes see better than mine. What color is that traffic light?" By pointing to the light, I directed her attention off the toy that she'd dropped. "Julie, I need to turn just after a big church – can you look on this side of the road and tell me when you see it?" Or, "Julie, we need to find a parking place, and you are so good at finding things – can you find an empty space for us to park in?"

I'm a firm believer in letting a child contribute. I will give him or her a job to do whenever I can. Getting your unhappy passenger to contribute to your job of driving will take their attention off any minor upset they may be having.

We've all told the kids to look for a McDonald's when they're hungry. Why not get them involved with driving every time you're in the car together? Not only will it keep them busy and stop them from distracting you while driving, but they'll also actually learn the skill of reading the road ahead starting at an early age – thereby helping to develop them into becoming safe drivers.

Drowsy Drivers

As of June 1996, drowsy drivers were causing more than 1,500 deaths a year.

The American Medical Association proposed that states consider regulating drivers with sleep disorders. A sleep-deprived driver can have just as slow a reaction time as a drunk driver.

"This is America's hidden nightmare, and particularly on the highways where accidents in the vast majority of cases are not properly investigated for [driver] fatigue," said Dr. William Demet, director of Stanford University's sleep disorder program.

Your children need to know about tired drivers. When you see a car wandering or weaving on the road, realize the driver may be drunk, or he may have just partially fallen asleep for a moment. If you have a cell phone you should call and report it. There may be a law enforcement officer nearby who can pull the car over to find out why the driver has trouble concentrating.

If you are near such a car, there's no reason not to blast your horn, especially if you think the driver could run into somebody. A horn blast just might wake him up or make him realize that he should pull off the road to take a nap.

Make your children very aware of the fact that, late at night, a driver can be doing fine and then all of a sudden be overtaken by the need to sleep. It's at this point he must pull over and get a nap or sleep all he needs to so as to be safe.

Usually a driver who pulls over and naps won't sleep for a long time and he may even wake up sore because of the uncomfortable sleeping position, but he will be ready to drive on safely.

Once they do start driving, get your kids' agreement that you would rather they come home later than planned if it's because they needed to pull over to take a nap. They may think you'll be upset when they don't get home on time. Let them know you'll be more upset if some official comes to the door telling you that they were killed in an accident.

When I was a teenager my mother always insisted that if I were tired at the wheel I should pull over and take a nap. This probably saved my life and it could save the life of your child too. My mother had it right 50 years ago.

The body has recurring daily cycles that affect body temperature. Recent research has shown how these temperature cycles affect sleep. The best time to drive is while body temperature is high because that's when we are most alert. When body temperature lowers we feel more inclined to sleep.

With most people the body temperature usually starts to rise at 5 am and continues to rise until mid-afternoon and then it slowly drops down until 6 to 6:30 pm. Then it will rise again until ten to 10:30 pm, and then start dropping again, reaching its lowest level at 2 to 2:30 am.

This helps to explain the mid-afternoon grogginess that some people attribute to eating too big a lunch. It means that mid-afternoon is a good time to take a nap just like the people who live near the equator have always done. In hot climates, their "siesta" is built into their work day schedule.

There's another thing you should know about body temperature cycles. The compelling urge for you to sleep are at their maximum during the hour just before you normally wake up. Hence, if you're driving late at night, you can find yourself fighting sleep (trying to stay awake) in the "wee hours" of the morning (1am to 4am) and even more so during the hour before you usually get up.

These timed body cycles explain why it's so hard to stay awake as we drive late into the night – but about 5am we seem to start waking up. If you have to drive late at night, a nap during those early morning hours will make you into a much safer driver.

Another point to note about these natural sleep cycles is this: The hour before you normally go to bed is the time of day you may feel the least need for sleep. The body's cycles are working to keep you awake. That's why going to bed an hour earlier on a Sunday night doesn't always result in going straight to sleep. That's been given a name: "Sunday insomnia."

Drivers need to know that starting a trip an hour before their usual bedtime is not a good time. Even if you feel very alert and bright, it won't last. You'll start feeling sleepy within an hour or two.

Recently it's been found that some drivers who were involved in accidents still had sleep aid drugs in their blood during the day. So if you take medicine to get to sleep, don't take too much – and never take it when you're going to be driving.

Driving is very serious business. It can be a matter of life or death. Keeping appointments or getting home on time is not the most important thing – driving safely is. Sometimes getting home late after stopping for a nap or arriving late for an appointment is the only sensible way. Make sure your children know this.

Teenagers and Sleep

Research shows that teenagers' body clocks are set to a different schedule than that of younger children or adults. This prevents adolescents from dropping off to sleep until 11 pm and waking up before 8 am. According to a National Sleep Foundation poll, 28% of all teenage students fall asleep during the first class of the day. This was only polling those who showed up at school; some kids were just too tired to get there.

Not surprisingly, when high schools in Fayette County in Kentucky delayed their starting time to 8:30am, the number of teenagers involved in car crashes dropped in spite of the fact that statewide, accidents for teens rose.

To be a safe driver you need sufficient sleep. An inexperienced teenage driver needs to be well-rested to drive safely or learn things in school. School schedules should be set to help the children. They are our future.

Try this for those sleepy morning teens. Pull the shades and let the sun in the moment they wake up. Eat breakfast in the sunniest room in the house. This will help reset their sleep clock, but it won't work if they have to get up while it's dark.

Bad Temper – Bad Driver

The student driver who gets mad whenever another driver does something wrong must be corrected. When the learner gets upset his attention is distracted from the job of driving and getting upset about another's actions is just stupid since it serves no useful purpose. A good driver expects some drivers to do silly things and will be constantly alert for such actions. A good driver doesn't have accidents because he's always on the alert for potential trouble. This is a vital part of what's commonly called "defensive driving."

The learner must dismiss the idea that another driver is in the wrong. It's his responsibility to get out of that driver's way and not just sit and get upset as he gets hit or runs into the other driver. He may be legally right but it's no good being "dead" right. A wise driver knows that even when he legally has the right of way it's not his right safely unless others yield to him.

A bad-tempered driver needs to change his attitude to a light and bright constructive approach. As traffic becomes heavier some drivers become increasingly impatient. Aggressive drivers are becoming a dangerous part of the traffic scene. Do whatever you can to encourage your children to be conscientious, thoughtful drivers. Aggression doesn't belong on the road. As a driver you should not pass on to your children the habit of being bad tempered. Teach your children to keep their eyes open and be alert for mistakes others make but not to get upset because of them. Make driving fun by keeping comments about the other drivers light and bright.

Chapter 13

Lanes and Passing

Looking for "The Gap"

Changing lanes and merging into fast-moving freeway traffic from on-ramps doesn't have to be scary. It's easy to do if you realize you need to look for a "gap" – a big enough empty space in the traffic for your car to move into.

When getting on a freeway, if a driver fixes his attention on a large truck and doesn't look at the gap in front or behind the truck, freeway driving will be a scary experience. Simply look where the car needs to go, and plan a path to follow. The car needs to go into a space between other vehicles, so look for a space you can move into, rather than fixating on the vehicles before or after gaps.

A new driver changing lanes can be inclined to slow down when he begins checking for a gap to move into. Before driving age, if you get your children to look for gaps to move into, later when they start to drive they'll be confident and won't feel a need to slow down.

In addition to a big enough empty space for you to move into, the main thing to do before changing lanes is to check for traffic in your blind spot. Always turn your head just before you change lanes, to check for any fast moving vehicle which may have just entered your blind spot.

Keep your eyes well up ahead of your car and aim for the center of the lane you intend to move into, so you gradually change lanes. If you look too close, your hands will follow your eyes, and your lane change will be too sudden and jerky. If there's a vehicle far enough ahead of you in the lane you need to get into, aim for the center of it and use it as your "tow" vehicle, to gradually pull you into the lane you need without any sudden jerks.

Once in your new lane, keep up your speed. Some drivers ease off their speed after changing lanes. When truck driving, I've seen that happen quite often. The only explanation for it that I can see is that an unconfident driver finally gets past a big truck and feels he can relax a little, and in relaxing, slows down. Let me tell you, it's not a good idea to pull in front of a big truck and slow down!

Let your child know the correct lane-changing procedure so they learn what to do. Once they've found a gap you can move into, ask them to check the blind spot to see that no fast moving car has pulled up beside you. With those extra eyes looking, you'll be teaching them the importance of checking the blind spot before changing lanes, and it will become a built-in habit long before they get behind the wheel.

Correct Passing

The rules of passing (including road markings) should be explained to your children, and they should be gotten involved whenever you pass. This is especially important if you don't do much driving on two-way roads, where you actually have to cross over and travel on the left side of the road, exposing yourself to on-coming traffic. The more your children participate, the better their judgment will be when they start driving.

The first rule is to stay back before starting to pass. Keep at least two seconds distance back from the car in front, so you have better visibility farther ahead. If you get right behind a large truck or RV (recreational vehicle), your view is reduced and you can't see far enough ahead. So always stay back, even if you have to slow down a little, until you think an opportunity to pass may be possible. By staying back, if you start to pass but find the road isn't clear up ahead, you can slow down and safely get back behind the vehicle in front of you until there's another opportunity to pass it.

The other reason for staying back is that your acceleration (speeding up) can begin before crossing the dividing line, and before being exposed to on-coming traffic. This will get your car already going faster than the vehicle in front before you start to pass it, so your passing it will be completed faster, giving you less exposure to any on-coming traffic.

Passing procedure: While staying back, you check ahead to look for traffic at least 12 to 15 seconds ahead. It takes approximately 10 seconds to pass another car, and 12 to 15 seconds to pass a large truck. Also check your mirror since you may have someone coming up to pass you. Signal that you're moving to the left. Always speed up enough to pass safely, as you move left, before you get too close to the car in front. Then pass.

LANES AND PASSING

If you're approaching a slow moving truck, stay farther back, so that when there's an opportunity to pass, you can then get up to normal cruising speed before you pass. Good planning by looking well ahead should enable you to adjust your speed, so that you're up to normal or slightly faster speed by the time any oncoming vehicle in your way goes by; and you're then ready to move left and start passing the slow-moving vehicle in front.

Passing is the most dangerous of all driving actions, especially on two-way roads, since misjudgment can result in a head-on collision. Teach your children early all the places the driver handbook says not to pass. Make sure they understand what the different yellow center line markings mean. When you come to a vehicle you need to pass, if there's no build-up of traffic behind, stay back of it and let the kids tell you when it would be safe to pass. If they're wrong, show them why. Try to ask your children if they think it's safe to pass before you do so. This will develop their judgment, which can be gained only by experience, so that when they start driving they'll have the judgment to pass safely each time.

Let me put this important passing procedure in sequence by numbers:

1. Stay back.
2. Check ahead.
3. If clear, check to see that no one is passing you.
4. Signal.
5. Accelerate and pass.
6. Watch your interior mirror to make sure you are well in front of the car you have passed.
7. When clear, signal and pull in front of the passed car.
8. Keep your speed up. Don't pull in front of a large truck and slow down.

Chapter 14

Trucks and Cars

Trucks Need More Space

Truck drivers are constantly looking out for "four-wheelers" (as they call cars) that are driven by inexperienced, drunk, or tired drivers who may do something unpredictable. According to police reports, 29% of fatal accidents between cars and trucks are the truck drivers' fault, and 71% are the car drivers' fault.

In November 2005, USA Today reported that a new highway law provides $10 million annually for five years to pay for more police patrols. These patrols were to target cars driving unsafely near trucks and to publicize the safety risks involving trucks. Also it has just enlarged a program which teaches people about the risks of driving near tractor-trailer trucks (Big-Rigs), to include teen and elderly drivers.

There are major differences between how the brakes on a car work as compared to the air brakes that trucks use. Because of this, plus their much greater weight, trucks almost always take longer to stop than cars. At 55 mph cars take an average of 225 feet to stop but an eighteen wheeler takes 335 feet, resulting in a huge 110-foot difference in stopping ability.

If your kids are old enough, have them figure out how many pounds each wheel of a car has to stop, if a car weighs 4,000 pounds. Then let them use a calculator and divide a truck's 80,000 pounds by the eighteen wheels of a fully loaded Big-Rig. They'll see that a loaded truck has more than four times the weight on each wheel as compared to the wheels of a car. A car has about 1,000 pounds on each wheel, and a loaded truck has 4,444 pounds on each wheel.

Of course, a truck's wheels are bigger and wider (more rubber gripping the road) and a truck's brakes are bigger and designed to do the job. However, if the brakes are not serviced properly, they might be out of adjustment and won't work as effectively as they should. Overheated brakes, even if they were recently adjusted can cause them to not work as efficiently as they should. For example, this can happen after an inexperienced truck driver has taken a truck down a mountain road. Even if there are no mountain roads where you live, a truck can travel over 3,000 miles (almost the distance from New York to Los Angeles) in only five days, so realize that big trucks may have recently had their brakes overheated while going down a steep incline.

When a car's brakes are not working properly the car will usually pull to one side because there are only four wheels with four brakes. However, with eighteen brakes on a Big-Rig, the driver doesn't know if some of them aren't working properly unless he gets underneath the truck and checks them. Most cars minimally have disc brakes on the front wheels because disc brakes are safer. Big-rigs have the less efficient drum brakes.

You can now tell your children all the things that can make a truck take longer to stop than a car. There's one more very technical reason. Your children need to know that trucks use air brakes – and that is the best way to create the force necessary to stop an 80,000-pound Big-Rig. When the driver uses his brakes, air is sent along pipes (brake lines) to each of the wheel's brakes. Once the air arrives the brakes begin to work. It's not like a car's hydraulic brakes where the brake lines are always full of fluid and the moment you touch the brake pedal the brakes begin to work.

A truck's air brake line is similar to a garden hose with no water in it. You turn the tap on and water runs along the hose and after a moment, water starts coming out the end of the hose. This is how a truck's air brakes work. You hit the brake pedal and pressurized air goes along the air lines and in a moment the brakes start grabbing the wheels. A car's hydraulic brake line is like a hose full of water so when you turn the tap on, the water comes out almost instantly – the instant you touch the brake pedal, the brakes start working.

A Big-Rig's brakes do have air in the lines but no pressurized air until the brake pedal is pushed. As a result the truck doesn't begin slowing until the pressurized air arrives at each of the wheel's brakes. This means that if the drivers of a car and a Big-Rig both hit their brakes at the same instant the car's brakes work at once to slow the car but it's longer before the truck's brakes begin to slow the truck. It takes about half-a-second after the driver has hit his brake pedal for pressurized air to flow to the truck's brakes. During that half-second, at 55 mph, the truck will have traveled thirty-two more feet.

Most truck drivers realize they'll travel a greater distance after they apply their brakes as compared to a car so they leave a bigger distance between them and the car in front of them. If car drivers understood this difference in braking time and distance they would never cut close in front of a truck. Make sure your children understand this.

Bigger Trucks

Size does matter! If you've been driving for many years, you might think that Big-Rigs have become bigger – and you're right. Their trailers were 45 feet long in the 1960s, then 48 feet in the 1970s, and up to 53 feet in the 1990s and later. Not only have they gotten longer, but also their widths have increased from eight feet to eight-and-a-half feet since the 1990s.

Most interstate highway lanes are twelve feet wide, not including the usual five to six inch width of lane marker lines. So even when a truck sits exactly in the center of its lane, it has only about one-and-a-half feet of space on each side of it – and its big mirrors, sticking out, will take up half of that space. If you measure your car, you'll find it's about six feet wide or less. Thus, as a car driver, you have about twice the space on each side of your car compared to what a truck has.

Trucks, especially the ones towing two trailers, can tend to wander. On tight curves, notably when getting on and off freeways, it's sometimes impossible for such a truck with trailers to stay within its lane.

A safe driver needs space all around the vehicle because, when things go wrong, space gives you both more room, and more time to think and take appropriate action. You need space in front too, so don't follow so closely behind a truck that it blocks your view. To have space to the sides, don't travel alongside another vehicle. Find an open spot away from other traffic. I know this can be impossible when traffic is heavy, but at least try to leave some space on one side, and don't travel alongside a large truck any longer than you have to.

Following Trucks

To keep safe you need space and visibility; therefore it's not smart to follow a truck too closely. In spite of what I've just said about cars being able to stop faster than trucks, sometimes a Big-Rig will stop faster than a car, especially at highway speed. If the road is wet, the truck will have better traction (due to bigger, wider and heavier tires) and better stability than a car. Its brakes may be perfectly adjusted and the weight a truck is carrying may actually give it a greater stopping ability than a car.

Also realize that with a truck close in front of you, you don't have enough of a view to read the road ahead. So if you have to follow behind a truck, leave plenty of space between you and him. Get out of the trucker's blind spot and stay back far enough, so you can see the driver's mirror. As soon as possible get out from behind a truck so you can once again read the road ahead and thus be in better control.

If you're stopped behind a truck on an uphill, stay slightly to the left of your lane so the trucker can see you in his mirror, and make sure you leave plenty of room in case the truck rolls back slightly when it first starts to move ahead again.

Please – and I say this as a truck driver – dim your headlights when you're behind a truck. At night, lights on high beam reflect from the large truck mirrors right into the eyes of the trucker. This can temporarily blind him. He doesn't have a dimming adjustment on his mirror like you have for your inside rearview mirror. When a thoughtless driver forgets to lower his lights, it also strains the trucker's eyes and can cause headaches. Have your children remind you to lower your headlights when following or passing a truck, and then put high beams back on only when you've moved up even with the truck's mirrors.

Judging a Truck's Speed

It's useful to know which trucks are carrying a heavy load and thus will slow down on hills and which trucks will drive fast.

Of course, if a truck is empty, it carries very little weight. This is easy to see with a flatbed trailer – it has no van enclosure, so you can see when it's empty. A "reefer" (refrigerator) truck trailer can be very heavy when fully loaded with vegetables or ice cream. You can tell if it's a reefer because at the front of the trailer there's a refrigerator unit that looks like a large window air conditioner. Also a reefer trailer usually has a very small door at its rear. If this door is open, the truck is probably empty. Fully loaded reefers are heavy and will slow down while going uphill.

There are two types of truck drivers: Those who drive trucks owned by a trucking company referred to as company drivers, and those who own their trucks called owner-operators.

As a rule, owner-operators drive more powerful trucks than company trucks. You can recognize owner-operator trucks by their large sleeper cabs just behind the driver's seat. Owner-operators tend to favor trucks with long hoods over the engine and two tall exhaust pipes (or "stacks") pointing up, one on each side of the rear of the tractor. Two large chrome air cleaners where the air is drawn into the engine are also outside. These trucks usually don't have engine governors, devices that control speed and prevent it from exceeding a certain speed. Whenever I rent a truck its governor-controlled top speed is 70 mph, so even when there's a speed limit of 75 mph the truck can do only 70 mph.

If you do a lot of freeway driving you will learn which companies govern their trucks to a slower speed than some speed limits. There is a transport company called "Swift" which governs its trucks to a slow speed and my granddaughter thought it was funny when I told her that some drivers think that "Swift" stands for "Sure Wish I had a Faster Truck."

Company trucks usually have smaller engines with only one air cleaner under the hood out of view and only one exhaust stack. They nearly always are governed. This is why you'll see a truck passing another truck so slowly; the truck doing the passing is governed at just one or two miles per hour faster than the one he's passing.

If you spend a lot of time on the highway with your kids, show them the different trucks. Let them learn which ones slow down a lot on hills and which ones have more power. Tell them when you have a truck coming up from behind at a fast speed so they can get to know the types of trucks that are driven faster. Also point out the trucks that slow down on hills.

Judgment depends on the ability to recognize similarities and differences. All the large trucks you see when driving are similar to the casual observer. To be really roadwise it's good to also know the differences between these large trucks.

Passing Trucks

A truck will lose speed as it goes uphill and this is a good time to pass it. When going downhill a truck's momentum will make it go faster so that can be a dangerous time to pass and pull in front of one – especially if you then slow down because your speed has crept up above the speed limit. Because of its greater weight a truck going downhill builds up momentum more quickly than a car and in this situation it will take longer for a truck to slow down or stop compared with a car.

On a level highway it takes about three to five seconds longer to safely pass a truck than it takes to pass a car. Allow for the extra time it takes to get past a long vehicle and complete your pass as quickly as you can. Don't stay alongside another vehicle for longer than you have to.

In many cases on four-lane divided highways (two lanes in your direction) the car should just stay in the inside (left) lane and not even move into the right lane in front of a truck. This is especially true when a road goes up and down hills. Trucks in the right lane will slow down going uphill and speed up going downhill. A modern car is barely affected by hills so it's able to maintain the same speed and it can do so in the left lane.

When a truck passes you, you can make it easier for him and safer for both of you if you slow down slightly. Never speed up when a truck is passing you. Sometimes a less experienced truck driver will try to pass you without realizing that, because of a slight hill, he may lose the momentum he had built up. It's very much in both of your interests for you to ease off your speed slightly and let him in. You don't want an upset, inexperienced driver running beside you. He will learn by his mistake – you don't have to teach him a lesson. It's also likely that another truck driver, seeing what happened, will tell the inexperienced driver what he did wrong and how to correct it, using their CB radios.

Running alongside a truck is a very dangerous practice. A tire tread could fly off and go right through your windshield. You've seen big tire treads lying on the road – they usually came off a truck. It's crazy for anyone to unnecessarily put himself in a position where one of those huge chunks of rubber could fly off a truck tire and hit his car.

If you're running alongside a truck, and its driver comes over a hill and sees a very slow moving or stopped car in his lane, the trucker will have no choice but to push you over if you're blocking his escape route. Truckers have been trained in defensive driving, including avoiding stationary vehicles, so he knows there's a better chance of survival if he hits a vehicle moving in the same direction (like yours) rather than a stationary vehicle.

Staying away from trucks could be a matter of life or death. Get a safe distance between you and a truck and never run alongside one for any longer than you have to.

Looking on the bright side, letting your kids wave at truckers as you move out of a truck's way can lessen their fear of trucks and raise their respect for truckers.

Another point about lessening the fear of trucks is this: When you're approached by a truck coming from the opposite direction on a two-lane highway, you should keep as far over to the right as possible. That will reduce the amount of wind turbulence between your car and the truck. The wind will push the two apart – it does not suck them together. So if the children get nervous about the car's shaking, caused by a passing truck's wind blowing the car, you can reassure them that they are being pushed away from the truck.

Truck Blind Spots

Even with all their mirrors, trucks still have large blind spots which can cause trouble. If a truck needs to swerve or change lanes quickly a car in the trucker's blind spot can be hit.

I know car drivers don't understand how big a problem, blind spots are for truckers; otherwise they wouldn't place themselves in areas which are totally invisible to the trucker and expect to be seen.

A car running alongside to the right of a Big-Rig – next to the truck's passenger door with the car's front end slightly in front of the truck can be completely invisible to the trucker. If that trucker starts moving to his right, the first thing that will tell him a car is there will be the crunching of metal unless the car driver is smart enough to realize that he can't be seen and taps his horn to tell the trucker he's there. If possible don't position yourself in a truck's blind spot but if you just can't avoid that be prepared to tap your horn if you see the truck start moving toward you.

Don't follow directly behind a truck – it is a blind spot for him. Realize a trucker doesn't have an inside rearview mirror like you do, so he can't see what's directly behind him.

When passing a truck don't even start to change lanes to in front of the truck until you can see the front of the truck fully in your inside rearview mirror – getting at least four seconds ahead of him. A truck even has a blind spot in front. This is what they call a "no-go zone" directly in front of trucks and buses. Don't ever go there!

A truck makes wide turns. Unlike cars a truck at times must move to its left before it turns right so that its trailer doesn't hit the curb or light poles. The trucker will be watching his right hand mirror to see if any unaware car driver is trying to cut in to his right. However, there's no guarantee the trucker's mirror will show such a car especially if the mirror is reflecting sunlight into the trucker's eyes. Just don't ever cut in between a right-turning truck and the curb. Explain this well to your children so they won't ride their bikes in that blind spot of a right-turning truck and later won't drive cars there either.

More about Truckers

Years ago truck drivers used to stop to help car drivers in trouble when they broke down. Today, truckers are instructed not to help drivers with car troubles for security reasons – truckers have been robbed and sometimes have had their trucks stolen. The other reason a trucker is instructed not to help stranded drivers is that he doesn't have the time, usually being on a tight schedule.

There are two different types of trucks. Ten-wheelers do local delivery and their drivers usually know the areas they're in. Long haul over-the-road trucks usually have eighteen wheels and often have a large "sleeper" area right behind the driver's seat, built into the trucks extended cab.

If you see an eighteen-wheeler on your local streets, realize the driver may not be familiar with your area. He may have driven 2,000 miles to deliver his load and be in the neighborhood for the first time, plus the driver may have been given incomplete or wrong directions so he could be lost.

Please be aware that an eighteen-wheeler may have gotten into a situation which makes it necessary to swing wide or move across to the wrong side of the road before making a turn. Don't crowd the trucker, please. Give him lots of room to turn. Back up if you have to. Friendly, helpful and cooperative drivers make everyone's day better!

When driving my Big-Rig, many times children will ask me to blast my truck's loud air horn. They do this by using a hand signal – they lift up their arm and then pull it down just like a truck driver does when he uses the air horn. However, because I usually drive with a co-driver who may be asleep in the sleeper cab I don't always oblige the kids since I don't want to wake up my teammate. So your kids should understand that if they ask a trucker to blast his horn but the driver doesn't it's probably because his teammate is asleep.

I think it's good for kids to communicate with truckers and it can be encouraged. There is an organization called TruckerBuddy.com you can find on the Internet. They organize drivers to be pen pals with your child's classroom and sometimes a driver will also come and talk at your school and show the kids his truck.

My wife enjoyed over-the-road truck driving so she encouraged me to write about it. See Driver Ed's Trucking Guide. Your complete guide to a career in over-the-road truck driving: www.DriverEdBooks.com

Chapter 15

Teaching Games for Young Kids

In the previous chapters many games are provided to teach your child driving skills such as reading the road and developing the sense of distance, sense of speed, etc.

In this chapter a few additional games are shown to help teach your child basic subjects such as counting while you drive.

Counting can be taught while traveling – there are always things moving past that can be counted. Even our great grandparents counted the number of rail cars hitched to the steam locomotive as they sat in their horse and buggy and waited for a train to go by. As the kids now see more trucks than trains, I've developed a game for counting wheels, explained here.

Counting Wheels Game

This game is one your children can use to learn counting and to look for differences in things. Not all trucks are alike. This game will bring up a child's ability to notice similarities and differences. What they see now, before you teach them this, is simply trucks on the road which probably all look very much the same to them.

You can get a game going in which your children have to first find a vehicle with two wheels, and then four wheels, six wheels, eight wheels, etc., up to 18 wheels.

Some highly specialized trucks have more than eighteen wheels, and it's fun to try to count the wheels when you see one.

A car transporter truck sometimes carries up to ten cars on its trailer. When the kids are older, counting the wheels of these Big-Rigs, plus the wheels on the cars, can be fun. You can start teaching your children to multiply ten cars times four wheels = 40 wheels, plus the Big-Rig's 18 wheels = 58 wheels. Not only can you get the children to count and add, this is also one way to help them understand the multiplication tables.

Once you start playing this game, the kids' observation will improve and they'll start recognizing differences in things.

Basic Math Words

My wife has been a school teacher and preschool teacher. She explained this data to me and now I'll relay it to you.

There are many words a child must understand in order to grasp the ideas of math. I'll give you some of the words here so you can have the joy of teaching them to your child while you're in the car together – using real life examples that you and the child can see.

Big and small are easy to show: a big truck and a small pickup. Use things you see while driving to explain all the basic math words: Big, bigger and biggest, near and far, long and short, many and few, high and low, above and below.

Other terms you can demonstrate, using real objects, are greater than and lesser than, short, shorter and shortest. You can teach all the words that apply to math very easily as you drive along.

Shapes

My elder daughter was taught shapes on her first day at preschool. She came home and excitedly explained to me what a triangle was. If only I had known what to do I could have taught her myself and shared her excitement as she discovered basic shapes while we were out in the car. It's simple if you use road signs.

Not only should children know shapes, they also need to know that road signs have certain shapes which tell what they mean by their shape.

If you teach them well you'll have other eyes watching to help prevent you from driving through stop signs and to remind you to look for trains. They should have this ability long before they drive.

Road Signs

A child can be taught to read by reading road signs. My eldest child started to learn to read at a very early age partly by looking at road signs. One of the ways a young child is taught to read is by the use of cards with a word written on the card in big letters. My eldest child used road signs as her cards and the very first word she read while on the road was "ICE."

Reading signs will give a young child the idea that words and pictures are a form of communication and watching for signs will get him looking ahead. Also by having your child read the signs ahead you'll be able to tell at an early age if your child has trouble with long distance vision.

Reading signs can be used as points to educate your children on other subjects too. My favorite sign is "Beware – ducks crossing." A delightful few minutes can be spent watching a duck crossing the road with its ducklings.

You can also use road signs to develop a sense of height. In most states many bridges on freeways have a sign giving the maximum height for vehicles. This is done so that oversized loads don't hit the bridge. The maximum height of a trailer which can travel through all states is thirteen feet and six inches.

To develop your child's sense of height, explain that the average height of most men is just less than six feet, that most houses have eight-foot-high ceilings, that a truck's trailer is usually thirteen feet-and-six inches or less, and that the overpass or bridge down the road is fifteen feet high. You can also have them look for maximum height signs at entrances to drive-through restaurants and parking buildings.

Riding in a car is an ideal place to teach your child colors – with cars painted in many different colors all around. You don't have to wait for some teacher to show them colors in a classroom. Why not point out the grass is green, the sky is blue and the car in front is red?

Even if your children are too young to learn the skills of driving, car trips can be made into an educational experience from a very early age. When they're old enough to take an interest in the road you can naturally continue teaching them all the observational skills needed to become expert drivers.

Learning the Alphabet and New Words

Children must learn the alphabet well to function throughout life. As you know, it's needed to efficiently use many things arranged alphabetically such as phone books, files, book titles in a library, etc., and for some employment tests.

While driving you can help your child practice the alphabet. Advertising billboards and road signs make this game easy to play in the car. It's a game that's been played over the years by parents trying to keep their children entertained. You can use it to help your child master the alphabet.

Simply start with the letter "A" and as you drive around have him look for an A, then a B, then a C, and so on – all the way through the alphabet. Keep a copy of the alphabet in the car for reference.

Once your child can go through the entire alphabet from A to Z then have him find the letters backwards from Z to A. Doing the alphabet backwards will give him certainty that, for example, T comes before U.

Unless you're a librarian you won't know the alphabet backwards – but don't skip this second step just because you can't do it. Young children can learn things a lot easier and faster than most adults.

A car is a good place to learn new words. As a parent you need to explain the meanings of new words to your child from an early age. The more words a person knows the better he will be able to communicate with others.

Driving in the car together is a good time to increase the number of words a child knows. As we drove, my wife or I would define any new words the kids didn't know and then use the word in a sentence. We would repeat this with different sentences until the kids had a full understanding of how to use the word. When they were older we showed them how to use a dictionary and encouraged them to look up words they didn't know.

Now my granddaughter reads a book out loud as we drive and if she does not know the meaning of a word we explain the words meaning and we use it in different sentences until she knows it well enough to make the word part of her everyday use.

Children learn differently depending on their past experiences. That is why if the word is used in a sentence in a number of different ways it will enable the child to understand it a lot quicker.

Farmer Counting

In my younger days I was a farmer who worked with dairy cows in New Zealand. Every morning and evening when we brought the cows in to be milked we would count them to see if every cow was present.

Counting one at a time (one, two, three, four) is not fast enough when a herd of 120 cows is coming toward you! Also your count has to be exactly correct down to the last cow in case one has fallen into a drain and gotten trapped. The cows are counted by adding the numbers of cows in each group.

TEACHING GAMES FOR YOUNG KIDS

Add the number of cows in each group: 4, 5, 5, 4, 5, etc.

Farmers are good at counting animals, and it became automatic for me. I could go to church or other gatherings and before I sat down I'd know how many people were in the building.

Many years later when out driving, I taught my kids what they still use and think of as "farmer counting." I asked them to count the number of cows in a pasture as we drove past them. The highest any of the children reached was twelve, before the animals were out of view. They had counted one, two, three. I had added up the groups and had the total of 23 very quickly.

When I explained to my kids how to count by adding up the groups, they learned to do it as we drove through the farming areas of New Zealand. It developed their math skills and my elder daughter gained the ability to look at small groups of things and just know how many items are there. The movie Rain Man showed someone with the ability to just look and know the number present. This skill can be developed in anyone to some degree and farmer counting will help develop it.

Since there are far more cars than cows to be seen while driving on American roads you'll need to count the cars in view at any one time. Don't necessarily expect to be good at doing this yourself. It's been over 40 years since I've done it so even I've lost the ability. However, don't use that as an excuse to not teach it to your children. Children at a very young age can master things that an adult finds impossible. If you don't teach this to your children no one else will – it isn't taught in schools. Perhaps only a few farmers have taught it to their children.

More Counting Games

My kids would invent counting games as we drove around. Each of us had a gas station assigned to us: Ed had Exxon, Cherry had Chevron, Shelley-Anne had Shell, Michael had Mobile and Sandy-Lee had Texaco. Each one would count the number of their gas stations we passed.

Shelley said she mainly played this game to stop Michael from beating up Sandy, and it worked. When Cherry and I would stop playing the kids would then have to keep the totals added up for us as well as their own. As a result the kids would be counting in their heads, first just for their own gas stations, and later they would keep the running total of our stations in their heads as well. Sometimes along roads with few stations, a second game was played in which the children all had a color assigned to them and the number of cars of their colors were also added up. This achieved many things:

1. It got their attention looking out, to develop their driving skills.
2. It developed their skills in adding and remembering numbers.
3. It prevented Michael from being a nuisance for his younger sister and us.

Sing Along

My elder daughter used to collect song lyrics and she'd put them together in a large song book for us to use in the car.

Once when we did a 2,000 mile trip our kids were eleven, twelve and fourteen. When the driving lessons were over and the counting games done for the day the kids would sing as we drove.

Now my grandkids download the lyrics of their favorite songs and have their own song book. Julie and Katie now know these songs so well that even a short trip becomes a musical interlude. My grandkids harmonize and sing songs: from musicals to the Costa Rican national anthem in Spanish.

Put together a song book for those long trips. Your kids will forget the expensive toys you bought them. They won't remember the summer you stayed home and painted the house. They will remember the summers you took them on trips and really communicated with each of them – and they'll probably remember the family singing together for a lifetime, especially if your singing is as bad as mine.

Chapter 16

Help Wanted

You Can Help

I know this book will save lives. I've written it for just that purpose and know of no better mission than to save our young people from the needless slaughter that occurs on our roads. To achieve this noble purpose, parents and grandparents must be aware that this book can prevent the tragic death of their young ones but it requires that the very simple information given in this book be used.

If you've found this book to be of value please get it into the hands of other parents around you, especially those with kids the same age as yours. One day in the future, your children may be passengers in cars driven by those other children. Why not do whatever is necessary to make sure those young people also have a copy of this book in their car and use it as they grow up? You can even give this to grandparents to pass on to their grown children who are raising their grandkids or for their use when looking after their grandchildren.

Request that your local bookstores keep this book in stock. School and local libraries need to be made aware of this book and where they can purchase it. Donate copies if you have to – it will likely qualify as a tax-deductible donation.

Whenever teenagers are killed needlessly in a car accident you can write your local newspaper to say there's a better way. Describe how you've used the clear and simple games and skill developing techniques given in this book while out in the car with your kids. Quote a brief excerpt from the book and give an example of how you applied it to your children to make them safer drivers. Say where the book can be bought giving the local bookstore and the Web site www.DriverEdBooks.com.

A *Teach your Baby (and Teen) to Drive* Foundation needs to be established to forward the aims of this book. This will enable people to contribute their time and money to get parents to take responsibility for their children's driving education. For those who have lost a child in a car accident this book and its Foundation may even give you a new direction and purpose in life – and your efforts could prevent another family from having to live through the tragedy you were forced to suffer.

You may be able to help me put together work books that can be used in conjunction with the *Teach your Baby (and Teen) to Drive* book. You can contribute to building my website by including things that you have developed and used to give your kids a better understanding of car safety and then have your friends link into this website. I am eager that I do all that is possible to gather your suggestions so they can be shared with others. Your help is needed and wanted.

Rest Assured

When I was a teenager one of my cousins was killed in a car accident. Later, a family friend had a teenager son die needlessly in a car wreck. My wife had four teenage school friends die in car crashes and I didn't want this to happen to my kids.

However, since developing what I've written in this book and also applying the data to my children I know that they won't kill themselves in a car wreck.

My kids who drive, have driven safely in both New Zealand (on the left side of the road) and in the U.S.A. (on the right side of the road.) I don't insist that they call when they've arrived at their destination because I know they'll arrive safely. I know that a phone call in the middle of the night is not some authority calling to tell me of a road accident involving a child of mine. It's usually a friend calling from overseas who has forgotten the time difference.

If you apply these simple principles you may rest assured your kids or grandkids will be in a better position to survive the dangerous teenage driving years.

To get your child "roadwise" and "carwise", keep this book in the glove box of your car and keep referring to it. Don't just read it and then do nothing. You must use the simple ideas and do the simple actions in this book to develop the senses and abilities of your children.

You and your children will enjoy working together, learning new skills – just like I did with my kids. Treasure the moments you have with them. I know you'll use them wisely.

Section Two

How to Teach Driving and Most Other Things

Chapter 17

How to Teach

Failed Drivers Taught Me How To Teach Driving

Driving instruction is very much a one-on-one learning situation with an instructor teaching only one student at a time. I discovered that driving instruction was an ideal learning experience to work out what is needed to teach any subject successfully.

I was raised in New Zealand which once boasted it was the most literate country in the world. More books were sold per capita than any other country. Maybe it was that TV was out of range for so many farmers and books were the only entertainment. New Zealand had an excellent library system and books were available from many different countries.

On becoming a driving instructor I read all the books about driving. There was an abundance of books from Great Britain, where the test to obtain a driver's license was designed to make a student fail. There were driving manuals from government authorities written by bureaucrats – not people who actually taught people to drive.

I tried to apply all that I had studied, including what the New Zealand transport agencies had written about teaching driving. To my great surprise I realized there was no system developed to teach driving.

While talking to the examiners who took the new driver for his driving test I found teaching was a very hit-and-miss process. Some driving instructors did a good job while others, even though licensed by the state and tested on how to teach driving, just didn't get results.

I taught a lot of older people who had attempted to get their licenses as teenagers and had failed. Many of these people had immigrated to New Zealand from Britain. Most had attempted to drive in Britain as teenagers and then on arriving in New Zealand as adults, got more professional instruction. But once again they did not develop enough confidence to even take the licensing test.

As discussed in more detail later, Sue Evans-Jones persisted for 27 years in England with 1800 lessons and ten different driving instructors before she got her license to drive. It proves a good point of persistence but it is also a reflection on the state of driving instruction. Too many driving instructors just don't know how to teach driving. All too often the following is heard: "We are going for another drive to give you more practice." They have no plan set out to improve one particular skill, so the student's progress is very uneven.

I seemed to be in an ideal place (New Zealand) to teach driving. As I explained, I had adults from England who had tried and failed. I taught people from the Pacific Islands where there was next to no contact with cars, and from Hong Kong where there was no need to have a car. Also I taught some drivers who had driven 45 years ago as teenagers then had never driven again.

It was those failed drivers who taught me how to teach driving. By listening to them, I found out what previous instructors had done that got in the way of the student becoming a confident driver.

Being raised on a farm my evolution as a driver just seemed to happen. I have no memory of learning to drive. When I started to teach driving I had to develop my own system of how it was taught. I just couldn't teach the way I was taught as a teen. I had to put together a system that worked.

I developed a system that corrected what other driving instructors did to slow down learning and developed a step-by-step method to get the student doing what was needed quickly and safely. I helped these failed drivers to obtain a license and the freedom a car provides.

Section Three of this book gives you exact steps to get your teen driving. But to my surprise, I found that the principles that apply to teaching driving are also applicable to teaching most other things as well. So Section Two covers how to teach driving and most other things. This section is summed up with an instructor's guide entitled, "A Parent's Guide to Teaching."

Why Almost Everyone Learns to Drive a Car

Some people are practical. They are good with their hands and are able to make and fix things. Then there are others who never learn to do practical, everyday things but are able to drive a car and do become good drivers.

Why is it that these non-practical types can drive a car but not sew on a button? Driving a car gives the personal freedom of unrestrained movement, so there is a huge motivation for someone to learn to drive. But is there more to it than that? I believe there is, so let me do my best to try to explain. If we can apply the same principles of teaching someone to drive a car to other practical training situations, we should be able to teach almost anyone to do anything. After all, whom do you know who doesn't drive a car? Now I know that this is a pretty amazing concept. To be able to teach someone to spell may appear impossible. But we all know that, even if a teenager spells car with a "K" he will still learn to drive one.

Of course the modern car with automatic transmission, power steering, and large mirrors is easy to drive. You might say that my logic is faulty because anyone can drive a modern car. I will point out that yes, a modern car is easy to drive, but driving conditions now are more difficult than, say, 60 years ago, with a greater number of vehicles on the road. People learned to drive cars 60 years ago that wouldn't always start the first time. These older cars didn't always have automatic transmissions – many had clutches that were heavy and the gears were hard to change. But men and woman did learn to drive. How?

A driver must first learn each action needed to drive a car. These individual actions get drilled or drummed into every driver until eventually the process becomes automatic. If a driver fails to look and pulls out in front of another vehicle, he may get a sharp reminder that he needed to check for traffic. A few close shaves will scare the driver into looking. It may be only the sound of another driver screeching to a sudden stop, or an angry driver making obscene gestures at the forgetful driver, but he will learn to look. The sound of tearing metal may be the impact required for a driver to finally register the fact that he needs to turn his head and look for other traffic. It seems that a car driver has instant peer pressure brought to bear on him to do it correctly.

If a driver does something wrong, it may come to the notice of the police. Then attending traffic school or a driver improvement course as the result of a ticket may be enough to get the driver corrected.

If pressure from other drivers and a fear of getting a ticket isn't enough to convince a driver that he must look every time before he pulls into traffic, next comes the economic threat of a damaged vehicle plus higher insurance premiums in the future. The force of the law comes into effect with fines and the threat of losing one's license, sometimes all too quickly, for the inexperienced driver who forgets to look and runs into another vehicle.

A new driver does not always have his mother in the car with him to check for traffic if he forgets to, even if she does pick up after him at home. The driver has no choice. He has to learn to do the needed actions himself.

Learning to drive has a clear objective – to get a driver license. With a clear goal to be achieved, people do end up as licensed drivers.

These are the steps a driver sometimes needs to take – which will produce a reasonably good driver. These same steps being applied in other areas would also produce a result.

Let the Student Do His Job

Sometimes it takes considerable effort and willpower to sit patiently and just watch another person do something slowly or badly – especially when you know that you could jump in and do it much faster and better yourself. To be a successful instructor you must resist that impulse. A good teacher must be able to sit back quietly and observe. You must learn to "sit on your hands" and "bite your tongue" if saying something in the middle of his action would distract more than help. Let him figure it out and let him learn from his mistakes without too much of your "help" interfering with him doing his job. Only then can he fully grasp what's needed and learn to do it well.

When I trained as an over-the-road driver while learning how to drive a Big-Rig, I witnessed an unusual teaching tool that allowed the instructor to simply observe without getting too involved in what the student was doing. The instructor would sit in the passenger's seat and read his newspaper as the student drove the truck. Or, at least that was the way it appeared to be. On closer inspection, I found the instructor had more attention on the road than on the newspaper. The instructor involved had driven trucks for millions of miles before he had become an instructor and his attention was never far from the road. He was also very familiar with the roads that his students drove on and was aware of all the danger points.

With the instructor reading his morning paper the student felt less under pressure and no longer had to worry about commands coming from the instructor. The student would now only have to ask where he should go and this put him even further in control of the vehicle. The instructor was less inclined to "get involved" with the driving because he had the newspaper to occupy his attention – as well as keeping an eagle eye on the road.

A student must do the actions of a task without interference in order to learn it. Having a teacher doing something else, like glancing through a newspaper, keeps him busy enough to not get involved and therefore interfere with the student. This is a good technique for teaching most things, but for driving instructions, don't try it until you have the experience needed to know what to expect from a learner driver.

Drivers learn to drive because they have a seat to sit in. It is very hard for the instructor to do the student's job, so usually the student does learn to drive. This is important, so I'll say it again: I believe that the most important reason that a student will eventually become a driver is that he has his own seat to sit in, and he has all the controls available to him.

I taught a young person to drive who'd failed to learn from a previous instructor because the instructor interfered and tried to do the student's actions. The instructor often used the controls on the dual-control car himself, rather than let the student handle it. That student and others had failed to learn to drive, because the instructor had interfered with what they were trying to do. They weren't given the opportunity to learn what was needed for themselves and were not allowed to do it without the instructor getting in their way.

Let's be silly for a moment and look at potty training. As mothers and fathers we've all been through this. Potty training is a bit like teaching someone to drive because the toddler has his own seat to sit on (the potty). Therefore the toddler, just like a driver, does learn to do the needed job because nobody pushes him off the seat and tries to do the process for him. By the very nature of potty training, patience is needed for the toddler to have enough time to do his thing. Also the parents persist because they want to get the toddler out of diapers. Whom do you know who can't drive and is not potty trained?

Whenever you are teaching somebody something apart from driving remember the relationship the student driver has with his equipment and the toddler has with his potty and how it is very hard for the teacher to take over. Somehow in your mind's eye keep the student in the "learner's seat" – don't shove him over and take the seat for yourself.

An Instructor Needs to Communicate and Ask Questions.

Kids, especially teenagers, don't always listen to what parents have to say. When it comes to learning about cars or driving cars, kids or even defiant teenagers, will pay attention as learning to drive is a high point in a kid's life.

Realize that learning to drive a car is a huge achievement. The teen has learned to handle a car where danger is involved. Also a driver's license gives a teen a new freedom of movement. As a parent this is a wonderful opportunity for you to get involved in strengthening the bonds you have with your children. The teenager's eagerness to learn also supports keeping an unruly teenager on track.

Good, calm, and respectful communication (by both you and your student) is absolutely vital for all effective learning and instruction. You must be totally honest with each other. Not only must you communicate with your student in a helpful and positive way, your student must also feel safe in your presence, and as a result, be willing and able to talk to you. Communicate your intentions about what you want to do in plenty of time for him to do the needed action.

When teaching you will make mistakes. When you realize that you have, explain the mistake to your student. Hiding mistakes is dishonest and to have a good relationship with your student you need to be totally honest with each other.

Don't teach a student who is unwilling to talk to you. If it's a short-term upset handle it before you start your lessons. If you have a poor relationship with your student perhaps the reward of a driver's license is an opportunity to establish better rapport. Spend some time together cleaning the car's windows and opening the hood and checking the car's fluid levels. The common interest should be enough to get you talking to each other. If not, start a conversation on a topic that holds your student's interest and get a dialogue going. It's natural for two people in a car to talk to each other. So go for a drive together if that is what it takes to get your student talking.

Talk honestly with him and get him to talk to you. Ask questions. The only way you'll find out what is going on with your student is to ask. Get him to ask questions too, and answer his questions to the best of your ability. If you don't know the answer, be honest and say so. Be willing, at a later time, to find the answer to his questions.

When teaching driving always ask questions about what is going on around the car, such as: "Did you notice that child?" or "Is there anyone behind you?" or "Did you see the brake lights just light up on the fourth car ahead of us?" The only way you'll know where he's looking is to ask him. If you feel that he isn't looking far enough ahead, ask: "What are you looking at?" I repeat – the only way to find out what is happening with your student is to ask him.

The time-proven questions salesmen use can also be used for instruction when you're trying to make a point. "Am I explaining this clearly?" "What do you think?" "Do you agree with me so far?" Ask questions often when you're explaining something, to see if what you've been saying has been understood correctly.

Also use a question such as, "Did I make myself clear on that?" That question implies it's the teacher's responsibility to convey the information. That's a better question to use than "Did you understand this?" which could be misinterpreted as questioning his mental ability to comprehend.

Let's see now if I've made myself clear about asking questions in this book. Did I clearly explain the need for asking questions? What do you think? Enough said – I think you get the idea. To get good results at good speed with your student, make sure that the two of you remain in full communication at all times.

Ensure good communication isn't hindered by misunderstandings of individual words. You've probably had the experience of using big words with a small child and getting a blank stare back as he wonders what the heck you're talking about – but this can apply to grownups too. Even simple little words can be the source of unexpected problems, such as with one foreign student I knew who spoke fair English but thought that "is" always meant an abbreviation for "island." It sounds wild, but irresolvable arguments can result from words which are unknown or incorrectly interpreted. As the famous French philosopher Voltaire once said, "If you would argue with me, you must first define your terms."

Explain the Meaning of New Concepts

If the student spends the time to learn the words and concepts that apply to a subject, he is well on the way to understanding that subject.

A student driver will learn that a DUI is driving under the influence of alcohol or other controlled substances because he will have to answer questions using the term DUI to pass the state learner's license. As a result, DUI and other new words will be perfectly clear to the student before he gets his license. Also the state driver's handbook that explains the rules of the road will need to be understood to get a driver learners permit.

In a lot of cases, road signs are only pictures so drivers do not get confused by the terms relating to the subject of driving. As a result even people who cannot read well actually learn the meaning of the terms they need to know in order to understand how to drive a car.

To grasp a subject quickly you need to learn any new words used in the subject as well as new meanings for old and familiar words that are used in the subject. A student or foreigner learning to use a computer would be awfully confused if he thought a mouse was only a small animal that cats chase.

All too often a student is introduced to a new subject without having to learn the new terms that apply to the subject. The student could then feel or act stupid because if he were trying to use the animal version of a "mouse" on the computer things would not make sense. It could only make sense after it was explained to him that "mouse" has a different meaning and what that meaning is.

A student will learn to drive a stick shift quickly if he understands the concept of what happens when he releases the clutch and the friction point is reached. If the student thinks friction is only an upset with another person, he will not understand what the instructor is talking about, and feel stupid and be hard to teach. A person can understand the definition of the words "Friction" and the word "Point" but may not understand the concept of what a friction point is.

Illustrations are a good way to show a new concept. See the illustration of friction point in chapter 22.

To help understand a new concept the person must envision or visualize what is meant. For example, when describing the use of the clutch when driving a stick shift, I have to explain in full detail what the friction point is. To demonstrate a friction point, the student can place the palms of his hands together then turn one hand in one direction and the other hand in the opposite direction. Keep applying force until the hands stop slipping against each other and lock up together. The hands slipping demonstrate the friction point. The hands locked together show the clutch pedal all the way out and the clutch plates are locked together. With the clutch pedal all the way in, he hands are not touching – the plates are not in contact.

To get across to a student a new concept you can also give an example of how the concept applies within an area of interest. Here is how you can get an idea of a friction point across to a bicycle rider. You just say the friction point is when the brake is being applied and the wheel is still spinning. If you would lock the wheel up and skid the tire on the pavement, it would be like having the clutch pedal all the way out and the clutch fully engaged.

You can also have your student tell you how he sees the concept. By listening to his view you can perhaps provide an example so that all of a sudden it will dawn on him what it is all about. Once your student grasps the concept he can get on with the actions needed.

As I wrote this book I attempted to explain each technical term that I used. I've also included a glossary so that a reader can find a simple meaning for some of the technical or slang words I've used.

People learn to drive because they have grown up with cars, and the concepts involved with driving are pretty well understood. The same person who learns to drive might drop out of other learning situations because he never took the time to learn the new words and understand the concepts of the subject he was learning.

Drilling an Action that Applies to all Learning

We all know the saying "practice makes perfect." When a person practices an action correctly, and continues practicing until he can do it without hesitation, the result is excellence. This is known as drilling.

Of course, practicing something incorrectly will develop bad habits that may be hard to break. Perhaps we could say that practicing an action correctly makes perfect. This is why it is important that when you teach something new you pay close attention to your student to make sure his mistakes won't turn into bad habits.

My daughter Shelley-Anne was about nine years old and hadn't learned to spell. I had the same problem and rationalized it by saying that Shakespeare was a great writer, and he couldn't spell – he even spelled his own name in various different ways. Shelley's teacher got her to drill the correct spelling of words and my daughter learned to spell. Even I started to drill words I used a lot, and my spelling improved.

The best way to learn a skilled action is to first grasp what is needed and then drill it, meaning to practice doing it or applying it. There are different aspects to drilling. For dangerous situations the action must be drilled until it is an automatic response. For example, throughout history the military has had their soldiers and sailors repetitively drilling actions so that they could do them without having to think about what to do. Airline pilots regularly drill handling emergencies in flight simulators. Actions done only in emergency situations, that may never happen, need to be drilled in a flight simulator on a regular basis. For example, if a pilot ever needs to land on water recent simulator training will ensure he knows the routine.

Other actions that do not involve danger need to be drilled only to a point where the person can do it smoothly. For example, salespeople drill their sales pitches. Actors drill by rehearsing their parts. You and I often rehearse an action we intend to do in the future – sometimes just running through the sequence of steps in our minds.

A different type of drilling or practice is used to obtain great skill in a subject like music. A musician will practice his scales over and over again to develop an even greater skill. Gymnasts practice their routines every day for hours to become world champions. Only a dedicated few become champions where this type of continued practice is required on a regular basis. For driving and most other things, once we have learnt the action no further drilling is necessary.

Because one's life can be at stake, the action of hitting the brake must be drilled until a new driver doesn't need to think about what to do. It must become an instinctive automatic action. But usually your student needs to practice performing an action only until he gains a little more confidence and then move on to a new action. Drilling can be overdone.

Visualizing What Needs to Be Done Will Achieve Your Goals

There's a step that's needed before we actually attempt to do something, if we're to do it successfully, and that's to mentally visualize the exact steps to be done before starting them. Picture in your mind what needs to be done, and then do it.

The best future drivers have, from an early age, played with toy cars and envisioned driving them. Teaching some alert teenagers to drive is very easy, as they appear to have done it all before. In a way they have, as they have mentally driven all sorts of cars and even raced them in their imagination. The teenager who is hard to teach is usually the one who has no affinity for cars, and has seldom played a game where he imagined he was driving a car.

To actually be a good driver you must visualize your planned action before you do it. While waiting to turn at a traffic light a good driver looks to where the car needs to go and plans his course before he begins to move.

At times, not only will the student not envision in his mind the correct procedure, but he will envision doing it backwards or incorrectly. If you do get a student to visualize what is needed before he does an action, and he still can't easily do it, find out if he is visualizing something different than what he actually needs to be doing. He may be envisioning an earlier attempt that resulted in failure.

The student may have been taught how to do the action incorrectly at some earlier time. When you try to teach him now, he is still visualizing the earlier incorrect way. Make sure you get the student to envision newly what needs to be done, not just remember how someone showed him how to do it in the past.

The less a student driver envisions what he is going to do the longer it will take him to learn how to drive. It's time well spent to run through in your mind what needs to be done before you do it. And if needed, spend time to remove any earlier preconceptions of how to do the job. A driver needs to visualize being a safe driver. Apply visualization to everything we do, and a lot more things will get done.

Whatever you are teaching, insist the student first runs through what needs to be done in his mind. This basic law can be summed up in a little poem: "Before you do something, think it through, you'll be able to see what you're trying to do."

*****

Cartoonist Scott Adams, creator of the Delbert comic strip that appeared in more than 1,500 newspapers, believes that to live big dreams you must first visualize them. He would write, "I will be a syndicated cartoonist" 15 times a day. Adams says, "Wish good things for you that are not overtly bad for someone else. Write it down 15 times a day. Amazing things will happen."

If visualization does work this well, maybe I should envision that I have a "Driver Ed, Keeping You Safe on the Road" column syndicated on radio and in newspapers worldwide. If I write it down 15 times each day and each of you wrote to your local newspaper and radio stations requesting that they run my column, it could happen. Not only will this be good for me, but it will not be overtly bad for anyone else. It could, in fact, save many lives.

Why Patience is Necessary

When we understand that a student must first envision what needs to be done, we can then see why patience on the part of the instructor is so important. A student must be given enough time to think things through. If an instructor is impatient and tries to hurry up the student's actions, the student will feel pressured. He'll try to do things quickly and skip that important first step of visualizing the correct way to do things. Because he's skipped the visualization step, he'll fumble and make mistakes as he attempts to do the action. It's like a young child being told to hurry up and throw the ball. Under pressure he may throw the ball in the wrong direction because he didn't think of where it was supposed to go.

It may appear to an untrained person that a student is goofing off if he doesn't instantly do as he is told. But the careful student isn't being disobedient – he is just taking the time needed to sort things out in his mind. The instructor needs to be patient while the student comprehends the problem and visualizes the solution. If the instructor is patient, the action being taught can be mastered.

My young brother taught my mother to drive as he was the only one patient enough to spend the time to seat her correctly behind the steering wheel. By doing this my mother could finally envision herself driving. Before this she believed that it would be impossible for her to ever master the controls of a car.

Please be patient with me as I say this again: Patience is granting others enough time to run through in their minds what they need to do or say before they do or say it.

Persistence Pays Off

Drilling is not all that is involved. Persistence is also very high on the list of why nearly everyone learns to drive a car. The reward one gets from having a driver's license makes even the most uncoordinated, absent-minded person persist, and eventually he will become a licensed driver.

It takes time to learn all the actions of driving – it doesn't happen overnight – so your student must persist until all actions are learned. It also takes time to teach driving, so you as the instructor must also persist.

Stories of persistence in getting a driver's license often come out of England where the actual driving test is difficult and most people fail it the first time. In early 1997, after 27 years, ten instructors, 1,800 driving lessons (and that is correct: 1,800 driving lessons) and $30,000 in costs, Sue Evans-Jones qualified for her driving license. It was only her fourth attempt at the test. On her first attempt she hit the clutch instead of the brake. Then, during the second, she pulled in front of a police car that was trying to pass her with lights flashing and sirens blaring. The third time she went the wrong way around some traffic cones. She may have been a slow study, but she sure proved the point of persistence.

In a lot of cases the ingredient that is missing in getting someone to learn a skill is persistence. Many times it is far easier to do it yourself, than to make the effort and persist long enough to get someone else to learn to do it. Don't take the easy way out. Persist. It will be worth it in the end.

Be Predictable

Whatever actions you take, as a driving instructor, they must be predictable. If you do something unexpected this will make your student nervous, because he will then worry that you will do something else unpredictable in the future. For the student to feel safe and confident in your ability to help him, you must not do anything to throw his attention off what he is doing.

If you get over-excited easily, explain this to your student, so if you happen to overreact it will not come as a surprise.

The more predictable you are, the less your student will need to have his attention on you. One professional driving instructor told me that he once slammed on the dual control brakes to "punish" a student for not stopping at a stop sign. For the instructor to slam on the brakes would have been something the student had no way of predicting, because he was not about to hit anything. The instructor should have drilled the student to stop at stop signs. If the driving instructor had persisted and continued to drive around a block that included stop signs, the student would have learned to look for stop signs and learned where to pull the car to a stop.

When you start an action, finish it. Your student needs to know that if you are doing one thing, he won't be jerked away from what he is concentrating on. The more predictable the teacher is, the more the student can concentrate on what he is doing, and will not need to worry about the next thing he will be asked to do.

As well as an instructor being predictable, and doing nothing to throw the student's attention off his driving, the progression of the lessons must also be predictable. An instructor should only have the student do new things in a common sense way.

One instructor I know would get the student driving, and on about the second or third lesson, "throw the student into the deep end," putting him in a situation far beyond his capabilities. This would overwhelm some students so much that they would stop their lessons and not attempt to drive again until they found a more predictable driving instructor.

If you plan to gradually teach a student the things he needs to know, it will work far better than "throwing him in the deep end" and "hoping." This applies to teaching a child to swim – or any other skill they need to learn.

Another prediction point is simply having and following a schedule. Professional teachers give exact scheduled lessons. Too often when a parent attempts to teach his child, little or no learning occurs because no set schedule is arranged and followed; time has a way of slipping by and opportunities to practice and learn are lost.

Whenever you are teaching people, especially children, try to establish a safe routine and don't do anything unpredictable. The more predictable the lessons are, the better the learner will feel, and he can then put his attention on visualizing what needs to be done, and then on doing it.

Have a Goal and Work toward That Goal

When a person doesn't have a goal to achieve something, then usually nothing gets accomplished. This applies to both teachers and students.

When asked what is going to be taught today, instructors who fail to teach their students say, "We're going for another drive to give you practice." They have no plan and don't set out to improve one particular skill – so their students have no sense of progress or achievement.

Once you set a goal you will have something to work towards. A goal seems to create enough energy to get something done. A goal with the privilege of the right to drive seems to energize even the most non-practical person. By having a goal that is achievable you can get most things done. Just needing a license to drive establishes a definite goal.

When you are teaching driving, have both a long-term goal and smaller goals for each lesson. Having an achievable goal in mind helps to get things done so that progress is made. Set a goal for what you want to achieve in each lesson.

Realize that you can't get your student's agreement on some goals until he's made some progress, because he won't be able to easily envision achieving them at the start. However, after you've guided him to some initial success, voice the goal and work toward it – and most importantly, get his agreement to achieve that goal.

For the first time on the freeway, have him get on and off the freeway once. Then say, "We'll continue getting on and off the freeway until you can do that confidently and are no longer nervous about it. Do you think you can achieve that today?" He'll now know the goal and go about achieving it.

As your new driver becomes more familiar with what is needed, after all the basics have been taught, let him start to set lesson goals. If he has a goal to achieve some improvement on an item, or some point, agree and let him practice it.

Even when he's driving confidently, and is close to taking his driving test, you both should still agree on what you're trying to achieve. For example, you might say, "Today, we are going to go driving – and I'm going to talk while you drive, so you can learn to drive while handling the distraction of someone talking to you, but only if you laugh at my jokes. Okay? Do we have a plan?" He should agree, so long as you promise not to repeat any bad jokes.

Keep things very close to the present. Although you should set goals, don't put the student's attention on things too far in the future. Even if I wanted to achieve three or four goals in the lesson, I usually mention only one at a time and get that done.

You need your student to concentrate on what needs to be done now, not worry about something he's going to do in the future.

When I first started teaching driving, I'd tell a student, "We're first going to straighten out what you had trouble with in the last lesson, and then we'll start on freeway driving." He'd instantly tell me that he feared getting on a freeway and didn't want to drive that fast. I had put his attention on something too far ahead – so in that lesson I never did straighten out what he'd had trouble with earlier. I'd distracted his attention from the job at hand and onto something in the future he was afraid of – and that made the job at hand more difficult to teach. (It was two or three lessons later that we finally started freeway driving.)

Quite often I have worked with a student who had failed to learn to drive after many hours of bad instruction. I would teach him more in one hour than he learned in the previous twenty hours. The biggest difference between other instructors and my instruction was that it followed a gradual plan: I got into good communication with my student and ensured that he always understood what was needed. I was calm, patient, predictable and persistent. I did not interfere with his job and did not endlessly chatter at him, but I did answer his questions. I broke down every action into its simplest steps, concentrated on his learning one thing at a time and I set goals and had him work towards each goal.

This of course applies to teaching anything successfully. Whatever you're teaching, don't just go out and "have some more practice." Decide on what one particular thing needs to be learned or improved and work on that.

The learner driver has a very well defined goal to work towards. The end result is a definite achievement, the right to drive a car after passing a test and getting a license. Whenever you are teaching someone something, have a goal and work towards that goal. With a clear goal, progress is possible as everything else seems to fall into place.

Expectations

Always expect improvement. When you see improvement, tell the new driver he's doing better, or tell him what you feel he's achieved. For example, after he's learned steering, say, "I feel you're now in control of the car. How do you feel about it?"

You are not the final authority when you've noticed that your student has gained an ability. Check with him and see if he feels he's gained new confidence in doing an action. If he's happy with his new ability, say, "It's great that you've achieved that," or otherwise let him know in some way that you're pleased. If he still wants to accomplish more from the exercise, discuss with him what he still wants to achieve – and go ahead and let him work on that.

If he's a perfectionist who demands too much from himself, let him continue for a while and then get his agreement to move on. Sometimes all that's needed is for you to reassure him that he has the required level of ability needed at that point. Of course, practice does make perfect, and you'll tell him he'll continue to improve.

Whatever you're teaching, expect not only improvement; also expect him to learn the different actions quickly, "You can do it" should be said often.

When you get a result, be willing to get excited about it. Show him by words, expression, actions, body language, or all of the above, that he is doing well.

After a Success, Move On

Have your new driver do an action only until he can do it – don't make him continue past the point where he can do it well, or makes a substantial improvement on it. When he can do it well, move on to another action.

For example, he needs to learn to stop the car at an exact point. You have him practice that, as given later in this book. When he can do it you've accomplished what you've set out to teach him. Go on to teaching him something else.

Even if he weren't stopping close to the line, but showed improvement after spending 15 or 20 minutes on the drill, go on to something else. If needed, make a point of returning to that drill at a later time to get a better result.

If you continue trying to get a new driver to do something perfect every time, he'll feel you're not satisfied with any progress he makes. He will feel he is not winning. It's far better to return to an action several times, such as at the very start and the very end of the lesson period. It's better to get an improvement and stop rather than to continue an action for a long period trying to get a perfect result. In teaching, trying to achieve perfection is an enemy of progress. Perfection is achieved through experience when you actually put into practice what you have been taught.

Get a good improvement and make sure he knows that you're moving on to another action because you're satisfied with his result. This will keep him winning, build his confidence and keep him progressing much more rapidly.

No Unnecessary Talking Since the Student Has a Job to Do

I was fortunate early in my career as a driving instructor. I almost lost my voice, so I continued teaching by saying as little as possible. I noticed that my students progressed faster, without my constant chatter that distracted them from the very difficult job they were trying to do.

From those students who had professional instruction, before they came to me, I found their biggest gripe was previous instructors talked too much about themselves.

You, as the instructor, are also the navigator and give instructions on where you want the car to go. Your student knows this and will try to listen to you for directions because he may not know where he is. The student is very dependent on you for giving him directions so what you have to say is very important to him because in a way he is lost. Therefore don't chatter at the student. He only needs directions and help with his driving. If you talk too much he will shut off and then not hear your directions.

When I'm teaching I try to say only what relates to what the student is doing at that moment. The less advanced the student is the less chatter he needs, as his whole attention should be on the road and the car. As it is all new to the student, any talk must be directed only to assist his driving.

In later lessons when the student is driving well and there is not much traffic around I will at times start to chat with them. After all they will be driving a car in the future with a passenger chatting at them and I want them to be able to handle that situation. So I get to know the student a little and the student finds out a little about me.

All of us like to talk about ourselves and once we start it never seems to stop, so as soon as the traffic gets heavy again and the student needs to have his attention on the road I say, "That is enough talking. With all of this traffic around you need your attention on the road, so I will stop chattering at you." I make sure the student knows the chatting has stopped because of the road conditions, not because I am not interested in what he is saying.

My rule is the following: No chatter to start with and only controlled talk later. All talking ends when the student has to put his attention fully back on the road.

I never talk to a student about a mistake he has just made if he needs his attention on the traffic ahead. I will bring up a small driving error later once driving conditions are safe enough for him to give me enough attention to understand what he did wrong and what he should have done. For a major error I stop the car at the first opportunity so that both of us can take our attention off the road.

Now that I've explained this, it all seems quite obvious. Although it is traditional to talk when in a car with an experienced driver a conscious effort has to be made to stop the chatter and let the new driver get on with driving the car.

A student learning a new skill needs to be envisioning what he needs to do next, not working out in his mind a response to or a way to stop the teacher's unnecessary chatter. Whatever you are teaching let the student get on with what he needs to do. He can't do this if he is being distracted by unnecessary talking.

Answer the Student Driver's Questions

The next biggest gripe heard from students is that instructors won't answer their questions. For example, the student stalled the stick shift car when starting to move the car forward and then asked the instructor why it stalled.

For the instructor to say, "You are doing fine. This simply happens when you are learning. Just try it again and you'll get it," is simply just not doing his job. An instructor who knows his business knows that if a stick shift car stalled when starting, either the clutch was let out too fast or the motor was not turning over fast enough, or both.

If a professional instructor can't answer such basic questions it means he doesn't know enough about driving and how a car functions to teach – or most probably he wasn't paying enough attention to what the student was doing. In either case he shouldn't be instructing for a living.

At odd times a student would do something that he felt he needed help with but I hadn't noticed what he did wrong. If this happened I would explain what I had my attention on and why I wasn't paying attention to what he was doing. After that I would give him the usual reasons for that particular problem having occurred.

Driving is a known skill. If the student does something and doesn't get the correct result, the driving instructor must be able to tell the student what he did wrong and how to get it right the next time. In this way, the student learns by his mistakes.

For a student to be told hour after hour that "the reason he stalled when starting off is because he needs to practice it some more and he will get it right", is no instruction at all. My firm rule is: answer every question specifically, and if I didn't notice what the student did wrong be honest and say so.

If you are teaching your own child to drive you probably will not know the answer to all the questions that he could ask you. I have tried to lay this book out so that you can easily find the answers. The fastest way is to refer to the book's index and go from there.

Your own driving experience will enable you to answer most questions. The time a student will ask the most questions is while learning how to use a clutch when driving a car with a stick shift. Even if you are an experienced stick shift driver you probably learned to drive years ago and have forgotten how you picked it up.

When questions come up about driving a stick shift, use this book to find the reference to answer the question the student has.

Whatever you are teaching, if the student has a question, do your best to answer the question. The student must be lacking some understanding to be confused enough to ask the question in the first place. By patiently answering the question and letting the student ask more questions you will handle any confusion or misunderstood concept that the student has. This misunderstanding would remain a mystery to the student and continue to slow his progress if you didn't answer his questions.

At all times an instructor or parent needs to respond to a student's or child's natural curiosity and take the time to answer his questions or promise to answer the question in the future if it is not possible to do so at once.

Teaching is Divided into a Series of Small Actions

An experienced stick shift driver makes driving a stick shift look very simple. It is like a tennis player hitting a ball. A good tennis player makes it seem like a very simple action. But he might not have any idea how to teach it, especially if it was years ago that he learned to play tennis.

A tennis coach, teaching a right-handed player to hit a ball coming in on the right side, will break the action down into these steps.

1. With the arm outstretched move the racquet back.
2. Step back with his right foot. This action will be practiced until it is an automatic response. Then the "racquet back" and "foot back" will be practiced together until the learner can do it well.
3. The student will then be taught to swing forward to hit the ball and complete the follow-through (where the racquet keeps moving after the ball has been hit.) Once this step is mastered, all of the steps will be put together: swing back and step back, swing, hit the ball and follow through – all done in one smooth action.

I'm not trying to teach you to play tennis. I just want you to understand that something you can do without any thought may be hard to teach another. All the small steps that go together to teach an action must be broken down into separate actions. These small actions must be drilled and learned before the next one is tackled. When this is done it is very easy to teach.

It is the same with teaching someone to drive. I have taken every action a driver needs to do and given a step by step guide of how to get the action taught quickly. Not only will you be able to teach these actions quickly, you will get the job done with the least amount of stress on you, your student and your car. You will be able to get your student driving quickly and confidently.

You will be able to do the job a lot better than some professional driving instructors who have not developed an exact method to teach every action needed. Whatever you need to teach, take the time and break the needed actions down into simple steps. Teach one step at a time and you will have your student winning in no time at all.

It's easy once you know how. Go to it.

Teach One Thing at a Time

When teaching someone to drive a car, it's very important to concentrate on one thing at a time. This of course, applies to anything you do – try to improve only one thing at a time. The student should know exactly what is being taught and be allowed to have his attention on doing that particular thing.

For example, a student is driving around the block, learning to do right-hand turns. When pulling up at a stop sign, you notice that he doesn't stop the car exactly at the correct place. Learning how to pull a car to a stop and stopping at an exact point takes practice, and is another separate exercise you can take up in a future lesson. As long as the student has stopped the car in such a position as to be able to see the other traffic, he is doing fine. If the student didn't use his turn signal to indicate the direction he intended to turn you would have to bring this to his attention because this is part of making a turn.

I've had students who previously had poor instruction. They were constantly nagged at every time a turn signal was not used but the important actions like clutch control were ignored. As a result, unless we are practicing making turns, I do not constantly remind the student when he forgets to use the turn signal until he has learned the basics.

There are many different actions a driver does, or should do, as he drives a car. The beginning driver can easily get confused and forget one of the actions, or do something incorrectly. If every time this happens he is told about it, he can get overwhelmed by the complexity of what he is trying to do and want to give up.

Another example would be, if you were out driving, with the intention of getting the student in the habit of checking in the rear view mirrors more often. All the small driving faults would be ignored, and the only faults that would be corrected would relate to the student being aware of what was happening in the rear. I would ask how far the car behind is and expect the student to know because of having checked recently. I would correct for over or under use of the mirror, and for fixating on the mirror.

I would make sure the student could look in the mirror and recognize if a car was directly behind him. He needs to know what lane the car behind is in because once he can do this the mirror will no longer be a scary place to look.

Dangerous driving faults would be handled at once if they could result in an accident. Of course you would make a mental note of the small faults you did not mention, to bring them up for improvement in future lessons.

You, as an experienced driver, will often have to make a big effort to not say anything that doesn't apply exactly to what you are doing.

It is not just in driving a car that you concentrate on developing one thing at a time. A teacher must have the student's attention on what he is doing, not distracted over several areas. The only way to place the student's full attention on what he is doing is to teach one thing at a time.

Yelling Will Get You Nowhere

I never got a result with a student driver by yelling at him. The only time I became angry with a student, his parents found him another driving instructor.

While being trained as an over-the-road truck driver, I did see driving instructors yelling at student drivers. The instructors would yell at mature men learning to drive large trucks. Three students rode in the truck with one instructor, each student taking turns at driving.

One student had a pilot's license and a large boat that he towed on a trailer, and had a lot of experience backing down steep boat ramps. He also had a good feel for handling equipment. After being trained by one instructor (in my presence), he went to pieces to such an extent that he failed his driving test three times.

In addition to yelling during a major error, this instructor constantly picked on every small fault. The instructor talked so much he was losing his voice. He would distract the student from his job. This would result in the driver making more errors and the instructor yelling more. Of course the student became discouraged and had trouble passing the test.

I also experienced some excellent instruction from other instructors. They did not raise their voices once, and only spoke when they could say something to help the driver.

There is no excuse for losing your temper as a teacher. I've never seen that do anything but make an unconfident, nervous, mistake-prone driver. Students will not learn under duress.

Stay Calm (It Can Be Done)

I know it is very easy for me to say stay calm. I have encountered almost all the possible situations a driving instructor could possibly end up in. As you may have never done this before, let me explain why you must do your best to "appear" calm and in control of the situation.

Your student is going to make mistakes and get upset. If you also get upset it will add to the student's upset. By you appearing to remain calm and showing no upset, your student will quickly calm down and get back to the job at hand. My simple rule is – the more upset the student is the calmer the instructor must appear to be.

If you do get upset, just don't show that you are upset. If your student has done something stupid, he will feel bad about it. You don't have to yell at him for it. If he knew everything, you wouldn't be teaching him.

Realize that a mistake is an opportunity for you to teach, not a reason for you to get upset. If you expect the impossible "perfection," you will get upset when a mistake is made. If you expect your student to make mistakes (as he will) you will not get upset when he does so. Perfection is only achieved through experience. A driving instructor cannot expect to do a "perfect" job every time until he has taught hundreds of students to drive successfully. A learning driver will not achieve "perfection" without extensive driving experience. Demanding "perfection" from an inexperienced driver will only slow progress and cause upsets because mistakes by both an inexperienced instructor and driver will be made.

If you have taught your child to "read the road" while being a passenger the mistakes your child will make will have to do with handling the car. They will already have a built-in instinct not to pull out in front of a Mack truck.

If you expect a little bit of excitement and confusion to happen while teaching someone to drive you won't be upset by the unexpected.

If you expect your student to be perfect and not make mistakes, you will get upset for no reason when a mistake occurs. As a result your student will not learn as quickly as he should and he will lack confidence as a driver.

Even while teaching mundane things where no danger is involved you still must remain calm as a teacher. Learning only occurs in a calm environment.

Discover What the Student Driver is Doing Wrong

and Fix It

During teaching, a student's progress can bog down. At these times the instructor must find out what the student is doing wrong and fix it.

By working with a student, you can usually find the reason why he can't do something the correct way. A surprising number of times, someone doesn't try to do something – not because he is lazy but simply because he doesn't know what to do. So, instead of doing something wrong, he will do nothing.

If you take the time to find out what a student is confused about – or received the wrong information about – you can teach almost anybody to do anything. Once you've pinpointed the underlying confusion or lack of know-how, you can figure out pretty quickly how to handle the situation. This is what makes a good teacher. The results can appear miraculous, but anyone can do it if he keeps it simple and persists long enough to find out what the real problem is. "Seek and ye shall find" is very true.

Emphasize Improvement, Not Errors

If you're going to teach someone how to drive a car, it follows that you expect him to progress and achieve new skills.

As you teach, if you keep emphasizing the student's improvements and positive results, that's what you'll get more of – good results. On the other hand, if you keep nagging and focusing mainly on errors, that's what you'll get – more errors.

Don't use errors to criticize. Use an error only as a sign that there's still something more that he needs to learn. Don't focus on errors or scold the student driver for making errors. Find the reason why the error was made and then handle what caused it. When the same error is being made consistently, get into good communication with him. Ask questions and find out what's going on. Believe me, if you persist you'll find something the student simply didn't grasp or understand correctly – or didn't know at all. That's how you help him. Never make the mistake of assuming he knows even the most simple, silly things, just because you do.

Mistakes are part of learning – we all learn by making them. It is so much easier to teach successfully if you view an error as something which gives a teacher a reason to be present and to do the job of teaching. View an error as an opportunity to teach more. You can discover why the error was made, help him fix it, and then produce a confident student. Again, this applies not only to driving but to teaching any subject.

Demonstration Saves Time

It's far easier to teach if you show your student what to do as well as telling him. Even with something simple it's better to show as well as tell. Then have him do it. They say a picture is worth a thousand words. This is even truer if you demonstrate. Demonstration while teaching can keep you from losing your voice from over-use. Here's some of the ways I used to demonstrate while teaching driving.

In the beginning you'll be driving to a quiet spot for his first lesson. Before you get out of the driver's seat demonstrate to him what needs to be done. For example, you can drive the car around a parking lot showing him how to steer. Then he does it. If you're teaching him how to drive a stick shift then demonstrate how to use the clutch. Then let him do it.

Parallel parking should be demonstrated to most students. Angled parking may need to be demonstrated if the student has trouble with it. Some students have no idea how it's done until it is demonstrated to them while they stand outside, watching and seeing how the front and back wheels don't follow the same path.

If your student is not grasping how he's supposed to do something, even after you've asked him what he's thinking or visualizing, then you probably just need to demonstrate it to him. If you've done that, and he seems to understand but he still doesn't do it quite right, then probably all he needs is more practice.

It's not always necessary for you to take the wheel to demonstrate a point. Sometimes it's actually better, to demonstrate something by using a toy or making a simple sketch. Even small objects, such as two pens or two paperclips, can be used to show the idea of two cars, one following or beside the other. Use your hands to show one car in relation to the other.

If he's not swinging the car out far enough to do angle parking properly, you can sketch the angled lines on a pad of paper and show where he should steer. When I teach Big-Rig truck driving, I always use a toy truck and trailer to show what's needed. By using a toy the student can get a bird's eye view of it, something which is otherwise impossible to see. One student couldn't get the idea of backing a car around a corner so I had him do it on a bicycle where he could see what happens when the wheel is turned. Whatever you are teaching, progress can be faster if you demonstrate what needs to be done.

Lets Sleep On It

At times you will end up with an upset student. Your job as a teacher is simply to get the student through the rough spot and the upset will soon be forgotten. If you were to stop doing the teacher's job and take over the student's job he would have an even bigger upset. When teaching driving, if you have developed in your student all the skills of reading the road as described earlier, you should never have a situation where the student driver goes to pieces and for safety reasons you would be required to get behind the wheel yourself.

When teaching, if an upset occurs let your student get back in control and practice something the student is good at for the rest of the lesson. Only continue with what the student was having trouble with after your student has had adequate sleep. This also applies to a lesson where the student had trouble doing an action. For example, like practicing uphill starts while teaching a student to drive a stick shift.

The old saying of "Let's sleep on it" works. It provides time to sort out the events of the day and put them in a better sense of order. Also after a difficult situation do your best to follow up with a lesson the next day.

In teaching, sometimes you may feel you have failed unless the need for sleep is understood and allowed to occur before you continue the action the student was having trouble with. As a driving instructor several different students said that they dreamt about me after receiving a lesson. I eventually realized they weren't dreaming about me. I was just part of the dream where they were sorting out the problems they were having with driving.

As learning to drive involves danger and stress it is important that these students dreamt about it. I noticed that those who said they dreamt about it the night before improved rapidly in the next lesson. Hence, by letting students get a good night of sleep and hopefully dreaming about it, I was being helped in my task of developing difficult driving skills quickly and safely in them.

Practicing an action does "make perfect", providing you keep in mind that what you are trying to do may be too much for the student to grasp all at once. The student must be able to have a restful night of sleep before more practice occurs, so "Lets sleep on it" should be an important component of the learning process.

I am always amazed by what a good night of sleep does for the learning process. It seems the next day it usually comes together quickly without the problems of the earlier lesson.

Uncoordinated Drivers

You might have trouble teaching a student who lacks coordination. Before you give up, try the following.

Some learners can watch the road and see what's happening ahead, but sometimes it takes too long for them to make their foot respond to what's happening. The eyes and feet don't seem to work well together.

I have usually found that when there's not good foot and eye coordination, the student doesn't play sports but spends a lot of time surfing the Internet and watching TV instead. Occasionally, it takes more than just a walk to get the eye and foot coordination working well. I suggest using a skipping rope. Boxers need excellent eye and foot coordination, and they skip to achieve this. I once taught skipping to a boy who at first couldn't do it no matter how hard he tried. Then I skipped with him using a long rope that would go over his head and told him when to jump. With me skipping, and the boy now inside the rope, every time the rope came to the boy's feet, I would say, "jump!" This got his eye and foot coordination going and taught him to skip.

There's another coordination exercise done on stairs that can get feet and eyes working together; it involves walking up and down stairs and should be done slowly at first. It is done differently than the usual action of walking up stairs so it demands a higher degree of foot and eye coordination. Have him place one foot up on a stair and then bring the other foot up to the same stair, alongside the first foot. With the same first foot step up again and then bring the other foot up to meet it. Repeat this for several steps. Then have him repeat the exercise with the opposite foot taking the first step and do this several times. He will very quickly be more alert with his eyes and feet working together.

If there is a handrail to hold it can also be done backwards down the steps doing the above action. Since this is not a familiar action it really helps to reset the brain. It is vital you use the handrail while doing this as it is such an unusual action and you could fall if you were not hanging on to something.

I use this exercise myself whenever I've been writing for long periods and the brain has ceased to work, or when I'm driving and my coordination has slowed down because of too much sitting and not enough exercise.

With a student who loses coordination, I have also stopped the car near some steps and made him do this exercise for a couple of minutes.

Tennis coaches also use this method to get eyes and feet working together to improve a player's skill. If it's important enough for people playing sports to be coordinated, it should be far more important for a driver to get well coordinated before he drives by doing exercises like this. In most sports if your coordination is not very good, the worst you can do is lose your game. When driving, one could lose much more.

If you notice a young child has little interest in sports, it may be because he does not have good eye and foot coordination; some simple exercises such as skipping or climbing stairs following the above method may be all he needs to improve this.

Even so-called attention deficit "disorders" are now being effectively managed without the use of drugs by simply having the child exercise three times a day. Exercising gets blood, oxygen and hormones flowing better and that greatly improves the ability to focus one's attention. Improved nutrition, exercise and better learning methods can enormously improve or entirely eradicate such attention deficit problems.

Braingym.com offers a series of simple exercises designed to boost overall brain function. It has been reported that these Brain Gym techniques enhance learning and coordination.

Chapter 18

Driver Ed's Instruction Guide

Here is what I will call "A Parent's Guide to Teaching." This instructor's guide will successfully help you teach your kids driving or most other things. Your kids can also follow it when they teach you things they have learned that you never knew. Hope it helps.

A Parent's Guide to Teaching

1. Make sure your child is feeling safe and at ease. When learning to do something like drive a car or pilot a plane, your most important duty is safety.
2. You as a teacher must feel safe and familiar with the area you will be working in. A driving instructor must only operate on roads he knows.
3. Always remain in good communication.
4. Explain your instructing mistakes as soon as possible.
5. Answer your child's questions to the best of your ability.
6. Only speak if it is to help the child; no unnecessary chatter.
7. Always appear calm, do not show anger when teaching.
8. Remember you are in control of the lesson.
9. Let your child be in control of his actions. When teaching driving keep the student in control of the car.
10. Be patient and allow the child to envision in his head what he needs to do before he does it.
11. Drill – but only to an improvement, then move on. The one exception is to build an automatic response so the student can do something without having to think about it. Hitting the brakes must be drilled until it is an automatic response.
12. Persist. When you start an action, finish it.
13. Have a plan and follow it.

14. Establish a schedule, and follow it.
15. Break down actions you want to teach into their simplest steps.
16. Teach one specific thing at a time. Ignore all the other mistakes, and get an improvement on what you are teaching.
17. Always have a goal to achieve a new skill or gain improvement. Share the goal with your child only when he can see that goal is achievable.
18. Don't put the child's attention on something in the future.
19. Teach with high expectations.
20. Handle dangerous faults at once.
21. Realize that a mistake is part of the learning process, and don't get upset because of mistakes.
22. Spend the time to find out why a child isn't progressing.
23. Demonstrate: by driving, or with toys, or drawing, or sketching, or using your hands.
24. Get excited about the improvements. Tell your child when he is doing well. His good points need to be acknowledged.
25. Make instruction fun – keep it light and bright.
26. When an upset occurs let your student get back in control by practicing something they are good at for the rest of the lesson. Only return to the area of upset after a good night of sleep. "Let's sleep on it" needs to be understood to be a successful teacher.
27. Use exercise or coordination drills to reboot the brain when needed.

Section Three

Teach Your Teen to Drive

Chapter 19

How to Teach Driving

Congratulations!

You have taken the time to teach your children how to read the road and every other aspect of driving, except working the pedals and steering wheel.

Why not complete the job and teach them this as well? President Clinton taught his daughter Chelsea to drive in the summer of 1996 while living in the White House. If he could find the time then, you should be able to as well.

You have taught the kids the complex part. Why not grow together as you actually teach them the easy part? If you follow my teaching method, one step at a time, you will get them driving and keep your hair.

Easy to Teach

Most students who are about fifteen or sixteen years of age are surprisingly easy to teach, especially those who've already learned to read the road ahead as passengers. They will learn well and quickly.

Even students with poor eye and foot coordination can be taught without too much extra effort if the coordination drills in this book are used.

Of course there are exceptions to every rule and for some children it is better if they are not taught by a parent. Someone not involved with the family may be needed. If your student's lessons don't progress with steady improvements then I would suggest you get the help of a professional driving instructor. In some rare cases having a professional outsider can prevent unnecessary upset from occurring.

This Book is Your Teaching Plan

A good teacher has a prepared plan to follow. If there is no plan, you will end up going in all sorts of directions that don't necessarily lead to accomplishing your purpose.

This book is your teaching plan. It outlines the step by step actions needed to achieve your goal of a confident, safe driver.

Every person who drives a car will be quite willing to offer you all sorts of advice on driving. Most people believe they are good drivers, even if they have very bad driving faults. To get a safe, confident driver, stay with the teaching plan you have. Don't act on "helpful" advice offered by other drivers without thinking it through first and making sure they know what they are talking about.

Whatever you are teaching, be certain you have a teaching plan to follow. If necessary, find a book on the subject and follow the plan it suggests.

Licensing Age

I am a firm believer that a student should start driving at an early age and get many miles of driving experience while still under parent supervision. It is only by driving and spending time behind the wheel that a driver gains experience, learns from his mistakes, and develops an automatic response for handling emergency situations. Even if it's another driver's fault, an emergency situation does not have to result in an accident. A good driver learns to anticipate the actions of other drivers and takes those into account.

I often hear teenagers say their parents won't allow them to get their license until they're eighteen, even when it's legal to do so earlier. However, I believe this is an incorrect approach.

If you let your teenager get his license at the earliest possible date allowed by law and then you let him drive you around it will build his confidence. He will also gain the experience so necessary for today's driving. Some experts think it takes 10,000 miles of driving to become an experienced, safe driver.

Young drivers have a disproportionate share of car accidents. The California Highway Patrol reports that drivers 19 and younger – who make up fewer than four-percent of all drivers – account for more than nine-percent of drivers involved in fatal collisions.

Another advantage of letting your teen learn to drive at fourteen, fifteen or sixteen (whatever the youngest age is your state legally permits) is this:

If he later decides to drink alcohol with his friends, he will already be an experienced driver. When one combines an inexperienced driver with an inexperienced drinker, you've created the most deadly mixture. The more driving he has done before he chooses to drink or not, the more responsible he will be as a driver. He would have had some close misses and gained a lot more control over his actions, more than an eighteen-year-old who has driven for only ten hours before getting his license.

The eighteen-year-old who has only ten hours of driving experience and has just passed his driving test thinks he's a capable driver who can do no wrong. Such a driver is a menace after drinking alcohol even when he's below the legal intoxication limit, especially if he's also inexperienced with alcohol and has no idea how it affects him. This is why many states first give a restricted license with a low or no alcohol limit.

A parent who is worried about their teenager having car accidents should make sure their teenager gets a drivers license or permit as young as the law allows. The advantage being that this is still at an age when a parent has the right to restrict the time and circumstances under which the teenager can use the car.

I've found that when the average fifteen- or sixteen-year-old is learning to drive, he or she is not out drinking or trying to impress the opposite sex and is actually easier to teach than two or three years later. The sixteen-year-old is often an excellent student, learns quickly and if allowed to get a license or permit, will be an experienced driver by the time he gets heavily involved in dating.

I was amazed when I lived in California and sold a car to an out-of-state buyer. He said his son was going to drive the car to school once he got his driver's license at eighteen. It turned out that since the age of sixteen his son had been flying himself to school in his own plane! I've always wondered how a state's lawmakers and the DMV think that an airplane is safe in the hands of a sixteen-year-old but a car isn't. This shows that not only some parents have it wrong but a state motor vehicle department can have it wrong too.

When your teenager has his license don't return to the driver's seat – let him remain behind the wheel. To become an experienced driver he has to drive. So every time you go out, invite your teen to drive you. Not only is it good experience for your child, these may be almost the only times the two of you spend together. This time together may give you and him opportunities to communicate about teenage problems that wouldn't otherwise be shared.

Choosing a Car for Teenagers

As I write this, I am watching a wrecked Mustang on TV that two boys died in. The driver was eighteen and his passenger only sixteen.

Kids can do silly things in any type of car but choosing the correct car for an inexperienced teen can reduce the risk.

Do not buy a powerful car like a Mustang and let an inexperienced driver loose in it if you want him to live. Horsepower does count. The more of it, the more dangerous a car is in the hands of an inexperienced driver. Of course, if your teenage boy is a NASCAR fan he will beg you for a powerful car. Any car you select will not be his first choice so be willing to hold your ground.

If you are buying new, get anti-skid control. The anti-skid control helps the driver stay in control of the car by reducing the chance of a sideways skid during turns. It is especially useful if an inexperienced driver takes a corner too fast.

Anti-skid control was only available on expensive cars but now some compact cars have them because the car manufacturer realizes the system makes a car a lot safer in the hands of a young inexperienced driver. So if you can get an anti-skid system, pay the extra cost. It could save a life.

Buy a car, not an SUV. Cars sit lower on the road and due to the lower center of gravity they are less inclined to roll over in a skid. Don't hand down the family SUV to a teenager to drive. Cars keep kids safer than SUVs.

Teens and Sticks

Even though in America automatic transmissions are becoming more popular and fewer stick shifts are sold, there's a very good reason why your kid needs to know how to drive a stick shift.

Many young males still favor stick shifts. It's those young males whom your daughter or son may ride with in their stick-shift sports car or pickup. If the driver of a stick shift has been drinking and it is no longer safe for him to drive your teen will need the skills to drive the stick shift. Otherwise their lives may be put in danger simply because they never learned this skill. Have you ever seen a photo of a pretty, full-of-life teenage girl who's just been killed in a car accident while riding with another? Whenever I see this I wonder to myself if the tragedy might never have happened if she'd been the one driving.

Our children need to know how to protect themselves from the destructive actions of a drunk driver. At times the only way this can be done is for them to assume responsibility for driving and to take the wheel even when it means driving a stick shift.

There's no reason for your teen not to be able to drive a stick shift. If you have to, you can rent or borrow a stick shift car, or pay for driving instruction if you don't have access to a stick shift. Better yet, own a stick shift car and get your kids shifting gears as passengers before they get behind the wheel.

I put a lot of time and care into raising my kids and I had no intention of placing them in a position where they'd be the victim of someone who doesn't know how to handle liquor or drives while intoxicated. I taught them all the skills of staying alive and that included driving a stick shift.

Automatic Transmissions and Stick Shifts

Automatic transmissions make driving easier. Some drivers need them. If the student is older before learning to drive, he may find it difficult to put his attention on the traffic while also remembering to shift gears. He should be encouraged to drive an automatic. It will be a safer car for him since he can concentrate on the traffic, without his attention being involved with changing gears. I've also found that small cars are easier to learn to drive for older drivers, since they're a lot easier to maneuver and park.

The most important rule for driving an automatic is to use your right foot to operate both the gas and brake pedals. This lets you drive an automatic the same way as a stick shift is driven – except that there is no clutch pedal to push with the left foot. If you do use both feet in an automatic and accidentally push the brake at the same time as the gas, you could go into a dangerous skid.

The only exception to the right-foot-only rule is when you are turning the car in a very limited space. Sometimes in tight maneuvering, it's easier to use the left foot on the brake – but don't do that while driving on the road.

Some automatics are inclined to creep forward when the car is stopped so you should always keep your foot on the brake.

At times with an automatic you may need to shift down to a lower gear to get more acceleration (speed up) especially when you are passing or on a freeway on-ramp when you have to speed up quickly. For more acceleration in an automatic you can shift down to a lower gear – without moving the transmission lever – simply by stomping down on the gas pedal as far as it will go. This is known as "kicking down," because one kicks the gas pedal down hard.

A new learner can be hesitant to put his foot down hard and if so, should be taken to a quiet area to practice the kick down. If he doesn't master this, he may find himself on a freeway on-ramp, not going fast enough to get up to the speed of traffic he's trying to merge with.

Most automatics allow the driver to select the gear he wants by moving its transmission lever, similar to a stick shift. When going down a very steep hill you can move the lever to select a lower gear (such as "D2" or "D3") to help slow the car and the car will stay in that gear until it's shifted back to Drive.

Make sure the vehicle is fully stopped before putting it in Park or Reverse – otherwise the transmission can be damaged. Also never leave the driver's seat until it's put in Park. If the car is on a slope also put the parking brake on.

To change from an automatic back to a stick is relatively easy. After driving an automatic for a long time the main problem you may have once you are back driving a stick, is forgetting to push the clutch in before coming to a complete stop and thereby stalling the engine. Have this happen a few times and you'll soon learn to use the clutch again.

Saying that one doesn't want to be confused by the two systems is no reason not to learn to drive a stick shift. Once you have learned to drive a stick, you'll keep this skill even if you spend most of your life driving automatics.

Young people have no trouble driving a stick shift. They enjoy shifting gears and like having the extra task to do.

Safety – a Driving Instructor's Duties

You as the driving instructor of course must teach the learner what he needs to know, but there are safety factors which any driving instructor must keep in mind. High on the list of safety points are, for example, don't teach when you're upset – and don't try to teach a student who is upset, tired or hungry. Always make sure these conditions are fully handled first.

Each time a new action is begun, safety must be considered. If you usually have him practice parallel parking in a particular spot, and this time there are children playing nearby, go to a different place rather than risk your student backing over a child.

Whenever he's driving always keep your eyes on the road ahead. Always look for yourself before he turns, to see if any traffic is coming – don't just leave that up to him alone. You need to be totally alert all the time just the same as if you were driving the car yourself.

Don't relax and leave it to the student once he appears to be driving well. This is the point when accidents can occur – the student makes an error or misses seeing something the instructor should have been alert to and should have advised the student about what to do so as to prevent an accident. He will learn quickly but he'll still be inexperienced, so don't expect too much from him. Don't relax – keep your full attention on the job every minute of each lesson.

The longer the lesson has gone on, the more alert you must become as an instructor, because the student can get tired and make an error. Realize that you must end the lesson before he makes a serious mistake due to fatigue and before you, the instructor, get tired.

Never assume anything! Just because there's a stop sign a hundred yards from your home don't assume that your student knows it's there.

One time I put my attention on my paperwork just before a lesson ended, when the student had only to turn right at a stop sign a hundred yards from his home. I assumed he would know there was a stop sign there because he had lived there all his life. Because I assumed that it was safe to stop looking he drove straight through the stop sign into another vehicle!

I did two things wrong: I relaxed my attention just before the lesson fully ended – when the student was tired – and I also assumed he knew there was a stop sign and would stop and look for traffic. The sound of tearing metal shouldn't be what gets your attention back on the road.

Only Let a New Student Drive in Areas You Know

You should be familiar with the roads you let a new and inexperienced student drive on. Map out your route in advance and have him drive only on roads which you are familiar with. If a new learner-driver is directed into heavy traffic that's moving very fast, he can be overwhelmed very easily.

The service I provided as a driving instructor included picking up the student from his home, school or work, and returning him after the lesson. When I first became a driving instructor I would take students into areas where I didn't know the roads. After twice overwhelming a student by directing him into traffic beyond his abilities to handle, I decided to never let it happen again. It seemed to me that it took another three driving lessons before he got his confidence back.

From that point on I checked out the streets around a student's home, became familiar with them, and found an area where we could drive safely – before I gave the lessons. For driving instructors reading this, it's very easy to check out a new area. With one of your advanced students who needs more driving practice, drive around where a new student lives looking for the busy streets to avoid and a quiet area to give a lesson.

While I was being trained as a Big-Rig truck driver I saw the difference between a good and a bad instructor. A bad instructor would let us drive down streets he'd never been on before. One instructor who was teaching my wife, let another of his students drive into a situation where the only way to get the Big-Rig out was to disconnect the trailer! The corner the truck had to turn was too tight and there was no way a Big-Rig could get around it. The instructor was simply not in control of the lesson. He had never taken the time to discover areas where it was safe and manageable to practice driving a Big-Rig.

A good instructor would have already found an area in which to teach each action a truck driver needed to learn. The instructor would be totally in control of the lesson.

As the instructor you'll feel a lot more in control of the situation if you have your student drive only on roads you're familiar with, especially if your student is very new to driving. If you're not totally confident in your directions, your student will sense that, and he'll start to worry that something unexpected may happen.

An Instructor must be in Control

Professional instructors give exact, scheduled lessons. Too often when a parent attempts to teach his teen, little or no learning occurs because no set schedule is arranged and followed and as a result few lessons are given.

The fastest and most economical way to teach a student driver is by giving a one hour lesson every day, at least five successive days a week, every week. Doing it that way enables the student to keep moving ahead, without slipping back between lessons. If you give a lesson only every now and then, what you last taught him will have to be repeated – because he will have forgotten what was taught earlier. Faster progress is also made by giving lessons closer together. For example, on weekends or while on vacation, two or three lessons given throughout the day will really get results.

Well ahead of time, set a date and schedule an appointment for your student to take his driving license test. If you have that deadline to work toward you'll be more inclined to keep the lessons going. If there's a required waiting time before he can take the test, find another deadline to work toward, such as preparing him to drive your whole family to a wedding or another special event that's coming up and then stick to your driving lessons schedule.

As the driving instructor, you need to be in control of the lesson, including control of the areas where the student is driving. Also make sure you don't let a new student drive when there's extra traffic. For example, don't have an inexperienced driver go past a school when the children are leaving for home. Be in control of the condition of the car, such as keeping windows clean and not leaving objects sitting where they might fly forward during sudden braking.

Stay in control of yourself at all times. If you overreact and upset the student, the lesson will go out of control very easily.

Even though the student needs to be in control of the car, you are in control of the lesson. If you think it's unwise to continue you take charge and make the decision – don't let the student talk you into continuing if doing so would put you less in control. You don't want the situation going out of control because the student is overly tired and lacking concentration. Act in a positive and helpful way to make sure that doesn't happen.

The last thing you want to do is take control of the car away from the student. Make sure you don't get into a position where you have to take the driving over because he's too overwhelmed by unexpected traffic or too upset to drive because of being yelled at.

Think "good, positive, helpful control," and be in control of the whole situation; think how you can get him to be in better control of the car. This applies to any teaching situation, but it is particularly important when giving driving instruction where danger could result from lost control.

Keep the Student in Control of the Car

As the driving instructor you are in control of the student. Make it very clear that if you shout "Stop" the student is to stop, as you will only shout stop to avoid a collision. However, realize the student is in control of the car and try to always keep the student in the driver's seat. In other words, don't get in and drive if the student gets confused. Let students stay behind the wheel and sort it out for themselves.

Only take control of the car away from a student after you get the student's agreement for you to drive the car yourself to demonstrate how something is done.

Your student may be overconfident at lesson's end so for the first few lessons get an agreement at the start of the lesson on when you will take over driving to drive home. For example, if you are teaching in a quiet area, have an agreement that you will drive home at the end of the lesson.

Students need to feel secure behind the wheel, knowing they are in control of the car and that whatever situation they get the car into, they can get out of. A driving instructor who takes over driving the minute a student gets a little confused is making a huge mistake. The student will stop being in control of the car because he feels that at anytime control may be taken away from him.

Never attempt to steer the car when the student is driving unless it is to prevent a collision. It is very disconcerting for any driver to have someone grab the steering wheel. Let the student feel that he is in control of his own learning situation.

Is the Student Handling the Car Better?

Your main guide to any action you teach is improved control. Is the student more in control of the car? If a student is not in control, things go wrong.

A student must be in control of his steering. First the student must master the mechanics of turning the wheel and being in control of his hands as he does so. Practice steering until the student is in control of turning the wheel.

You are also looking for the student to have control over the gas pedal and he must be willing to put his foot down hard to get out of the way of other vehicles. He must be in control when braking, he should know how to do an emergency stop as well as how to pull the car up to an exact point.

For the car to be steered smoothly around corners the student must also be in control of reading the road ahead. You can judge how well your student is doing by how safe you feel in the car. If you are not feeling safe, figure out what the student is doing wrong. It will usually be that the student is not looking far enough ahead and is fixating his attention on things close to the car. The student must view the whole scene to be in proper control of the car.

When driving a stick shift, it is necessary to get control over the friction point of the clutch. Good clutch control is vital otherwise you will be spending a lot of unnecessary time and effort trying to get the car moving without stalling and it will not resolve until the student gains good clutch control.

Occasionally a student can feel pressured by a driver crowding him from the rear and the student will drive faster than he should. If this occurs, then the student has allowed another driver to control him. Don't let this happen. Whatever the driver in the car behind him wants to do should not bother the student.

When you are teaching, whatever the student does not control well should be taken up as soon as possible.

Dangerous Faults

Most of the time you shouldn't chat or interfere with your student while he's driving, but give needed directions only. However, there's one circumstance in which you should open your mouth and do so quickly: when he does or fails to do something that could result in an accident. Those instances you speak up at once and calmly correct him.

When a dangerous situation occurs have him pull over and park the car as soon as it's safe to do so. Then he can give you his full attention. Explain to him what he did or didn't do that could have caused an accident.

Mostly such dangerous situations are the result of forgetting to look or not reading the road ahead. If you, as an instructor or parent, have worked with your student or child while he was a passenger and taught him the data and skills written in the earlier part of this book then such situations won't happen.

As an instructor I used to teach the skills of reading the road, working the pedals and steering the car, all at the same time. That's too much all at once so it's not recommended even though that is the way driving has always been taught before the advent of this book. Some students had no habit of looking left, then right, and then left again. So when approaching a stop sign, this student would get so involved with bringing the car to a stop and making sure the turn signal was used, that he'd forget to also look before moving on. As this was a dangerous fault I would correct it at once.

I'd ask, "I didn't notice you look to the right. Did you?" If he'd looked (but I hadn't notice him do so because I was also looking to see if it was clear to the right), that was fine. However if he said he had not looked or gave me an evasive answer, I'd have him park and then find out why he hadn't looked. It may have been as simple as having too much attention on the turn signal lever and not being too sure which way to move it.

If that was the case, then, still parked, I'd drill him on it saying, "turn left," have him remove his hand from the steering wheel and move the turn signal the correct way for a left turn. I'd continue drilling him on this, for both left and right turns, until he did it correctly and instantly, without thinking about it or even glancing at the signal lever. I'd then have him return to what we were working on before the dangerous situation occurred.

Anytime you're teaching, be willing to stop what you're doing and handle any student fault which could lead to a dangerous situation.

Student Correction

As a driving instructor, you must constantly repeat and remind your student of the basics about where and how far ahead to look, as explained earlier in this book. For the student to be looking far enough ahead, he must aim his eyes high enough.

You will very quickly get a feel for when the student is not looking far enough ahead. The car's motion will become slightly unstable and you won't feel quite as safe as those times when the driver is looking the correct distance ahead.

Every time you feel the student doesn't have complete control over the car, ask him where he's looking, and you'll soon realize that he's not looking far enough ahead. You'll often find that the learning driver has been distracted, and has fixed his attention on something too close to the car.

Your student driver can sometimes get into trouble, and his progress can bog down. At that point, you the instructor, must find out what the student doesn't understand and fix it. It's of great importance to get him eventually doing all of the actions required to drive safely – but there could be a problem he hasn't yet resolved. For example, he might have his attention stuck on using the turn signal correctly, so he forgets to also look for traffic. That must be corrected, before he pulls out in front of a city bus.

Sometimes he'll have a simple idea which is getting in his way. For example, he may have heard that he should signal 100 yards before he turns, and someone else may have told him it should be 50 yards. He may be thinking about those things, instead of putting his attention on a present traffic situation – such as realizing he should stop now to avoid hitting another car. If that's the case, have him look in the state Drivers Handbook to see if a distance to signal before turning is given. In many states, it's "within at least the last 100 feet before you turn." Then, knowing the correct distance, he should be able to signal and make his turn without being confused or uncertain about when to start signaling so he'll have more of his attention on the traffic.

Driving has clearly defined written laws; rules of the road that describe what should and should not be done. These are necessary for safety and for keeping traffic moving in an orderly fashion. You need to refer to your state driver's handbook to sort out any road rule your new driver might not fully understand.

If you take the time to find out what your student is uncertain or confused about, or simply doesn't know, or in some cases has been given wrong information about from others, then you can figure out a way to handle the situation and teach him successfully. Anyone can do this if he keeps it simple and persists long enough to find out what the real problem is. "Seek and ye shall find" is very true in this situation.

Let's Start

After you've carefully read this chapter, skim through the upcoming driving lessons just to see how they're laid out and what data they include. At first, it's not necessary to read exactly how to do every type of action in those chapters.

All the data about driving a stick shift is presented in this style of font. This is so you can easily see it and skip it for now if you are not teaching a stick shift.

After you've quickly reviewed the driving lessons, start again at the beginning and closely read and start doing the actions in the book.

Have your student also read all of the earlier chapters, if he hasn't done so already. This way, your student will know the layout of the book, and know where to turn to in the book when help is needed. By doing this, your student can predict what will be done next, and can also practice some things on his own. For example, if he knows he didn't automatically hit the brake when he needed to during his last lesson, he can find out what to do. That is, sit in the car and practice working the brake without your suggesting it and without your help since the car will be parked.

Later, when you're ready to teach your student to drive a stick shift, closely read and start using the chapter devoted exclusively to stick shift driving.

There you have it. This is your game plan. Follow it well, and I predict that at least nine out of ten parents can proudly achieve very competent and safe young drivers.

Chapter 20

Behind the Wheel

Seating Position

Before starting each driving lesson, time must be spent with the student to get the seat adjusted correctly. His seating position is very important.

The seat should be up high enough for good visibility, especially for a small teenager. I think this is why minivans and SUVs are so popular with women drivers – the higher seat gives them a better view of the road.

This is even more important when you're teaching someone to drive a stick shift because the left foot must be in the correct position to work the clutch. The clutch is pressed all the way to the floor with the ball of the foot – not the toes. The seat should be adjusted so this can be done easily. If the student's seat is too far back he'll try to work the clutch with his toes rather than with the ball of his foot and this will not give him the same degree of control over the clutch.

To be able to work the gas pedal smoothly, place the seat so that he can put his right heel on the floor near the gas pedal. He also must be able to brake with his foot, not his toes. The seat needs to be adjusted so he can apply firm pressure on the pedal. Also, have him wear light shoes – not big, heavy boots that don't give enough sense of feel of the pedal, *especially if it's a stick shift*. High heels, flip-flops, or backless shoes also are not driving shoes. A learner needs flat heels for driving.

If your car has a tilt-adjustable steering wheel, find the most comfortable position for your student. The air bag, should it explode out of the steering wheel, must be aimed at his chest and not at his head. Your student may be smaller than you and the tilt on the steering wheel may need adjustment every time he drives.

If there's a choice of cars to teach with, it's easier to use an automatic shift car at first. When he's driving well, teach him in a stick shift. A student will also find a small, modern car easier to handle and park than a big car or

SUV.

New Safe Way to Teach Basic Car Control

The way driving has always been taught to teenagers was to get them behind the wheel and have them perform the actions of driving, sorting out problems as they came up.

This worked very well in places with little traffic. I taught my kids to drive on their uncle's farm in New Zealand long before the driving age. I have had my granddaughter behind the wheel on deserted country roads in Costa Rica. I also had my kids sitting on my knee steering the car. This is no longer safe to do because of airbags. A child or baby should never be on the driver's lap because an air bag could explode on impact and severely harm or even kill the child. So, it is no longer safe for a child to learn to steer a car while sitting on the driver's knee.

Most of us today do not have a safe place like a farm or a back country road to teach. We live in congested cities. I have therefore developed a system whereby your student can gain control over the foot movements needed to drive a car while it is sitting parked in the driveway. This will make him a safer student driver regardless of who teaches him to drive.

These are great drills for a timid student or a student who lacks coordination. Sometimes it helps an over-confident student by slowing them down long enough to learn what is needed. They are excellent drills for someone with no driving experience.

Driveway Lesson Zero

Since the first drills are performed while the car is parked, we'll call the very first driving lesson, "Lesson Zero." This lesson is comprised of eleven different drills in a specific order. All are done while the car is parked in the driveway. If you have taught them how to go from gas to brake before the driving age don't overdo these drills. Your student will be bored and will protest the action.

Sitting parked in the driveway with the parking brake firmly applied, first have the student sit in the driver's seat and adjust the seat so he's sitting in a comfortable driving position. The mirrors, tilt steering wheel and headrest may also need to be adjusted. Have him look up as if he were driving and focus ahead.

While he's inside the car, if you haven't already taught this, walk around the outside of the car positioning your body in and out of the blind spots so that he'll understand where the blind spots to the left and right are and where he'll need to turn his head to look instead of using the outside mirrors.

(1) With the engine off, have the student practice working the gas and brake pedals. Have him move his right foot very quickly from the gas to the brake. He can either brake hard or lightly touch the brake. Work with your student and drill him by saying, "touch the brake – touch the gas – hit the brakes hard – give it gas to speed up – touch the brakes – speed up," etc., until he has good control over his leg movements. Please note this very first exercise has to do with stopping correctly. That's how important this drill is.

(2) With the car in "Park" (*with the clutch pressed down in a stick shift*), teach the student how to start the car's engine and to watch for the "check engine" light to turn off. The student should start and stop the car engine repeatedly, until he can start it without having to think about what to do.

To repeat – this has to do with safety so please bear with me – the parking brake must be firmly applied during these drills, even if your driveway has no slope.

(3) Then have him start the engine and repeat the "gas to brake" drill with the engine running. But this time, as he moves his foot to the gas, he will get a feel of how far to push the gas pedal down for the engine to speed up. If you have a rev-counter (tachometer), have your student rev up the engine to about 2,000 rpm. This will give him a good feel of how hard to press down on the gas pedal.

(4) With the key turned on (engine not running), get him to signal left and right turns while looking up ahead; have him do this until he can do it correctly in both directions, confidently and automatically, without looking down at the signal lever.

It is "second nature" for you to use the turn signals, so don't rush this step or assume it's too basic to teach. A remarkable number of new drivers seem to want to move the turn signal in the wrong direction. This tendency could be given a long Latin name by some "behavior expert" who'd like to make a big problem out of it, but really all that's needed is some practice, and the new driver will soon get it right.

(5) Once he has a good feel for using the turn signals, then include doing the brake-gas-brake drill, and have him work the pedals as well as signaling left and right turns.

(6) Once these actions become automatic and are being done smoothly

without thinking, add the action of checking the rearview mirror to see what's behind him. Get the student used to glancing in the mirror correctly, without fixating on it, but also make sure he is looking long enough to see what's going on, and make sure he is focusing on what he sees, as given in the earlier chapters. Then get him used to checking all three mirrors.

This will probably be the first time he's practiced using mirrors while in the driver's seat. Even if you've taught him to read the road while a passenger, he wasn't able to practice using the mirrors from the passenger seat, so this is an important drill. Keep coming back to it until the new student can glance in the mirror quickly and take in the whole scene to the rear.

(7) Once he's doing all these actions (gas, brake, signal, mirrors) smoothly and without having to think about them, add the use of the horn. This of course could upset your neighbors so have him just touch the horn to get the feel of how hard to push it. Only do it once or twice and then continue the drill with him hitting the horn but not pushing it hard enough to make a noise.

(8) Next, if your kid hasn't learned this already, have him work the controls for the air conditioner, the heater and the windshield defogger. He must be able to operate these with only a quick glance at the controls. Except for quick glances, the student's eyes must remain looking ahead and not fixate on any controls.

(9) Once the a/c and heater controls can be quickly and correctly adjusted, have the student turn on the windshield washer. (Don't turn the wipers on unless the windshield is wet – otherwise scratching can occur.) Then add the actions of positioning the sun visor, changing radio stations, turning on the headlights, changing headlights from low to high beam and back to low and any other controls that your car may have, such as a sun roof, cruise control, etc., until all of the above control actions can be done without the student being distracted from his most important job of keeping his eyes on the road ahead.

While the car is parked, get him familiar with all the actions he will need to do as a driver. Once he's doing those correctly, have him sit in the car and practice the actions he's learned – without your supervision.

Continue drilling until all of those physical actions of driving a car are under the student's control and are all being done correctly, confidently, smoothly without looking down but keeping his eyes up ahead.

(10A) Next, if you're teaching in an automatic transmission car, get him to practice moving the transmission to different positions. With a foot on the brake, and the engine running, have him practice moving the shifter:

a. Park into Drive (and back to Park)
b. Park into Reverse (and back to Park)
c. Park into Drive and then into Reverse (and back to Drive)

Have him practice the above three positions – in different sequences – until he can do them with certainty and no mistakes. This must be learned because neither of you wants the car shooting off in the wrong direction – that's just like hitting the gas pedal instead of the brake! Make sure the new driver has drilled putting the car in Drive, Reverse and Park until he can do those without having to think about it.

Most people never learn to shift an automatic into drive or reverse without looking down to see what to do. It's a good idea to learn and be able to do this without looking down, just like drivers of stick shifts need to do.

(10B) *If you're teaching him to drive a stick shift, he must be able to quickly re-start the engine if he stalls it because of letting the clutch out too fast. Have him start the engine, then stop it, then restart it again quickly. Keep coming back to, and drilling, turning the engine off and on, until he knows he has to put the clutch in to re-start the engine and does so every time. (Note: according to U.S. safety laws, modern American stick shifts won't start unless the clutch is first depressed.) With the engine turned off, add changing gears. For example: "Put the clutch in, shift from first gear to second gear and let the clutch out. Check mirrors, put the clutch in, shift from second gear to third gear and let the clutch out. Signal a left turn. Brake hard – a child is on the road."*

(11) Once he can do all of the above actions 1-10 such as hitting the brakes and moving the turn signal the correct way – without thinking – then the next step is to repeat those drills while adding some distractions. But don't do this until he's confident and smooth with all those actions, without distractions.

Drill all of the actions while you add in some distractions. Do the following: Talk to the student about something not related to the lesson and add some driving instructions, and see if he can carry on a conversation with you while he correctly follows your added instructions. You can turn on the car radio and have him pay attention to what's said on the radio (make comments or ask questions about it), while he also follows your instructions to hit the brakes, signal a left turn, etc. – all of the above actions in 1-10.

Once the student can smoothly, correctly and quickly do all of those actions – while being distracted – he is then ready to start learning to actually drive the car on the street.

The drill of moving the foot from the gas pedal to the brake can be done again for a few times before every street driving lesson, and should be done again if he hasn't driven for a few days. Most people drive their car two or three times a day, and the actions become second nature. A young new learner doesn't drive that often, but he can sit in the car in the driveway and practice two or three times a day.

The more these drills are practiced, the safer your student will be when he takes to the road. If he's developed an automatic action to hit the brake pedal, he'll do it and not "freeze" and fail to stop in an emergency situation. "Practice makes perfect," and all of the basic actions needed to drive a car can be practiced while the car is parked in the driveway at home.

Do not overdo these drills. In teaching, "perfection" is the enemy of progress. So just get your student to a slight improvement and move on. Kids pick up new things really quickly and will gain perfection with experience.

Even if your student is going to do his school's drivers education program, he should be drilled on these actions before starting the school program.

Can you now see how easy it is to teach, if you break down all the many actions into separate single actions and drill each one? That's one of the secrets of good instruction and successful learning– for any subject.

Short Lessons to Start With

Driving requires doing a number of different actions, all at the same time. Until all those actions become "second nature," done without having to even think about what to do next, intense concentration is needed. Because of that, the student gets tired very quickly.

At first, give short driving lessons. As a pro driving instructor I used to give an hour lesson, but I found that the student's concentration would diminish after forty to forty-five minutes. If you're teaching a family member, don't make the lesson any longer than forty minutes to start with. I've found this is about the longest time a teenager can maintain the intense concentration needed to learn to drive a car.

First Lesson's Location

You need some safe places to give beginning lessons. You probably already know some good locations to give your first, actual in-motion driving lesson. Check them out before you start. The first lesson should be done in areas with little traffic.

An empty parking lot is a safe place, because there will be no other vehicles in it. I've found that church parking lots are usually empty during the week. Some industrial and commercial businesses have empty parking lots on weekends. I've even taught driving in a downtown parking building using its empty top floor. A new housing or industrial area, where roads are in place but building has not been started is perfect, if you can find such a spot.

If you're teaching a stick shift, look for a parking area on a slight slope where you can also have him learn to do downhill starts and uphill starts, so he will get the feel of when the clutch starts to grab.

You should use the same location at the start of each lesson until the student has achieved total control over steering. Even later, if he hasn't driven for a while, start him in the same place to get him accustomed to driving again.

Steering While Turning

The steering wheel is not gripped tightly but ready to do so.

There are two methods of steering a car on tighter turns. One is called the "hands-over" or "hand-over-hand" method and the other is called the "push-pull-slide" (or "shuffle") method. I will describe how each is done.

Push-pull-slide steering on turns: Many of today's older adults learned hand-over-hand, but that method was developed when steering wheels were larger. Before we had power steering it took many turns of the steering wheel to turn the wheels completely. Today we have smaller steering wheels that don't have to be turned far to change the car's direction and nearly all are assisted by power steering.

We also have airbags positioned in the center of the steering wheel, and those can explosively inflate outward with great force. Because of this, some safety experts suggest that instead of hand-over-hand turning, we should learn and use a new push-pull-slide method (called "the shuffle" in England), and even older drivers should learn it too. With this new push-pull-slide method, the arms are never over the airbag, but are kept away from the path of the airbag. Hence, the arms or hands can't be slammed against one's face by the airbag.

The other technical advance that has changed steering technique is the anti-lock braking system or ABS for short. With ABS, you can still steer a car while you have your foot stomped down hard on the brake pedal. With the push-pull-slide method in an emergency stopping situation, you'll be less inclined to over-correct when steering (turn too hard, too far, too fast) and overturn the car. So for this reason, I believe you should teach your kids the push-pull-slide method. It will make them safer if they ever get into a position where they may be using anti-lock braking in an emergency.

The usual driving position for the hands on the steering wheel using the push-pull-slide method is at eight o'clock for the left hand and at four o'clock for the right hand, or slightly lower. (O'clock positions relate to the hands on a clock face.)

To turn right: with the left hand grasping the wheel at eight o'clock or lower, push the wheel up clockwise to ten o'clock or higher. At the same time let the wheel slide through the right hand and bring the right hand up to two o'clock or higher.

If you need to turn the car wheels even more, next use the right hand to grab and pull the steering wheel down clock-wise from the two o'clock to the four o'clock position or lower and at the same time loosen the left hand and let the wheel slide through it while keeping it up near the ten o'clock position.

After the turn, to straighten the wheels out do the opposite – push the wheel up counter-clockwise with the right hand and pull it down with the left – or just let the wheels straighten out mostly on their own while letting the steering wheel slide through both hands.

You can see why it's called the push-pull-slide method, though it might be more accurate to call it the push-slide-pull method.

To turn or steer sharply left, it's the other way around. With the right hand firmly grasping the wheel at the four o'clock or lower position, push the wheel up counter-clockwise to the two o'clock position or higher. At the same time let the wheel slide through the left hand while bringing it up to the ten o'clock position or higher. If you need to turn the car wheels even more use the left hand to grab and pull the steering wheel down counter-clockwise from the ten o'clock to the eight o'clock position or lower and at the same time loosen the right hand letting the wheel slide through it while keeping it up near the two o'clock position. Then to straighten out, reverse the action or let the wheels straighten out mostly by themselves, while letting the wheel slide through both hands.

As the instructor you should demonstrate the push-pull-slide method to show how it's done. If you've never used this method, you should sit in the car while parked, start the engine so the power steering works and practice this a couple of times while reading this book – and then practice it a few more times without reading. This is a good example of how you doing the action in the car will make it much easier to learn rather than me just trying to explain it with words.

Today's teenagers are used to doing small, quick motions with their hands because of the time spent playing computer and video games so they should learn the push-pull-slide method quickly. In case your student just doesn't want to do the push-pull-slide method I will describe the following old method.

Hand-over-hand steering on turns: For this method the correct positions to place the hands and hold the steering wheel are at the ten o'clock and two o'clock positions. Slightly lower, closer to nine and three o'clock positions, are also satisfactory. For shallow, slight turns, the hands don't need to be lifted off the wheel; just turn and straighten again, keeping the hands in the same place.

Here's how the hand-over-hand method is done for sharp turns. Start from the ten and two o'clock positions. For a left turn, the right hand pushes up the wheel counter-clockwise (right to left). While doing that, the left hand reaches over the right hand and grabs the wheel at two o'clock and pulls the wheel around even more in the same counter-clockwise direction until it's back to ten or nine o'clock. This is then repeated, turning the wheel more and more, until the turn is completed.

To then straighten out the car, the same method can be used in reverse, or one can lightly hold the wheel at ten and two and let the wheel slide through the fingers back to its straight-ahead position. Let the beginner use the hand-over-hand-hand method in reverse to straighten out the car, since this is easier to control and gives him more practice using this method.

With the student driving very slowly, have him practice going around a chosen course or pattern. Be willing to let him try to do it himself, but if he's not quickly doing it right, you can correct anything you see that he's doing wrong.

I instruct the student to drive around the lot until he is very much in control of the car or until I get car sick. I even like to see him get adventurous; for example, not only steer around the corners, but also steer toward and away from the curb if there is one as he goes around the pattern. Doing this, his confidence will increase, and he'll gain good control over the car and also learn to judge close distances better. Especially when you tell him how far the front wheel is from the curb as you go, he'll learn how close to the curb he can drive.

This exercise is not taught just once. Come back to it every time you feel he's not handling his steering confidently enough. You should also make it the first exercise of the day's lesson for those who are hesitant or nervous, because this gets them in control and brings up their confidence. Also do it as the first exercise for a minute or two with a student who hasn't driven for a while so you get his confidence back. It's important to find an area close to your home (or his, if you're not his parent), where he can practice steering for a few minutes at the start of each lesson.

Braking

The student driver must have an automatic and instant response to quickly move his foot to the brake pedal whenever needed. You now need to drill this while the car is moving to build an automatic response at the first sign of trouble ahead.

Because you don't have a car with two sets of brake pedals, like some driving schools have, the student must learn very early in his lessons how to stop without him having to think about what to do. Until you feel confident you've gotten him to practice this enough, make it a part of every lesson. Ask him, "Did you cover the brake?", every time it looked like he may have needed to stop quickly due to a traffic situation ahead.

Don't take your eyes off the road to look down and see if he has his foot touching the brake. When something happened, and he should have moved his foot to the brake, ask him if he did so. After a while he will say, "I saw that up ahead and I had my foot on the brake just in case" without you having to ask. Continue doing this drill during each lesson until you have firm evidence that he has built an automatic response of "covering the brake", every time it is needed.

While driving, the student may encounter a small emergency in which he does hit the brakes automatically, just as he should. If you're lucky enough for this to happen, you can now relax a bit knowing that he's gained that ability.

My daughter's dog became extremely excited when the family came home. The dog ran in front of the car as my ten-year-old granddaughter was driving through the gate. Julie hit the brakes without thinking about what to do and as a result stalled the car. Julie's mother was excited that this small emergency had occurred because she now knew that Julie's brain was wired to hit the brakes.

As a minor emergency may not happen, or until one does, you'll need to find out from the student if he automatically moved his foot to the brake if it looked like he might have to stop.

Once you get the student driver moving, it's very important to teach him how to stop quickly. Practice emergency stops. Make sure there's enough room to the side in case the car skids. Explain it's an emergency stop, and no signals are needed (you will be watching for traffic). *If the student doesn't engage the stick shift's clutch and stalls the car, that's okay. You just want to know that the car can be stopped quickly, if it needs to be.* It's a simple action; you the instructor look behind to make sure there are no cars that could run into you. Then shout stop, and the student hits the brakes. Continue this exercise until you're confident he has no reservations about putting the brakes on suddenly and hard, if he has to. This exercise will greatly boost the confidence of a nervous driver, but stop doing it once a good result has been achieved – it can be overdone.

In a later lesson when the student is driving more confidently, again have him do more emergency stopping. Have him do it at 30 mph. This time, train the student to glance in his rearview mirror as he stops, to see if someone behind may rear-end him if he stops too suddenly. In the real world, all you need to do is stop fast enough to avoid hitting the car in front. If you can stop a little slower, and not hit the car in front, and not get rear-ended, you'll save yourself a lot of trouble.

Your student can also practice braking hard, and then easing off a little, and then braking hard, etc. This will develop very good control over the brakes.

Exact Point Stopping

Once he has good braking control, have him bring the car to a stop at an exact point ahead. This should first be done at slow speeds, such as 15-20 mph.

The easiest way to do this is to find a wide street with little or no traffic and have him stop even with each street light pole. If a shadow of the pole is lying across the street, have him bring the car to a stop right at the shadow. Keep doing this exercise with him until he does stop at the correct place.

In later lessons, if the student doesn't stop the car at the correct point, repeat this exercise at the same speed he was driving and when he missed the stopping point. For example, if the student overshoots the line at a traffic light and stops too close to a pedestrian crossing, or undershoots and leaves too much space between him and the car in front, then as a separate drill, you need to have him stopping at an exact point – starting at 30 or 35 mph.

Usually, to have the student practice stopping at an exact point at a slow speed, have him pull up even with each light pole he comes to. To drill at a faster speed, get him up to 30 mph and then tell him what point to stop at. It should be a wide street with little traffic where stopping for no reason won't interfere with traffic. It may also be just a street with many stop signs, where he has to legally stop often and therefore won't interfere with the traffic flow.

Finally, if you have anti-lock brakes, make him hit the brakes hard enough to activate the anti-locking action so that as a new driver he gets the feel of how the brake pedal pulses under his foot. When doing this, also have him steer the car, so he knows he can still steer away from trouble when he has to slam on the brakes. It's stomp, steer, stop! This applies only to anti-lock brakes. This exercise needs to be done away from traffic.

Right Turns

Once the student has the ability to start, stop, and steer the car in parking lots, you can then start him driving on streets in a quiet area. Have him first practice right hand turns. Right turns are easier to do than left ones, and when he first starts driving on streets, try to plan lessons so he makes only right turns. Simply have him drive clockwise around a block so that he'll always be turning right. Insist that he use the turn signal correctly and obey all stop and yield signs.

Pay very close attention yourself to see if the way is clear to your left and right, and also make sure your student looked. If you didn't see him look, ask if he did. You may not have noticed him checking.

As a rule, this is not a long exercise, especially if you've earlier had him practicing looking out as a passenger and telling you when it's safe to turn. If needed, re-do right turns in the next lesson.

If he has problems with the turn signal, realize he may not be sure which way to move the signal lever – in which case, have him stop the car, and you drill him on using the signal. If he doesn't stop in the correct position before turning, make a note of it so you can later drill or re-drill him in a lesson on stopping at an exact point.

Left Turns

Left turns are done only after right turns. Left turns are a little harder. Now the student must look for cars coming from both directions. At first have him do left turns in a very quiet area with little traffic, usually driving around and around the same block. Then later repeat this exercise where there's more traffic. You check to make sure he now looks to see if the way is clear in both directions before he makes left turns.

Once he can do right and left turns confidently (and the earlier stopping actions), then he's ready to drive in light traffic.

It's a good policy, even for an experienced driver, to plan your route so that you mainly make right turns rather than left turns, even if you have to go a longer distance to get to where you're going. You'll also expose yourself to fewer chances of having an accident and you will be more relaxed.

Backing

Backing up can be made to look very easy by a professional driver using his mirrors. However, when first learning to back-up, it's better to turn the body around and look straight backwards – leaving the mirrors till later. Many safety experts say even a pro should always turn around and look back, never relying on mirrors only, because there can be a small child whom you couldn't possibly see in any mirror.

To see if it's clear to the rear, your student should be taught to first check mirrors. If it's safe to back-up, have him leave his left hand on the steering wheel and his foot on the brake, then hold himself with his right hand on the seat and turn around to look straight back, focusing on whatever he sees, before he has his foot coming off the brake pedal.

When backing in a straight line, have him apply the "look ahead" data to looking well behind the car in the direction he wants to go and finding a point to aim for. This will keep the car from wandering as he reverses. But don't let him become fixated on any one point – he should also make occasional glances to the side.

Similarly, to back into a driveway positioned on the passenger door side, he places his hand on the back of the seat and he does basically the same as when backing up straight. He turns around, and then he backs and turns the steering wheel while aiming into the driveway so the car turns into it.

To turn into a driveway positioned on the driver's door side, he does the same action except he should turn his body around the other way, toward the driver's door.

Sometimes a driver can see better by looking in the mirror(s) on that side of the car that needs to be watched. He can also look out the driver's window if needed. He may also need to take off his seat belt so he can turn around.

When backing-up, he should keep his speed down to a walking pace. Truck drivers have most of their accidents while backing-up, so realize that it's a dangerous action. If there's any slightest doubt about where young children are, one should always put the car in park, get out of the car and look all around the car before starting to back-up.

The two most common faults in backing-up are 1) the student doesn't turn his body around far enough to see both sides of the car's rear while he is backing, and 2) he doesn't find a point behind the car to aim the car toward.

He also needs to know where the rear of the car is so that, when he backs into a parking lot, he knows when to stop. Since he may not have his seat belt on at this point, the quickest way for him to learn to judge the distance is to get out and examine the area he needs to back into. Then he should back, stop, park, get out again and check to see how close he got. Once again, safe backing is always a slow action.

Parking

Teach angle and straight-in parking as early as possible in order to teach the student how to shift the transmission back and forth between Drive and Reverse. *For stick shifts, it's a better way to teach clutch control than any other way I know. The student isn't concentrating on the clutch, but rather on the angle parking, so clutch control can be developed without the student making a problem of the clutch.*

Some students will learn angle parking very quickly, it will be no problem. Others find it hard to understand that when parking, the car's front must swing outward. The back wheels don't follow in the same path as the front wheels. The back wheels "cut the corner," and because of this, the front wheels must swing outward to allow the rear wheels to "cut in."

Have the student stand outside the car while you turn a corner and have him watch how the front and rear wheels track differently. If you can drive on sand or with wet tires on a dry road, the tire tracks will show the front and rear wheels having two separate tracks when turning. You can also sketch this on paper, showing the two separate tracks the front and rear wheels make as a car turns, or use a toy car to help demonstrate this to the student.

Three-Point Turns

A three-point turn is one way to make a U-turn (turning around to go back in the direction you came from) on narrow streets, in three steps: a) move forward while turning, b) move in reverse while turning and c) move forward again. These steps should be taught so that the student knows how to turn around when a street is too narrow to allow a normal one-step U-turn. This is especially important when it's not possible to go around the block.

Don't make three-point turns on a curved street, or where there's a hill in the road which could prevent another driver from seeing you or, prevent you from seeing approaching vehicles.

Here is how a three-point turn is done: Have the student come to a complete stop close to the right side of the road as possible. Signal a left turn and check for traffic both ways. Then:

1. Let the car start moving forward and at the same time turn the steering wheel sharply left all the way. Move the car slowly forward and just before the front wheels hit the curb on the other side of the road or just near the edge of the road, straighten the wheels, and stop.

2. Shift into Reverse, let the car start moving back and at the same time, turn the steering sharply right all the way, slowly backing the vehicle and just before the rear wheels hit the curb or just near the edge of the road, straighten the wheels and stop.

3. Shift into Drive (forward), check for traffic and then move forward – completing the turn. This really is not difficult and with practice all three steps can be done quickly.

If the road is extremely narrow, it may require another backward and forward move to complete the turn without running over the curb. If this is necessary, do so. *Three-point turns are something the student can practice in a stick shift to develop his clutch control, providing you can find a safe place to do it. Just like angle parking, the student should have his attention mostly on the three-point turn, and so not make a problem of using the clutch.*

Parallel Parking

In some states, parallel parking is not part of the driver's test, because it's more embarrassing than fatal if done wrong. Since the development of shopping malls with their angle parking, parallel parking on Main Street is not as important as it was fifty years ago.

Do have your student practice parallel parking, by all means. It teaches a driver to be in control of the car when backing, but realize that time spent on making turns and changing lanes is far more important. *Parallel parking helps to develop clutch control when learning to drive a stick shift.*

For the student's first time practice of this, find a parked car with plenty of open space behind it – no other parked cars. Here's how it's done:

1. The student signals right, and pulls up even with the parked car (the back bumper of his car even with the back bumper of the parked car), and close to the side of the parked car, with only about three feet or slightly less space between them.
2. Put the car in reverse, and slowly move straight back – until his car's rear wheels are even with the parked car's rear end bumper.

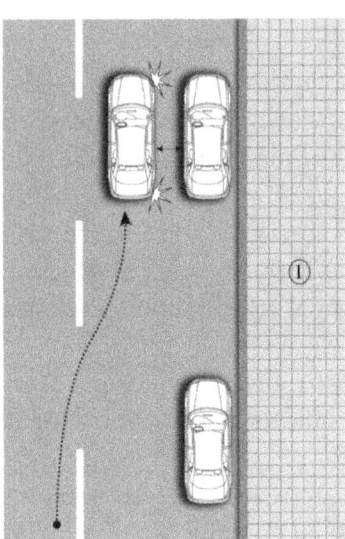
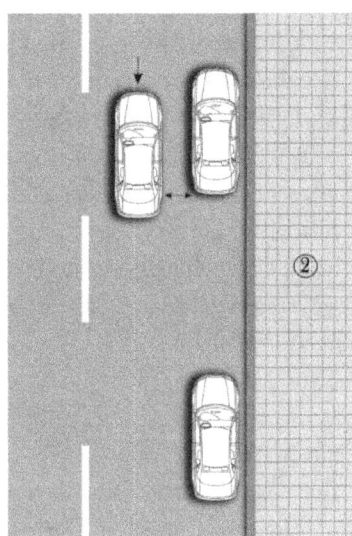

3. Turn the steering sharply right while backing very slowly.
4. When his car is at about a 45-degree angle to the parked car (see the picture below), straighten the steering and continue farther back at that angle.
5. When there's room for his front bumper to clear the parked car's rear bumper, start turning the steering left while backing slowly, to move his car's front behind the parked car's rear. Continue backing until

the car is parallel with the curb, and the front wheels have reached the curb, or nearly so.
6. If needed, pull the car forward, with the front wheels near the curb, both to get closer to the curb, and to put the car in the center of the parking space. If either of the right side wheels gently touch the curb, that's fine, but not necessary.

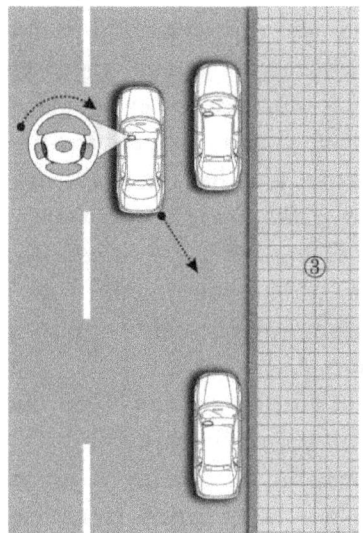 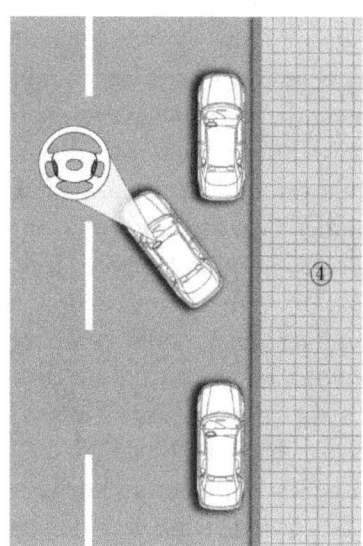

The basic steps you take when parallel parking.

The car's final position should have the front and rear wheels close to the curb. Ideally, the wheels should be only six inches or less from the curb. The closer to the curb, the more protection the car has from being "side-swiped" by other cars. It should also be far enough from other parked cars (ahead and behind) so that both you and they can pull out without too much trouble, or simply positioned evenly between any marked parking space lines.

With some practice, parallel parking is easy if the student driver follows the directions above. If the student is not succeeding even when following the directions, he's not moving the steering quickly enough, or he's moving too fast – both of which make parallel parking difficult.

Driving Around Busy Mall Parking Lots

Shopping mall parking lots are an ideal place to develop a student's ability to control a car, after he's learned the basics. By having him drive around a busy lot, he'll learn to steer, judge distances and handle the brake and gas pedals. *A stick shift driver also learns more clutch control.* The student learns to signal correctly. Pulling in and out of angle parking develops several skills. The driver must learn to look all around, and this trains him to not fixate the eyes on any one thing. In a busy lot, there's something happening every moment that he may have to respond to. He must keep his eyes moving, since traffic and pedestrians can come at him from any direction, at any time.

Take the student to a busy parking lot only after he's learned to angle park in a quiet area. He needs to know how to park in case he needs to stop and have something explained to him. His steering *and clutch handling* must be satisfactory (not perfect), and he must have drilled covering the brake in case a shopping cart or child comes at him from nowhere, and he must quickly stop without having to think about what to do.

Do this busy parking lot lesson before he's tired, since a lot of concentration is needed. It's not a long exercise, about fifteen minutes at most.

If he leaves the lot and drives too slowly for the conditions, remind him that he's been driving very slowly in the lot – and he needs to remember to speed up.

Not all students drive too slowly after driving around a busy lot slowly for fifteen minutes – but the ones who do are also the ones who have trouble speeding up after getting onto a freeway, or slowing down after coming off the freeway. So take this opportunity to repeat the data about adjusting one's speed, relative to what he was doing earlier, with particular reference to speeding up when entering the freeway, and slowing down when exiting one.

Judging the Car's Position

During the beginning lessons, while practicing steering slowly around an empty parking lot, see if you can find one with a curb so you can tell the student how far his front wheel is from the curb. Just say, for example, "You're six feet away from the curb," and the student will then quickly get to know where his car is positioned. (For anyone who has trouble quickly grasping this, have him stop the car, put the transmission in park, get out and see for himself exactly where he placed the car. Such students are rare.)

You should also open your door whenever he places the car too close or too far from the curb, to show him where he actually placed it. You can usually indicate how far away from the curb he is by holding your hands up facing each other and spread them apart the same distance that the car is from the curb. Doing this in early lessons gives him a good idea of where the side of the car is.

Later on if the student is still not judging the car's position well, you can do the following drill. Have him sit in the parked car behind the wheel. You stand outside the car and hold up a book in the air, a bit higher than the hood or trunk where he can see it, with its wide side facing the student. At first, hold the book about three or four feet away from the car. Then start to slowly move the book closer and closer toward the car. Have him tell you when he thinks the book is up to (exactly even with) the car. Then you show him, using both your hands spread apart, just how far the book really is from the car.

Do this drill several times in different positions; on the car's side, front, and rear, until he learns how big the car is. (This drill can also be done before the student is old enough to drive.)

He should also know how close to stop behind another car at traffic lights. The correct distance is reached when he can just see the other car's tires touching the road, over the car's hood. If he can't see that, then he's too close.

Painted line markers can be used for teaching your student how to correctly position the car while driving in lanes. Have him position the car in the center of the lane (according to both side mirror views), and have him note which point on the hood lines up with the lane markings to the left or right in front of the car. Or, if the hood is out of view, use a point on the wiper arms. If needed mark the position with a piece of masking tape that can be removed once the student driver is judging the car's position correctly. This is also an ideal way to judge the distance the car is from the curb for those beginning drivers who need to move closer to the curb. I haven't had to use this technique very often, but if a student doesn't quickly learn to place the vehicle in the middle of the lane, you should work with him like this. It gives him a reference point on the car or wiper arm that lines up with lane marks on the road.

My wife wouldn't keep the truck close enough to the center line when she first started driving an eighteen-wheeler on narrow roads. It was only after she had a reference point, by lining up a point on the wiper arm with the center line of the road that she learned to position the truck to within an inch of where she wanted it.

While driving our Big-Rig, my wife was pulled over once by a cop for speeding. The policeman showed some amazement when he realized the Big-Rig was being driven by a woman. She didn't get a ticket because the cop was quite sure she wasn't the driver – the cop said that only a man could drive a truck as well as she had been driving it. The above technique allowed her to keep the truck exactly in the center of the lane even when she was speeding.

Cardboard boxes can also be used to get an idea of the car's position. Stack up the boxes high enough to be seen by the driver and put them in front of the car. Have the driver move slowly toward them until the car touches the boxes. Then place the boxes far enough apart so they can be driven between and let the student practice going through a narrow gap. Also close the gap so it can't be driven through and let the student gain the ability to know what gap is too narrow to get through.

If your parking spot is tight, it's important for you, as the experienced driver, to figure out the best way for your student to get in and out. For example, watch the mirror as you move back past the garage door, and then look behind and aim for the distant mail box.

Too Fast! Slowing Down an Over-confident Driver

The most difficult student for an instructor to teach is an over-confident learner who drives much too fast and won't slow down when you tell him to. You tell him to slow down but it doesn't make any difference.

Just after I became a driving instructor, one husband called me in desperation, saying his wife was a crazy driver and he asked me, "Can you please teach her?" The husband was correct – she was a crazy driver!

She drove at a very fast pace, with almost no control of the car, and asking her to slow down was of no use! I needed to quickly get her off the road. A large busy shopping mall was nearby, and I immediately directed her to drive into its parking lot – not because I thought that driving in a busy lot would slow her down for good, but because I feared for my life and wanted her to slow down immediately. For about twenty minutes, I made her drive around the very busy lot in low gear, at a slow speed. The lot was extremely busy so she had no option but to slow down. After this, she slowed down at all times while driving.

I also found that a "speed demon" driver will slow down if made to drive in a small empty parking lot, such as the places I described earlier for giving your student the first street lessons.

From my experience, I've found you shouldn't tell a new driver more than once that he's going too fast. If you have to tell him he's going too fast for the conditions, and he doesn't instantly slow down to the correct speed, then if no busy parking lot is available immediately direct him to an area where he can practice steering at a very low speed, in first gear. Such a place may be totally empty, unlike a busy mall, but driving slowly while practicing steering gets him slowed down and back in control of the car.

A student learning a stick shift can drive too fast because he's afraid of stalling the car. The too-fast new driver has usually stalled the car when going slowly, and as a result has decided he's not going to let the car stall again – so he keeps the engine revving and he drives too fast for his limited ability.

In such a case find a large parking lot and instruct him to slow way down before a corner, and then speed up once he's completed the turn. After ten to fifteen minutes at most, he will drive slower and eventually go around the pattern at an idle in low gear. Have him practice the slow down and speed up lesson until he does slow down. I've found this applies more often to stick shift drivers. The "crazy driver" I mentioned earlier was learning to drive her husband's stick shift.

Also make a point of reassuring the stick driver that stalling won't be a problem in the future, because within a short time his clutch control will be perfect. Explain that you'll work together until the "hit or miss" approach to the clutch is handled, and he has the ability to always get the car moving under good control, without stalling.

Another reason a student may drive too fast is that he's afraid of the car slowing or doesn't know confidently how to speed the car up if it does slow down. He may have gotten into trouble with the car suddenly shooting ahead when he attempted to speed up. As a result, he keeps the car going too fast all the time to avoid having to speed up and risk shooting ahead out of control.

While driving in a parking lot, the adding of slowing down before turning a corner and speeding up once around the corner will give the student better control over the gas pedal – good control he may not have had before. This will develop the skills needed so that he won't have to drive fast because he doesn't know how to gradually increase the car's speed.

Probably the most common reason for a student's driving too fast is that a speed is "relative" to other speeds. For example, when coming off a freeway after doing 65 mph, it's hard to keep speed down to 35 mph in a residential area. If you're used to traveling at 65 mph, then that speed seems "normal", and 35 mph seems too slow. The same applies to a new learning driver. He tries to drive at what he thinks is the correct speed, but for some, that's too fast for the conditions and his poor ability to control the car.

When I checked what speed the "crazy driver's" husband drove at I found that he was a very fast driver. Therefore, when his wife started to drive, that was the speed she drove at because that was the "normal" speed she was used to while being driven around by her husband.

I know that following these methods for getting a speed demon student to drive slowly works, as described above. It always slows down driving that's too fast for abilities. It's a technique I might have used twice a day, as an instructor. I'd definitely use it on a new student who makes me feel unsafe because of his speed.

Also use this parking lot technique for a progressing student who is starting to get a little over-confident and is driving faster than he should be. Using this to slow down an over-confident student is a very easy way to handle the problem – and it works. You can have a student over-confident at the start of a lesson, slow him down with steering at slow speeds, then go for a drive in the country, and at the end of the lesson he'll be driving a little faster than he should – but doing so safely, in full control of the car.

If a student is in very good control of the car, and driving extremely well, but his speed is a bit higher than your comfort level, providing it's within the speed limit, do your best to accept that and just let him get on with it. Let him enjoy driving.

Foot Down! Pedal to the Metal

Some students are reluctant to put their foot down hard enough on the gas and won't speed up to get out of the way of other vehicles. This may not be apparent until you ask him to speed up quickly. It's no good telling him to speed up, he just won't.

To handle his reluctance, do the following. First, explain that being able to speed up quickly is just as important as being able to stop quickly. If, for example, he makes a misjudgment and pulls out too close in front of someone, he must be able to speed up quickly to get out of the way.

In a quiet area, have him travel slowly (*in second gear for a stick shift*) and practice putting the pedal to the metal. You, as the instructor, make sure it's clear of traffic in the front and rear. Then tell him to hit the gas pedal hard – and then slow down, once he has sped up. Keep doing this repeatedly, until the student has no reservations about accelerating quickly, but don't overdo it.

If the student has real reservations about stopping quickly, as well as speeding up quickly, then combine the emergency braking drill with this accelerating drill. Once he's sped up, tell him, "When I say 'stop,' I want you to stop as quickly as you can." Usually doing this two or three times is all that's needed to get the student to both speed up and stop confidently.

If a stick shift student always puts the car into second gear too soon, without increasing the engine revs by giving it more gas while in first gear, I usually find he has reservations about accelerating quickly. Quite often the reason he gives is that he doesn't like the sound of the motor at high revs, and he may also be afraid it could hurt the engine. If this is the case, and you have a rev-counter, have him rev the car up to 1,000 rpm – below the red line or red numbers – and show him that it does no damage to the car. Do this while parked. If the car has no rev-counter, have him look in the car owner's manual and find out what traveling speeds are recommended before shifting up to each higher gear. Then have him practice doing that.

Not all students need this foot down drill, but when they do, it really works. Make sure you've gotten the student used to getting the car up to speed before you have him attempt freeway driving. If you think he may be unwilling or reluctant to speed up quickly, such as on a freeway on-ramp, then first drill him on putting his foot down!

This foot down drill can change the student driver's attitude toward driving. The reservations he has about accelerating quickly enough are getting in the way of his driving competently. This drill will break through those reservations, and while doing it the student will brighten up and become happier and more confident about handling a car.

Freeway Driving

Begin freeway driving lessons once the student is driving confidently. The first lesson should be done at a time when the freeway is not busy. Only after he's experienced at driving on the freeway during off-peak times should you have him drive in heavy traffic.

Don't tell the student you'll be doing freeway driving until just a few minutes before you start it. This won't give him time to get nervous, if he's a nervous type.

Before entering the freeway, make sure he knows what's required as he pulls onto the on-ramp and accelerates in the merge lane. He must know he has to speed up, signal left and watch for a gap in existing traffic where he can merge in.

Make sure he knows he must look for gaps, spaces in the traffic. He must not fixate on the vehicles he sees but look for a space to get into. Getting on a freeway will be less scary for him if he looks for a space to enter rather than fixing his attention on a big truck moving toward him. He should also realize that the car's speed may need to be adjusted, faster or slower, to move into an available space.

Usually freeway traffic travels at or close to the maximum legal speed. Getting the car up to that higher speed quickly is vital for freeway driving. Since this is probably the first time he's driven at this high speed, the learner must be encouraged to get up to speed quickly, so he'll be at the same speed as the traffic he's merging with.

Once he's gotten on the freeway, have him exit at the first available off-ramp – one which enables him to easily return to the freeway. Once off, then have him cross over or under the freeway, then have him re-enter the freeway and return, back the way he came.

Once back on the freeway, have him get off at the point he started. When this pattern is established, get him to get on and off the freeway a number of times. Do this until he has no reservations about getting the car up to the speed which other cars are moving and has learned to merge with traffic as he enters the freeway.

To start with, just direct the learner to get on and off the freeway. Don't have him do any other freeway driving, such as changing lanes, until you feel he's confident about getting up to speed and is willing to keep his speed up until he's actually at the exit lane for the off-ramp, and he confidently leaves the freeway.

You want him to be confident about getting on and off the freeway in one lesson, so this is all that is concentrated on in that lesson. Try to find on and off ramps close together – so you can get on and off quickly a few times and finish the lesson before the student gets tired.

In the next lesson have him practice freeway driving. Under your direction have him move to the center lane, and have him practice looking twelve seconds ahead. Get him to select a point he thinks is twelve seconds ahead, and tell you what he's looking at. Then count one thousand and one, etc., up to twelve, and see if he was looking far enough ahead. Continue doing this exercise until he's looking the correct distance ahead.

Once the student is confident with entering and exiting the freeway and is looking far enough ahead, then start him on changing lanes. Make very sure he checks the blind spots and makes a final check by turning his head to look for a car which may have appeared in the lane he'll be changing into. This is important because sometimes a car traveling well above the speed limit will suddenly be alongside, just as the student starts to change lanes. So he needs to make a head-moving final check before changing lanes.

Next, steering around curves can be learned and practiced at freeway interchanges. Have the student put his attention twelve seconds ahead, and get him practicing keeping the car steady, as if it were on train rails, by going around the curve and moving his eyes near and far to keep the car centered in his lane. These are well covered in earlier chapters which I recommend you review before drilling him on this. Get him to practice going around long, sweeping curves, using a "tow" vehicle in front of his car to learn that technique, as also covered earlier in this book.

Once he's confident on the freeway in off-peak times, let him drive it at busy times. When entering or changing lanes on a busy freeway, make sure he looks for gaps to move the car into and doesn't fixate on vehicles in his way.

Before ending the more advanced freeway lessons, again have him practice getting on and off the freeway a few times, and see if he can do it without any advice from you. You're now close to getting the student tested, and if the licensing test includes freeway driving, the examiner won't be telling him how to do anything, only what he wants done (e.g. "take the next exit"). So have your student practice getting on and off the freeway without you saying anything.

Make very sure your student is looking far enough ahead. Freeway driving is usually at twice the speed he's been used to driving, and twelve seconds ahead is now about a quarter of a mile – not the one block ahead for driving on surface streets.

More Turning Practice

When your student has gained confidence and is in reasonable control of the car, have him practice more turning. Turning requires practice because it involves eye, hand and foot coordination, and this will improve his control of the car. Turning at a light takes coordination.

Let's see what is involved when waiting at a light. When turning left, he needs to have his eyes on three things at once: the light, the cars approaching from ahead and the area where he wants to go. He needs to watch the street he'll be turning onto, to avoid any pedestrian who may be crossing. Once the way is clear, the eyes must aim ahead, up the path the car needs to travel. At the same time, the feet and hands must work together to drive the car around the corner.

Don't just take your student driving on long, straight roads. Have him turn left and right into as many different turning situations as you can find. When it's not possible to make turns, have him practice changing lanes.

The car should be slowed before curves and turns, and slowly sped up once in the turn so as to push the car around the corner. It's too late to brake, once in the turn. He should brake while the front wheels are still pointed straight ahead. Braking while in a turn will "dig in" the front of the car, and make it harder to steer, and it may also make the car skid in slippery conditions.

Have him steer around a curve with his eyes looking up in the direction the car needs to go. He should help the car steer around the curve by slowly increasing its speed. He should have his eyes leading the way by looking ahead, not too close to the car. He slightly increases the pressure of the foot on the gas, and his hands will steer around the corner smoothly, steering the car exactly where it needs to be.

When he takes his licensing driving test, the examiner will want to be certain the new driver is in control of the car. The more turns and lane changes you can get him to make, the greater his control of the car will be.

Driving Test

Familiarize your student with the area in which his driving test will be done, and tell him what will be needed during the test – especially if he has a history of "going to pieces" under testing conditions.

Find out what his local driving test comprises of, and make sure he has practiced all the actions the examiner may ask the student to do. If parallel parking or three-point turns are part of the test, have him practice those as well. Have him practice all of the test actions – without you giving any advice. Only give directions when needed, just as if you're the examiner.

He should also practice driving and parking in the place where he'll be tested. Familiarize him with how to get in and out of the actual testing location, and have him spend time getting into and out of the place the car will be parked as he waits for the examiner. If the testing area is busy during work hours, take him there in the evening or on the weekend.

Practice makes perfect. The more you let your student drive before the test, the more in control of the car he will be. I've met many test examiners who have told me they know within the first few minutes whether or not the student is in good control of the car. Only if he's in control, and the examiner feels safe as a passenger, will the student be passed.

Chapter 21

Lessons Plan

Lesson One

Drive the student to an empty parking lot and demonstrate what the student needs to do – by you, still in the driver's seat, doing it first. First show him how to get the parked car moving. In an automatic, with the foot on the brake, it's as simple as changing the vehicle from Park into Drive, and then removing the foot from the brake, and pressing the gas pedal. *In a stick shift, demonstrate how to start moving in first gear.*

Use the markings of the parking lot to establish a pattern to follow, so you have some control over where the student drives. You should keep driving until you've established a pattern the student can follow. The area needs to be only large enough so that a normal corner can be turned and the wheels straightened up before the next turn is made.

If it's a big parking lot, while you're still behind the wheel, demonstrate speeding up and slowing the car. Find a place in the parking lot where you can speed up, and then slow it down quickly with the brakes. Figure out what speed it's safe to reach before applying the brakes, so the student can get the car up to that agreed-upon speed. This can be done only in a big parking lot.

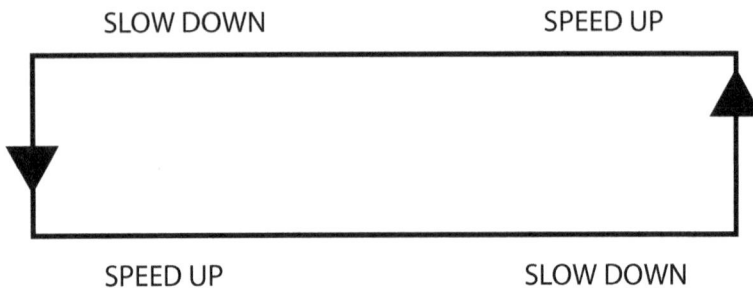

You also need to steer the car toward the outer edge of the lot, and have the student observe from the passenger seat how far the car is from the edge.

You have now established control and a pattern (a route to follow in the lot), and the student now knows what is expected. Once you've done that, then stop, park and let him take the wheel. Have him start the car and have him steer the car around the agreed on pattern.

He can practice coming close to the edge and you can tell him how close he is, so he gets a sense of the car's position and how big the car is.

When the new driver is progressing I state the goal of the first lesson. It is that he'll keep driving around until he has the ability to start, steer, slow, and stop the car at slow speeds. At this point the student can see what needs to be done and can agree on achieving that goal. If the parking lot is large enough, he can also learn how to speed up and slow down the car. If the lot is really big, you can have him speed up and slow down using the brakes.

The whole purpose of lesson one is to get the new driver to be able to start, stop and steer the car confidently at a low speed. By also having the student stop next to the curb and telling him how far away he is, he will learn to judge the car's position on the road. *When using the clutch while driving a stick shift, this exercise will take more practice, and you may not get it all done in one lesson.*

Lesson Two

At the start of the second lesson, you drive the student driver to your chosen spot and stop the car on a gentle slope facing downhill. Then, still driving, you demonstrate to the student how to start the car when going downhill. *In a stick shift, put the car in first gear with the clutch in and the right foot on the brake – then let off the brake and as the car moves forward, slowly let the clutch out fully.*

LESSONS PLAN

After you've demonstrated downhill starts, put the student in the driver's seat and get him doing downhill starts. Then go over what was done in his first lesson and have him practice, in an empty parking lot, steering for a few minutes driving around the same pattern you used in lesson one. Now he is ready to drive on streets with very little traffic.

Have him drive around on quiet streets and practice using his eyes to steer while looking up ahead. Then have him aim the car between any parked car and the road center line, looking up ahead through the gap where the car needs to travel. He must not fixate on the parked vehicle but be able to confidently look to where his car needs to go. See the illustration in Chapter 5.

Then go back to braking and have him practice some more light braking. While he's driving, have him touch the brake, then put his foot back on the gas and speed up a little, then move the foot back to the brake and if you're moving fast enough, then have him brake to slow the car. No matter how well the student drilled that action with the car parked, it will need to be drilled while in motion, once he starts to drive, so he can actually get the feel of how much to push the gas and how much to push the brake. If he drilled it well in the driveway, this will be a very short exercise. He should now be able to start the car moving, know how to speed up and how to stop at a faster pace. Get his agreement that you can achieve that goal in lesson two.

In a stick shift, if the student isn't too tired at that point in the lesson, have him start shifting gears from first to second. At first give exact directions, such as: "Put the clutch in and move the stick from first to second. Good, now let the clutch out and speed up a little." By giving exact directions the first few times, you can make sure he's doing what's needed correctly. Repairing a transmission is expensive, so you must be on the alert to see if he uses too much force on the stick – which can cause damage – or is riding the clutch not fully let out, wearing it down quickly.

Next have him practice emergency braking from 15–20 mph. Have him do this several times until you feel he knows he's in control of the car and can stop it quickly.

At this point, as in the first lesson, he has again practiced how to start, steer and stop though at a faster speed – and he will usually show a sort of relief. His fear of the car fades when he realizes he can control the car and stop it very quickly. If you don't have a very happy student at this point, have him do emergency braking again in his next lesson.

In a stick shift, teach and have him practice clutch creep to gain more clutch control. This needs to be taught before doing uphill starts. Don't overdo it at this point. Clutch creeps demand a lot of attention, so once he understands how it's done, stop before he gets too tired.

End the lesson by having him drive around a block where there is little traffic, making only right turns (for which he has to watch for traffic from only the left). Then have him practice making left turns, where he has to watch for traffic from both the left and right. All this can usually be done in the second lesson if you are driving an automatic car. *For stick shifts, you may need to have him come back to practicing clutch creep. A stick shift will take longer.*

Lesson Three

Lesson three is mainly going over what was done in lessons one and two and getting the actions done more confidently. You still drive the student to the practice area, even if you'd let him drive home after the second lesson. After several days of not driving, he will probably have forgotten some of what he'd learned, or at least need a warm up period on a quiet road to "put his eye back in." Before you leave the driver's seat demonstrate uphill starts on a gentle uphill incline.

In a stick shift you would put the car facing up a gentle slope and you would demonstrate to him how to do an uphill start without using the parking brake. Do this by simply moving from the foot brake to the gas pedal as the clutch is let out, without using the parking brake. Then put him in the driver's seat and have him practice uphill starts.

Spend the rest of the lesson going over what was earlier covered to speed up his actions. If he isn't already doing it, have him practice letting the clutch out quickly until he reaches the friction point. Then have him change gears quickly, if his actions need to be sped up. He needs to practice doing these actions quickly, because once he gets into traffic, his attention should be on the conditions around him, not on trying to do the basic clutch and gear shifting actions faster.

Have him spend a few minutes on clutch creep, and no more than fifteen minutes on uphill starts. Intense concentration is needed for him to learn uphill starts, so if you stay with it too long he'll start making mistakes because he's tired.

For the last twenty minutes of the lesson, have him drive around away from traffic and do more right turns. Once he's doing right turns confidently, have him do left turns. If he's too tired or hasn't progressed quickly, don't have him practice left turns but leave it for the next lesson.

Lesson Four

For a stick shift have him again drill uphill starts to develop that skill further. Of course, once the student actually hits traffic and needs to do an uphill start, he'll rush it, get flustered and stall the engine. Reassure him this is normal and explain that he must now learn to do uphill starts under pressure.

Put steering practice and *uphill starts for a stick shift* at the beginning of each lesson, if he's had difficulties with those or trouble with coordination.

Next, have him drive along a street and practice exact point stopping. Look for a wide and quiet street to do this, so he doesn't interfere with traffic.

Next, have him practice angle parking and backing out of angle parking spaces in a deserted parking lot. This will teach a new skill because of the extensive use of stopping and starting. *At this point, his clutch control won't be perfect and this parking exercise further develops it.* Not only will he gain the ability to angle park, he'll also learn to shift an automatic from Drive to Reverse and back again, *and in a stick he'll improve clutch control.*

The last fifteen or twenty minutes of the lesson should be spent on his driving around on streets, even encountering some traffic.

Country Road Lesson

If this is possible where you live, take the student for a long drive out of the city and onto country roads. Ideally when possible, use narrow and winding roads. The student will gain confidence and start to enjoy driving.

Each time you don't feel safe know that he's not looking far enough up ahead. To handle this, tell him to look ahead near and far.

Hopefully he has practiced looking ahead while being a passenger. Even so, he could now have his attention fixed too close to the car, after concentrating on the physical actions of handling the car, so he'll probably need to be reminded about looking ahead near and far.

Even if earlier lessons ended with the student driving around and looking ahead, the speed was slow, so this longer and faster drive is dedicated to getting him to look farther ahead. Have him, review the pictures in the earlier chapters and the data about looking ahead and aiming, before going on this long drive. You may even encounter a situation where the road is obscured and he needs to look into some trees to see where the car needs to go and then back to the road in front.

By constantly reminding him to look ahead, and keep his eyes moving while driving on narrow, winding roads, he will gain excellent control over the steering. His confidence will come up – even the most fearful students should begin to enjoy driving.

When you first start to teach driving, you constantly tell him to keep his eyes up. However, I've found this sometimes results in the student fixating his attention ahead. So now tell him to look up ahead and also keep his eyes moving both near and far.

If there are no hills with narrow, winding roads nearby, put this lesson on hold. He can even be a licensed driver before doing this lesson, but do make a point of having him drive someplace where there are narrow, winding roads so he can learn this skill.

Later Lessons

From this point on it's a matter of his learning to drive better by doing more driving and noticing what he needs to be corrected on, and having him work more on those things. Don't spend too much time on any one thing – get an improvement and then come back to it later, if more work is needed.

Three-point turns and parallel parking need to be in your lesson plans. *Both of those actions require great control over the clutch*, plus ability to turn the steering wheel quickly. This shouldn't be attempted until those skills are acquired.

If parallel parking is difficult for the student, it's probably because he's not steering the car quickly enough to get it in the correct position, *or in a stick he's not using the friction point to slowly reverse*. Don't continue with parallel parking if he's not getting it; have him practice more steering at slow speed, *and in a stick have him practice more steering and more clutch creep*, then come back to parallel parking at a later time.

If he has difficulties shifting gears, get him driving around and shifting from third gear to fourth gear and back down, on your instruction. Take him to a parking lot and have him change from first gear to second gear and back down. Keep this up until he has no difficulties doing this, and no reservations about putting the car into a lower gear when needed.

If his handling of shifting is bad, especially if he looks down to shift, have him park, turn off the engine, and practice putting the stick in different gears with the engine off. Make sure he doesn't look down at the stick while practicing.

Have him practice backing. Having him back along a road for 100 yards while keeping one yard from the curb, and make sure he's got good control of the car while backing.

Once he's driving confidently, during every lesson check to see if he's using the mirrors by occasionally asking what is behind him. This will encourage him to keep checking his mirrors.

For a student who has trouble putting his attention out and is inclined to fixate on things, have him drive around a busy parking lot, preferably at a large mall. Do this at the start of every later lesson. Driving around a busy parking lot will make him learn to look all around, since traffic and pedestrians can come at him from all angles at any time.

If he doesn't stop the car exactly where it should be stopped, have him practice "Exact Point Stopping" described earlier in this book, and keep coming back to that exercise until he can do it consistently. If he doesn't pull the car up to the correct position at traffic lights – overshooting the road lines or stopping too far away from the car in front – have him practice exact point stopping from a faster starting speed, up to 30 or 35 mph.

Then return to emergency braking to add to his stopping skills. Get him to also look in the mirror just before or while he brakes, to help him decide if he should stop a bit more slowly to prevent being rear-ended.

For the student who's driving too fast, take him to a busy mall parking lot and get him slowed down – anytime during the lesson – as given in the earlier "Too Fast!" section.

When he's gained more experience, direct him to drive in heavy traffic.

Later, when you have him practice freeway driving, make sure he gets up to speed on the on-ramp. *In a stick shift, he must be able to change gears quickly and confidently before freeway driving is attempted.* The first time you have him go on a freeway, be prepared to insist that he gets up to the speed of the flow of traffic. When changing lanes on the freeway, make sure he turns his head to see if anything is in his blind spot, just before moving over, since some are inclined to forget this – especially when moving to the left.

Whenever you're teaching, and you feel the car is not following the road smoothly, tell your student to look farther ahead. If you tell him only to look ahead, he'll do so but his eyes will become fixated on something ahead. You must say, "Look near and far."

If you're in doubt about where he's looking, get him to talk to you as he drives and tell you what he's looking at, as in the "Say What You See" chapter earlier in this book. By using this "commentary driving" technique, you can find out if he's looking ahead the correct distance, and you'll know whether or not he's seeing the whole picture.

As the date of his licensing test approaches, have him drive in the area of the testing facility. Make sure he can park in and back out of the place where he'll pick up the driving test examiner. In your last lessons, stop giving advice – give only directions, just as an examiner will do.

Chapter 22

Stick Shifts

How the Clutch Works

The "Clutch" is what engages the engine to the transmission. It also the name of the pedal that is worked with the left foot as you change gears in a stick shift car; hence the name "clutch pedal."

How the clutch works needs to be known and understood for a student to easily grasp stick shift driving. The clutch can be simply described as consisting of two discs or two round "plates" whose flat surfaces are facing each other. Each disc is attached to its own metal shaft or rod.

These plates can be either pushed together or pushed apart so that they are not touching each other. One of the rods is attached to the engine and turns at the same rate the engine is turning. The other rod is attached to the gear-box which in turn attaches to the wheels of the car. When the plates are pushed together fully and the car is in gear, the power of the engine is transferred via the gears to the wheels thereby causing the wheels to turn. When the plates are apart the power of the engine cannot be transferred and as a result the wheels are not being made to turn.

Whether these plates are touching or not is controlled by the driver pushing the "clutch pedal". When the clutch pedal is fully pushed in, the plates are pulled apart and are not in contact with one another. When the clutch pedal is fully out, the plates are in full contact with one another.

Stated differently, when the driver's foot pushes down the clutch pedal, thereby releasing the clutch, the clutch plate moves away from (separates from) the engine disc. When this is done, the engine disc turns but the wheels are not being made to turn.

When the driver puts the car in gear, and lets the clutch pedal all the way up, the engine disc is put into full contact with the clutch plate and the wheels of the car are made to turn and thus the car will start to move.

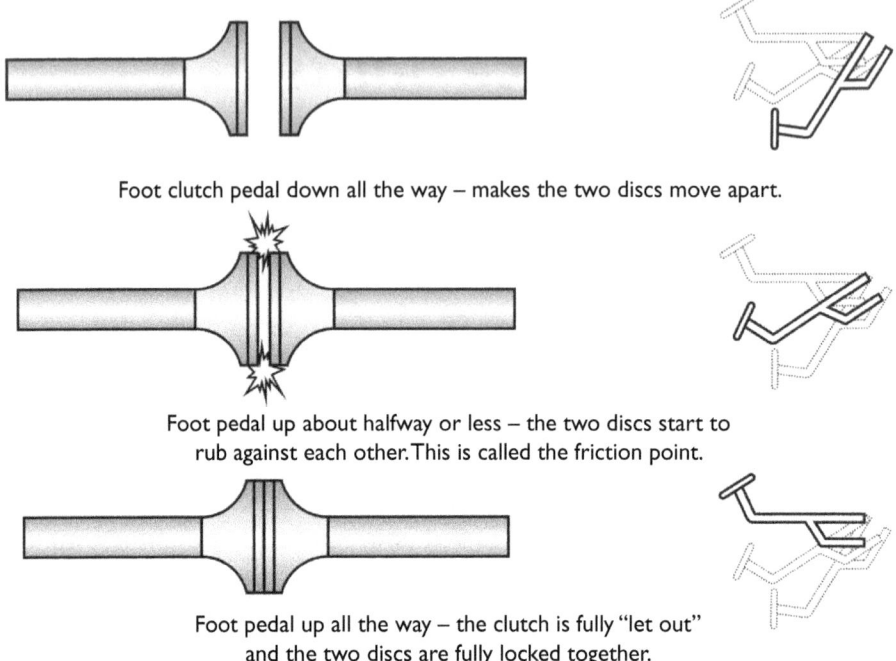

Foot clutch pedal down all the way – makes the two discs move apart.

Foot pedal up about halfway or less – the two discs start to rub against each other. This is called the friction point.

Foot pedal up all the way – the clutch is fully "let out" and the two discs are fully locked together.

Friction, as used in "friction point" is the rubbing together of one object against another when one or both objects are moving. For example, rubbing your hands together to warm them is a demonstration of friction.

Matches are lit by friction. Another meaning of the word is "friction" between people – for example, friction between the family members led to a heated argument.

In a stick shift the clutch is a friction clutch and by having the plates slowly coming together and creating friction a smooth change of gears becomes possible.

Point as used in "friction point" is a location, a certain place or position. So the friction point is the place or position in the travel of the clutch pedal where the clutch plate starts to engage. On different cars, the friction point may occur at different places as you let the clutch out (engage) but it's always in the same place for any one car.

What's called the clutch "friction point" is the point where the clutch is partly let out, and the first contact is made by the two discs. The two discs start rubbing against each other, but they're not yet fully locked together. At this point, usually the clutch disc is moving slower than the engine disc. The friction point is also known as the "contact point" or "biting point" – the point where first contact is made and the clutch starts to "bite."

The two discs rubbing against each other at different speeds cause friction. The amount of friction is determined by how much the two surfaces resist being rubbed against each other and the speed difference between the two surfaces. Two smooth pieces of plastic rubbed together don't resist each other much, as compared to rubbing a piece of sandpaper against a piece of wood. The speed or rate at which the sandpaper is being rubbed against the wood also determines how much friction is being generated.

Friction between two surfaces makes the surfaces wear down and it also creates heat. The more two surfaces resist one another when in contact and the greater the difference in rate and direction of motion between the two surfaces the more heat that is created.

The clutch plate is covered with a material that is designed to wear efficiently, but the more one "slips the clutch" – making it rub but not lock in full contact with the engine disc – then the faster the clutch plate wears out and the sooner it will need to be replaced.

When the driver lets the clutch out and it starts to bite the car wheels begin to turn, and thus the car begins to move. When this happens the engine has to work harder, and you will hear the sound of the engine change.

On a car with a dashboard RPM counter (tachometer), you'll notice the rpm (or revs) fall slightly lower when the friction point is reached. This is because more strain is being put on the engine at the friction point. The resulting change in engine sound is what most drivers use to know that the friction point has been reached.

Drivers must understand how the clutch works and learn its friction point. They must be able to picture in their minds the actual mechanics (moving parts and motions) of the discs making contact when the clutch is let out. Understanding this greatly improves their ability to quickly master using the clutch. If one can envision in the mind what happens as the discs come together, he'll understand what's happening and quickly get a good feel of how to correctly use the clutch.

This is the most important skill a new driver has to learn about driving a stick shift. It must be well learned or else his starts can be very "hit or miss" with the car stalling often and the new driver losing confidence.

To get the car moving with the engine running and the stick in first gear, the gas pedal is lightly pushed down to increase the engine speed to a fast idle, and held there. Then with the engine at a fast idle, the clutch pedal is let out (up) until the friction point is reached, then the clutch is slowly let out more to make the wheels start moving and then the pedal is let all the way out.

To practice finding the friction point, have the student do this exercise: While slowly letting out the clutch pedal (up), as soon as the engine sound changes, stop releasing the clutch and hold the pedal right there. The car should not move forward, or only barely start to move. If the car starts moving more than a tiny bit on a level road, he's let the clutch out too far beyond the friction point. Once he's found the friction point, have him hold it there for a moment, then put the clutch in (pedal down), and try it again. You, as the instructor, should show him how this is done – first on a level road.

During the first lesson, you might ask why not have the student let up the clutch fully after the friction point is found? Answer: a) If the student is taught to skip over exactly finding the friction point, but only finding it "hit or miss," he will constantly stall the engine – especially when under pressure in traffic; b) The ability to bring the clutch to the friction point and use it to hold the car stationary must be learned. Starting forward uphill will be very hard to teach without that skill – not only hard on you as the instructor but also hard on the student's nerves and confidence not to mention hard on the clutch of the car.

Next, teach him to use the clutch on a slight uphill which makes the car want to roll backwards. A road with a slight upgrade and without much traffic is a good place to practice this. For a student in good physical shape, have the student move the car forward and then stop it repeatedly.

For a student whose leg tires quickly while working the clutch, driving around a parking lot before the action is attempted again will give his leg a rest between each action. It will also let him practice steering as he rests his leg.

Next on a slight incline, have your student find the friction point. Then have him slightly push the clutch down and let the car roll backwards. Have him stop the backwards motion by letting the clutch out (letting the pedal come up) more until the friction point is again reached.

You need to demonstrate this exercise until your new student knows what is expected. Do it until he can see that, by understanding the friction point, he can achieve complete control when starting to move the car.

Clutch Handling Faults

Bunny Hopping

At times, the car may do "bunny hops" on take-off. When this happens, the student needs to promptly put the clutch back in. The hopping is caused by lack of smooth control of the clutch, and it can be made worse by causing him to pump the gas pedal at the same time.

To handle bunny hopping, first check to see if the seat is adjusted correctly. If it's too far back, he'll use only his toes to push the clutch in. He should use the ball of the foot, not the toes. Having the clutch pedal under the ball of the foot gives more control and less chance of jerking the foot up and down, and so can prevent bunny hopping.

Have him practice slowly letting the clutch out – and adjust the seat to different positions, until the most comfortable position is found for him to work the clutch. Then make sure he always puts the seat in that position every time he drives.

Shoes can be another problem contributing to bunny hopping. Sometimes the soles are so thick that he can't feel the clutch pedal. Shoes with thin soles should be worn so the pedal can be felt through them. Many times I'd have a student with clutch problems take his shoes off (temporarily), just to get a better feel of what was happening with bare feet.

If the seat is adjusted correctly, and the shoes aren't a problem, bunny hopping shouldn't be a problem providing the student also mentally envisions what's happening before letting the clutch out.

Poor Leg Control

For those few students who have trouble controlling their legs, practice makes perfect. One student had enormous trouble controlling the clutch. I told him to spend ten minutes every hour for the rest of the day, sitting in the family car and practicing letting the clutch out slowly. He did that, and the next day he handled the clutch perfectly.

Very occasionally, I find a student whose leg didn't have enough strength to handle the clutch. Asking some questions, I'd find she didn't do any exercise, not even walking, and just had no stamina to work the clutch for twenty minutes. After a week of regular walking, strength returned to her legs and lessons could be continued.

Avoid Unnecessary Use of Parking Brake

When starting the car forward on a level road, the hand brake doesn't need to be used when the student stalls the engine. Have him put the clutch in, restart the engine and bring the car to a fast idle. Again have him find the friction point, and when it's found have him slowly let the clutch out the rest of the way, and the car will start moving.

Engine Revs Need to Be Increased

Make sure he always increases the engine revs before letting out the clutch – otherwise he'll learn to get the car moving at very low revs by releasing the clutch very slowly. To get the car moving like that can be done, but it leaves no margin for error. When such a student gets nervous in traffic and doesn't increase the revs, he'll let the clutch out too fast and stall. If the revs are up, with the engine turning over fast enough, the car won't be so inclined to stall, even if the clutch is let out too fast. Having the revs up gives some insurance against letting the clutch out too fast.

No Riding the Clutch

The clutch is let out all the way when the car is being driven. If a driver were to "ride" the clutch pedal, resting his foot on it while driving, that causes the clutch plate to wear out quickly. Don't let him ride the clutch by resting his foot on it. Make sure he lets it all the way out. When not shifting gears, he keeps his left foot on the floor while driving.

Not Letting the Clutch Out is Another Fault

A new student may be inclined to keep the clutch in when he should have it out. For example, pushing the clutch in to change gears, when starting to turn a corner, but then not letting the clutch back up as he continues through the turn. If the clutch is left in (down), he won't have proper control of the car because he has to let the clutch out before he can accelerate.

The only time the clutch should be in is just before the car comes to a full stop, to keep the engine from stalling. About one car length distance from the car in front is when the clutch should be put in.

I had a student, taught by a parent, who had the bad habit of putting the clutch in every time she used the brakes – no matter what speed she was traveling.

When you first start teaching a student, the car is kept moving very slowly, and he begins by putting the clutch in at the same time he pushes the brake pedal – which is correct for very low speeds. If he didn't, the engine would stall. However, some students then continue doing that in all future driving. Even at high speeds, when the brake is hit, he pushes the clutch in also. An instructor won't notice this in the early slow-speed lessons, since he'll be too busy watching the road for traffic and ensuring the student doesn't hit anything. It's only in later lessons, when the instructor is more relaxed and the student is more in control, that he may notice the student always pushes the brake and clutch at the same time.

The use of the clutch must be explained properly at the start. Then, in early lessons (and again later), you watch the student's feet. If he always uses the clutch and brake together when he shouldn't, correct him right away, before that becomes a bad habit which would take more time to correct later.

The Stick

A modern manual transmission gearshift lever (stick) is very easy to use. The original car transmission had three forward gears and one reverse gear. The stick was moved in the pattern of a letter "H" to shift to each of the gears. We now usually have five forward gears, but the H-pattern is important because the stick has to be moved through this H-pattern for efficient use.

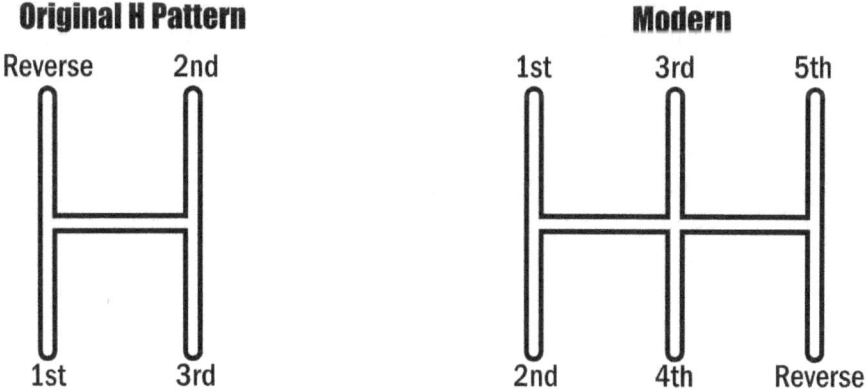

Three forward gears and reverse established the term H-pattern.

For example, if you're going to move the stick from second gear to third gear, it's moved along the path of the H-pattern. It's not moved diagonally in a straight line from the second to third gear position. It's moved from the lower left, straight up to neutral, then across to the right, then up to third. This is so basic that you know it but may not realize that your student doesn't know it.

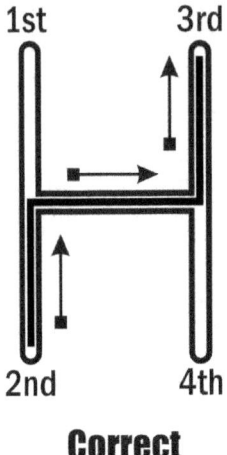 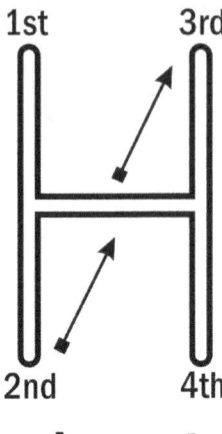

Correct   **Incorrect**

To shift a stick the H-pattern must be followed.

The H-pattern must be seen and envisioned by the student, and he must practice shifting through the gears by moving his hand (first without holding the stick), so you can see that he moves it in the required H-pattern. Once the student knows the correct pattern, then have him move the stick through the gears from 1st to 2nd, 2nd to 3rd, and 3rd to 4th – with the engine off. Then have him downshift the same way, from 4th (or 5th) back down to 1st. It can be made easier if there's a slight pause as the stick is moved through neutral. Get him to look up ahead – not down at the stick – and move the stick to the different gear positions. This is not a slow action – he can start slow, but encourage him to move the stick increasingly quickly.

Now that he knows the feel of the shifting action, have him again practice shifting in his mind by moving his hand without holding the stick. Make sure he has a slight pause as the lever is moved through neutral. Moving from 2nd to 3rd, the slight pause should occur as the stick comes out of 2nd to neutral, then again another slight pause after the stick has been moved across to the right side just before it's pushed up to 3rd.

When sitting in the driveway, have the student practice going through all the gears, both up and down shifting, so he gets a good feel for the actions needed.

Also have him turn the engine off, as if it were stalled, and practice re-starting the "stalled" car. A new student needs to be able to do this quickly, without getting flustered about what to do if it stalls.

He must be able to quickly know which gear the car is in, by the feel of the stick's position. To drill him on this, have him keep the clutch in, and have him keep looking up ahead – while you put the stick in different gear positions. Each time, after you move it, have him put his hand on the stick to feel which gear it's in, without looking down. Then you put it into a different gear, and again have him feel and tell you which gear it's in.

It's dangerous for a new driver to look down to see which gear he's in, when road conditions demand his full attention. Therefore, have him do this drill until he can tell by feel alone which gear the car is in, without looking down. He needs the ability to drop his right hand to the stick, and immediately know which gear he's in as he drives, while keeping his eyes looking ahead. (While driving, the engine sound also gives a clue as to which gear it's in.)

Next with the engine off, have him bring his right hand off the steering wheel to the stick while pushing the clutch in, change gears, then put his right hand back on the wheel – while looking ahead at all times. Have him continue changing gears up and down like this, each time putting his right hand back on the wheel.

No great force is needed to move the stick providing the clutch pedal is all the way down. Force should never be used. Just rest the palm of the hand on it, don't grab the knob tightly. The more force that's used the more trouble he'll have. I've had a woman use the stick as if she were stirring a large pot of thick oatmeal and it got her into all sorts of difficulties. I've seen big men grab the stick tightly and move their shoulders while moving it! If the stick won't get the gear engaged, let the clutch all the way out, then push it all the way back in, and try again – don't force it. Practicing using the stick and clutch with the motor off won't harm the car, and will definitely speed up future lessons.

The student should be encouraged to practice shifting through the different gear positions in his mind – he doesn't even need a car to practice in. He can practice the actions of working the clutch and stick as he sits on a chair at home – using the left foot to work an imaginary clutch, and using the right hand to move an imaginary gear stick. As part of this drill, he should practice re-starting the car quickly so he learns what to do when he lets the clutch out too fast and stalls the engine. Until he's practiced this action in his mind, he won't feel confident about driving a stick because of fear of stalling the car and not knowing how to re-start it.

He can practice that without requiring much of your time. Another child can help him drill the actions in a parked car, or at home while doing other things like watching TV. Even if you yourself choose not to teach your student how to drive a stick, this drill should still be done. If you can organize these drills to be done before he starts with a driving instructor, he'll learn much faster.

Starting Downhill

When starting downhill, you keep the car from moving with the foot brake. It is not necessary to apply the hand brake before starting to move forward on a downhill slope. With the stick in 1st gear, hold the clutch pedal down and keep the foot on the brake. When you are ready to move, take the right foot off the brake, and as the car begins to roll forward, move the foot to the gas pedal as you let out the clutch.

The student could take his foot off the brake, not let the clutch out, and start going down the hill with the clutch still in – but that is a very bad driving habit. It reduces his control of the car with the clutch kept in, because if he needs to speed up, the clutch has to be let out first.

Note that from a stop, when one starts going down a hill, you don't have to start in 1st gear. It's wise to start in 2nd gear or even 3rd gear for a very steep downhill.

Teach this action separately before teaching uphill starts. Otherwise, the student will make downhill starts difficult, trying to do it the same as an uphill start and using the parking brake. Get him totally sure of how to start downhill, before teaching uphill starts.

Clutch Creep

"Clutch creep" moves the vehicle forward or backward while in gear at a slower speed than when the clutch is let out all the way. The driver rides the clutch letting it slip so that the car creeps forward or backwards. In a stick shift, before you start the student on uphill starts, get him to gain more clutch control by teaching him clutch creep. A very slight uphill incline is the best place to teach clutch creep. First demonstrate this to him (do it yourself), showing how a car can be moved very slowly. This skill is needed for uphill starts, for parallel parking, and for positioning a car very close to something.

With the student at the wheel and the car moving very slowly in first gear, have him take his foot off the gas and push the clutch down past the friction point, to drive even slower. The friction point is found, and then the clutch is pushed down a little bit more so it doesn't "bite" all the way, but grabs just enough to slowly ease the car forward. The clutch is slipping when this is done. This should be practiced until the student can move the car forward at a slower speed than usual in first gear with no acceleration.

If he doesn't get a good result the first time, have him come back to this exercise again later. Don't stay with it too long because he will start to have trouble with it when his leg gets tired. Clutch creep takes a lot of concentration and control over the left foot.

Uphill Starts

After you have taught clutch creep, uphill starts are a natural progression of teaching clutch control. Uphill starts are taught as soon as possible after downhill starts and not left for later lessons.

Uphill starts should first be practiced on a very slight incline, just enough to let the car roll slowly backwards when the clutch is in and the brake off. The driver must learn to find the friction point and hold it there, release the parking brake and then move slowly forward by easing past the friction point. A slight incline will not put as much wear on the clutch as a steep hill, and will get the same learning result.

The exact sequence for doing an uphill start is as follows. Have the parking brake on, the engine running, and the stick in first gear. Then:

(1) Bring the engine up to a fast, steady idle.
(2) Let the clutch out to the friction point and hold it there without the car moving forward.
(3) After the friction point is found, release the parking brake.
(4) Slowly let the clutch out the rest of the way – not while releasing the parking brake but immediately after that.
(5) When the car begins to move, give it more gas.

All these actions must be kept separate and in-sequence: the friction point found, the parking brake released, the clutch slowly let out the rest of the way.

An experienced driver will release the parking brake, give it more gas and slowly let the clutch out fully at the same time. That's an impossible feat for most new drivers, who will release the clutch too fast and stall the engine or release the parking brake too soon and roll backwards. It's sort of like patting the head with one hand while making circles on the stomach with the other hand at the same time. Most people can't do that easily. So when training a new driver, insist that these actions are done in sequence, separately, and you'll quickly have a confident student.

A car will stall if the clutch is let out too fast, past the friction point, and/or the engine wasn't revving fast enough. The steeper the hill, the more revs the engine needs to have enough power to pull the car uphill without stalling.

The car will roll backwards if the brake is released too soon, before the friction point is reached. When using the parking brake, have it only on hard enough to keep the car from rolling backwards – and hold on to it while doing this, with your thumb pushing in its top button, so you can quickly release it.

Uphill starts usually need to be practiced again in a later lesson, even if the student got it the first time, to get him to speed up the whole procedure. The student driver should learn to bring the clutch to the friction point quickly, and let the parking brake off quickly. The only slow action that isn't speeded up, is letting the clutch fully out, after reaching the friction point.

At times, I'd get a student who'd previously been taught to release the parking brake and work the clutch at the same time. Trying to separate the actions of finding the friction point, and holding the clutch there, and then releasing the brake can be difficult to teach such a student – especially if he'd spent many hours trying to work the clutch and brake at the same time.

To correct that, get the student to put the brake on, and then put both hands on the steering wheel. Then get him to find the friction point, hold the clutch there, and then take one hand off the steering to release the brake. This gets him to do the procedure as two separate actions, rather than working the foot and hand at the same time. But you should use this technique only if all else has failed, because it can develop the bad habit of not having the hand on the brake, with the button pushed in, at the point when the brake needs to be released.

It must be pointed out to the student that on a hill he shouldn't hold the clutch at the friction point for long periods of time. To sit at a stop light and hold the clutch at the friction point will cause unnecessary clutch wear, and is done only by a driver who's too lazy to use the parking brake or foot brake.

Hill Starts with a Stick Shift without Using the Parking Brake

Using the parking brake while starting uphill is a skill the student should know, especially for very steep inclines. He should practice that until he can do it well on both slight and steep hills.

However, on slight uphill slopes, it's not always necessary to use the parking brake to keep the car from rolling. In fact, most drivers quickly learn uphill starts without ever using the parking brake. Here's how it's done.

In a stick shift, put the car facing up a gentle slope and show the student driver how to do an uphill start without using the parking brake. With the car in first gear and foot on the brake, find the friction point and hold the clutch there while quickly moving the right foot from the brake to the gas. Press the gas to rev the engine to a higher idle and then slowly release the clutch the rest of the way. This will need to be practiced by the student until he can do it quickly – it's a very fast action. Show him the clutch can be let out quickly at first, and only when the friction point is reached is it let out slowly.

Moving the foot from the brake to the gas pedal is done quickly. It's only letting the clutch out past the friction point that's done slowly.

If the student gets nervous and stalls the car when first using this technique, don't persist if he's holding up traffic; have him use the parking brake. Then later have him practice this again in quiet areas until he's got it.

Chapter 23

"Cars Kill Kids" Stops Here

Help the Licensed Driver

If you've spent time with your student over the years to develop his road skills, you'll find it surprisingly easy to teach him the physical actions of driving and his passing the license driving test will be well assured.

Even if he's learned to drive in a school program, during and after completing it, please realize that he still needs your help.

Once your teenager has his full license, he still needs your guidance. Don't abandon your job as a teacher. He still needs more practice behind the wheel to become a fully competent and safe driver. The more help your new driver gets at this time the lower his risk of a crash will be.

As parents, you should initially let your teenager drive with one of you in the car. Then after he has two to three thousand miles experience, let him drive alone. Also let him drive at night. He needs the experience, and in winter if you restrict night-time driving, very little driving will get done. Doing it this way, by the time he's eighteen he can have full use of a car with a full license, and he'll also have been through a two- or three-year apprenticeship supervised by his parents.

The whole plan must be based on getting the new driver experienced – that means he drives as much as he can within the restrictions of the law. To get experienced it will mean trying to drive every day and possibly going on trips on weekends. Getting a new driver experienced is your most important job as a parent, considering the serious consequences of an inexperienced driver having an accident.

Until your children have their own cars, they will not be driving two or three times a day like most people do. After first getting their licenses, most young drivers are still involved in study, watching TV and computer screens with their attention fixed at a close distance.

Your children must realize that a different skill is needed for driving and they must put their attention much farther out when behind the wheel. Also, even after developing the additional skill of taking in the whole scene on open highways, if they haven't done this type of driving for a while, that skill may have faded, so they need to practice looking at different things near and far.

You are the parent, not your child's friend. Realize you may have to show tough love if your teen driver is acting irresponsibly. If necessary take away his keys until he shows more maturity on the road.

Organize your life so that you do continue to help him. Take the family on weekend trips, and let your new driver do most of the driving – but not past the point that he's tired. Try to get him driving every day and do something special on the weekends to let him gain more experience.

I hope you enjoy the experience of keeping your teen driver safe and will always treasure the times you shared together.

Appendix

Driving in Other Countries on the Wrong Side

I have driven twenty-nine years on the left-hand side of the road and twenty-four years on the right-hand side, so these observations come from experience. In New Zealand, Australia and England, I had to drive on the left side of the road. In Europe, Canada, Mexico, and Central America, I've driven on the right. Most recently I've driven in the continental U.S. and have managed to stay on the right-hand side of the road.

The chances of making a mistake are worse when, for example, as a resident of the U.S., I spend a few weeks in New Zealand. The first change to the left side, I handle okay. It's when I come back to the U.S. that an error may be made. This means I have to be constantly aware that I can easily get confused. I've found we make mistakes when something reminds us of the country where we drove on the other side of the road. My wife and I have a policy when driving to not discuss things about a country where we used to drive on the opposite side of the road. We have found that when we do, we're more likely to end up driving on the wrong side.

In high-traffic areas, we have all the other vehicles to remind us which side of the road to drive on. When we do make mistakes, it's usually more embarrassing than fatal – for instance, when there's no traffic on the road to indicate which side to drive on, and we drive out from a gas station on the wrong side of the road because the station reminds us of another country.

Where there is no traffic and the road twists and turns like driving through a gorge beside a river, keep alert. Don't fixate on the beautiful scenery because if you do go around the corner on the wrong side, it could lead to a head-on collision.

Where there's no traffic on narrow two-way roads we can also find ourselves driving on the wrong side. When my daughter was tested for her Florida driver's license, she was failed, because she drove all the way down one street on the wrong side – a street that reminded her of New Zealand.

One-way streets can also be confusing, because they can make us feel we're on the wrong side of the road. Turning out from one-way streets can easily get us on the wrong side of the road unless we pay close attention.

Also, in some countries, especially England, cars will legally park on the wrong side of the road. These cars parked facing the wrong direction will make you think you are on the wrong side of the road. Unless you know this, it is very unnerving when you turn into a street where you expect to see taillights, and see parked cars' headlights looking at you. You instantly think you are on the wrong side of the road.

All the rules change when you go from one country to another. When you drive on the left, look right first; in New Zealand, it is "look right, then left, then right again." In the U.S., where you drive on the right, you look left first; it's "look left, then right, then left again." In New Zealand, it's "keep to the left" or pull to the left, if an approaching driver is coming onto your side of the road. In the U.S., it's "pull to the right" and hope the driver coming toward you gets back on his side. Things which have become instinctive have to be reversed when relating to left and right.

We always have the steering wheel to tell us which country we're in, because when a car should be driven on the left side of the road, the car's steering wheel is on the right. If you have trouble with left and right, the solution is simple. [Note: this advice does not apply when driving between mainland Europe and England in your own car.] Forget about left and right, and relate everything to the steering wheel, because it also changes sides in the car when you're in countries where you drive on the opposite side of the road. Keep the steering wheel closest to the center of the road. Be aware that the steering wheel is deliberately placed to be on the side of on-coming cars, you'll always be on the correct side of the road, no matter which country you're in. As an example, if a car were coming straight at you, you would immediately move your car in the direction away from the side of the car where the steering wheel is. As long as you keep the steering wheel away from the other car, you'll be correct, no matter which side of the road you are driving on.

If you pull forward out of a driveway, look out the driver's side window first and you'll always be looking in the correct direction first.

If you intend visiting a country where cars are driven on the other side of the road, while still at home start thinking in relation to the steering wheel, rather than left and right. Also, drive a car and not a motorcycle or scooter because you won't have a steering wheel to guide you. I likewise find it more difficult to adjust to being a pedestrian when cars are driven on the other side,

APPENDIX

because I have no steering wheel to remind me of where to look first.

If you drive in England, New Zealand or Australia, you'll encounter roundabouts (traffic circles) where there are no traffic lights. Cars enter the roundabout by yielding to cars on their right. With the steering wheel on the right, you just give way to cars coming toward you from the side the steering wheel is on.

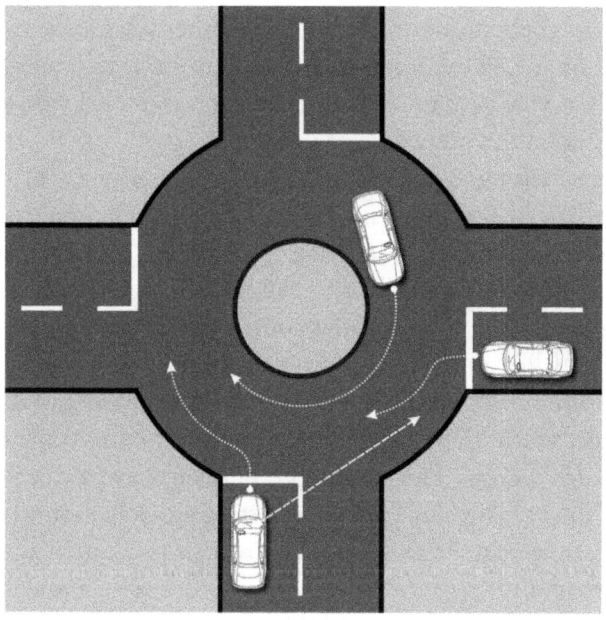

Keep left, go clockwise, and give way to traffic on the right.
This includes traffic already in the roundabout.

In Britain you will need to shift with your left hand, so if you have a choice, rent an automatic transmission rather than a stick-shift. For those of us who started driving by shifting with the left hand, it's no problem but Americans can be uncomfortable shifting with their left hands.

When you are used to driving on one side of the road and have to switch, do not drive unless you feel alert. If you are tired you can revert to the wrong side. I will, if tired, walk to the passenger door to drive; when this happens I know I have to be especially alert.

Don't arrive at the airport and pick up a rental car. On a long trip to New Zealand, I will wait several days before I start to drive. I wait till the jet lag is handled and my sleep pattern established in the new time zone before I drive on the "wrong" side of the road. I find it very unnerving leaving the airport while in the front passenger seat on the wrong side of the road, when suffering jet lag. My daughter says she finds herself screaming at least once and hitting a brake that is not there, but once we have a steering wheel to hold it all comes right. So don't give up when this happens to you. Once the steering wheel is in front of you, you will wonder why you doubted your abilities.

There is no gradient into driving on the other side of the road. You drive on one side or the other. The brain needs to be reset and a firm pattern established that you have the steering wheel on the other side of the car and you are driving on the other side of the road.

When first visiting Auckland, my wife makes a point of driving down Queen Street, the busiest street in New Zealand. On this major thoroughfare, she gets herself totally aligned to being on the other side of the road.

It is far easier to reset the thinking pattern when you drive in heavy traffic. There are always other cars to show you what side of the street you should be driving on. I like to drive in a busy city until I feel comfortable driving on a side I am not used to, before I leave the main road and drive on scenic country roads, where there might be no traffic to remind me of which side I should be driving on. This is not the popular view. I quote Mary Engel reporting in the Los Angeles Times about starting a trip around New Zealand in a rented camper van. "Kiwis, like their British Forbearers, drive on the left side of the road and we decided it would be better to start off on a lonely country lane than in a city, even a small one."

My daughter had a New Zealand friend arrive in the U.S., and I asked her how she found driving on the other side of the road. She said she found it very easy, because she remembered my daughter's rule: If a car is going to hit the driver's door – stop!

When I explained this idea to a friend who'd been denying herself the pleasure of driving a car in other countries where people drive on the opposite side of the road, she was thrilled and looked forward to this new driving experience on her next overseas trip.

Your kids could become international travelers and end up driving on the other side of the road, so make sure they understand that you have to look first on the side where the steering wheel is.

Alcohol – Let Me Confess

Every 15 minutes an American dies at the hands of a drunk driver. Traffic accidents are now the major cause of death for teenagers, and one quarter of those deaths involve alcohol.

The hopeful news is that the other 75% of teenage auto deaths are not alcohol-related and most likely are instead due to an inexperienced driver making a mistake. Remember, by applying the data in this book, you can give your teenager the skills and experience he needs to stay alive.

It seems that some teenagers who have trouble with alcohol and driving do so because of no experience with alcohol coupled with too little experience driving.

As a 15-year-old with religious parents, I'd had no contact with alcohol. Having just turned 15 and having a driver license for only a few weeks, I took an older neighborhood boy to a country dance. He got drunk and since I had never been involved with a drunken person I just thought he was sick. While hurrying to get him home I had an accident and rolled over the family car – five times! I was an inexperienced driver being distracted by a loud drunk.

In my late teens I started drinking and of course driving too. I'd had three years of driving experience before getting involved with alcohol. What kept me from speeding was the fact that as a new driver I'd already experienced a roll-over. I never had an accident while driving under the influence of alcohol and fifty years ago there was little enforcement of DUI or DWI laws – drinking and driving was more accepted as part of the culture. Now I know drunk driving is simply stupid.

When my son was going through the dangerous teen years, I had enough understanding of the problem of cars and booze to keep him alive. I made it safe so that he could be totally honest with me, and if he were going to drink, there was always a way to get him home without him driving. I acted as a parent. He had lots of friends, but he didn't need me as a friend, he needed me to be a strong parent who would be unrelenting if he drove drunk. I was ready to go pick him up any time of the night to get him home safe. Thank goodness he never needed my assistance.

I believe that the parents' most important job is to keep their children alive. We don't want to outlive our children. With strong support from caring parents acting in the best interests of the children this can be done. It helps if there is also a culture that doesn't condone drunk driving – and one in which the police actively enforce safe driving practices where teens gather.

You are the only parents your kids have. Realize you can influence their behavior and help keep them alive through these dangerous years when driving and alcohol form such a deadly mixture.

It's Crazy Out There

Jon loved his Harley-Davidson motorcycle. When I asked, "how's the Harley?" Jon responded, "I've sold it. It's crazy out there." After years of riding his Harley, Jon considered it to be too dangerous to ride in Los Angeles traffic.

What's changed to make an experienced rider give up on the pleasure of his Harley? Cell phones are distracting drivers. These distracted drivers are causing accidents. A cell phone is a great tool when you are driving to update your arrival time and keep in touch. It is not a tool that should be used to get into conversations handling problems that have nothing to do with driving, especially when traffic is heavy.

Americans are working long hours to keep ahead and some people just don't get enough sleep. As society goes 24-7 with more places open 24 hours, people are getting less sleep. Sleep-deprived drivers and distracted drivers using cell phones can have slower response times than legally drunk drivers.

Overwhelmed, sleep-deprived Americans seem to display anger when there is no reason to be angry. My daughter was lunching with a friend who was saying how angry her husband got toward other drivers when he was behind the wheel. At that moment her husband texted her this message: "the worst *!*!* driver ever." Here is an angry driver sending text messages as he drives. So we have an angry, distracted driver driving an over-powered car. An accident just looking for a place to happen.

"Road rage" wasn't known until recently. Road rage and higher horsepower cars seem to have arrived at the same time. Only ten years ago, few drivers had fast cars; now the majority of cars have enough power to encourage road rage.

I've driven with drivers who keep it light and bright with this type of attitude, "Ok girls and boys, you need to look further ahead." Or "You are in a car not a phone booth; please end the phone conversation and pay attention to the road." A driver needs to observe other drivers, and commenting on their behavior in a light hearted way is constructive. Reacting to other drivers with anger can lead to road rage.

Many more cars are on our roads, and very few new roads have been built. Congested roads grind to a halt when an accident occurs, making people upset about being late and adding to the possibility of drivers speeding to get to their appointments on time once the accident clears.

Cars have changed by becoming more powerful. One family car can now do 0 to 60 mph in 5.8 seconds. It was only a few short years ago that, if a sports car could do 0 to 60 in six seconds, it was considered a fast sports car. These fast sedans will be driven by inexperienced teenagers who can lose control of these overpowered cars.

The overpowered cars are being driven fast when there is no traffic congestion. The freeways in the Los Angeles area move at least ten to fifteen mph above the speed limit; there does not seem to be enough Highway Patrol presence to keep the traffic legal at 65 mph.

Because of economic necessity, law enforcement is not at the level it once was. As the baby boomers reach retirement age, these law enforcement agencies are going to be stretched even thinner with fewer personnel.

At times, all the law enforcement officers on duty are tied up with handling accidents, and no law enforcement is being done.

Traffic fatalities are the fastest rising cause of death – not just in the USA, but world-wide. Almost forty-one thousand Americans were killed in 2006, and 2.6 million were injured. Worldwide, 1.2 million lives were lost due to traffic accidents last year.

Between 1997 and 2012 the number of teenagers will increase from twenty-nine million to nearly forty million. Therefore many more teenagers will be on the road, driving while talking on the phone, sometimes sleep deprived, driving overpowered cars fast on freeways with inadequate law enforcement presence.

There will be laws passed to attempt to handle the problems I've outlined. This will not solve them because, for example, even if the use of cell phones while driving were made illegal there would not be enough law enforcement presence to enforce these new laws. Even with good law enforcement, you can't enforce unpopular laws. The most law abiding person will use a cell phone if he thinks it's an emergency situation, even if it's illegal to do so.

I wrote in the introduction that "Passing more laws is not always the best way to achieve more safety." I believe it is time for education to be applied to the problem of the pandemic of traffic accidents worldwide.

Maybe we should all listen to Jon when he says he can no longer ride his Harley because it's crazy out there. This book is an attempt to educate drivers. I hope it will keep you and your kids and grandkids safe on the road.

My Qualifications

I have driven for more than fifty years – from farm equipment to cars to over-the-road eighteen-wheel "Big-Rig" tractor-trailer trucks, long distance. I have driven on the left-hand side of the road in New Zealand, Australia and Great Britain. I have driven on the right-hand side of the road in Canada, the USA, Mexico, Central America and Europe.

I have been a professional driving instructor, teaching driver education to many young people. I have also made confident drivers out of older people who, despite many attempts to learn to drive, had failed to gain from their previous instructors the skill or confidence needed to pass the test.

My other qualification is that I taught my own children to drive; they got through their "first dangerous years" as drivers – and are still alive to prove it.

GLOSSARY

air bag: A cloth type bag in the center of the steering wheel which, in a collision, very quickly fills with air to form a sort of balloon, to help protect the driver from injuries. Cars also have an air bag for the front passenger, and some have side-impact air bags.

air brakes: The brake system of large trucks which uses pressurized air to apply the brakes, instead of brake fluid (a liquid) like cars use.

anti-lock braking system-ABS: Brakes which won't let the wheels lock up, thus preventing skidding. A computer eases the brake pressure so the wheels don't lock up. This improves braking control and sometimes also shortens braking distance and enables the driver to steer the car while braking hard. Hence "Stomp, Steer, Stop."

apprenticeship: A training program of months or years in which one learns a skill while working with and supervised by a skilled tradesman or artisan.

automatic transmission: A system/mechanism designed to change gears automatically for you as you drive. The driver needs only to put it in Drive for forward, Reverse for backing, or Park. Automatics do give the driver the option to downshift to "D2" or "D3" to use the engine to help slow the car down on long, steep hills.

axle: A rod or shaft which goes to and supports the wheels.

blind spot: Any area a driver can't see, either directly or in mirrors. The ones we are concerned with are to the left and right of the driver.

brake drum: A hollow, round, metal cylinder which the brake shoes push against to stop the wheel and thus stop the car. Most cars have disc brakes in the front, and drum brakes in the rear. Other more high performance cars have disc brakes on all four wheels. Large trucks have drum brakes.

brake lag: The time and distance a large truck travels after the driver pushes the brake pedal, before the brakes actually begin to slow or stop the vehicle. This applies to air brakes in big trucks. (The hydraulic brakes in cars act nearly instantly when the brake pedal is pushed.)

brake lights: Red lights at the rear of the vehicle which light up when the brake pedal is pushed even if only slightly depressed and the brakes are not being applied.

brake lines: The small tubes or pipes in which brake fluid is pushed along to the brakes at each wheel. In big trucks, pressurized air instead of fluid is pushed along the brake lines to each brake.

brake lining: Brake drums (see above) have two linings or "shoes" which push against the inside of the metal drum. That creates friction which slows and stops the wheels.

brake pad: The small, somewhat rectangular-shaped pads which push against a disc brake's surface, creating friction to slow and stop the wheel.

cable brakes: Brakes using a cable (instead of air or liquid), from the brake pedal to each wheel, to push the brakes against the wheels. These were sometimes used in cars many decades ago, and are still used today for only the parking brake.

car care: Looking after the car, keeping it clean, making sure all fluids are filled, tire pressure is good, worn tires are changed, all lights work, etc.

carwise: A word invented by the author to describe someone who understands how a car and its parts work.

CB radio: Citizens' Band radio; two-way radios on which people talk to each other while in close range, usually within one to ten miles. The "band" refers to the radio wavelength or frequency these radios use. Use of radio waves are regulated by the government, but no license is required to use CB radios, so they're for all citizens' use, hence they're called citizens' band radios.

clutch: 1) The part of a stick shift transmission which connects the wheels to the rotating motion of the engine, transferring the engine power to the wheels. (To be more accurate, the motion goes from the engine, to the clutch, to the gears, and then to the wheels.) The clutch plate is covered with a material that is designed to wear efficiently but just like brake pads, will eventually need to be replaced. See illustration Chapter 22. 2) The pedal operated with the left foot that is used to change gears is also known as a clutch or clutch pedal.

clutch creep: In sticks shifts, the action of moving a car very slowly by "slipping" the clutch, which means you let the clutch part way out, letting the two disks begin to rub against each other, but not fully locking together.

GLOSSARY

commercial drivers: People who drive professionally for a living.

cover the brake: The action of lightly touching the foot on the brake pedal without applying the brakes. The reason it's done is: (1) to make the brake lights turn on and thereby warn drivers behind that there is a possibility of slowing down or coming to a stop, and (2) to prepare oneself to slow down more quickly or suddenly stop with reduced reaction time because the foot is already positioned over the brake. This word is used more in England than in America.

cruise control: A feature where the driver can set a speed that he wishes to cruise at and the car's computer will automatically control the gas pedal instead of the driver. On a downhill, it reduces the gas given to the engine, and uphill gives it more gas. When the driver does push on the brake pedal or gas pedal, the cruise control immediately stops working and has to be reset to work again. It's only needed if you drive on the open road. It is not practical in traffic or on city streets.

crumple lines: The indented lines or small channels built into parts of a car, such as the underside of a hood, which make that part crumple (collapse or fold) in such a way that the force of impact is partly absorbed in a collision, instead of the hood being pushed into the interior of a car where the driver and passenger sit. Thus it reduces the impact force against passengers and helps to lessen injuries.

defensive driving: Recognizing that collisions can be prevented and doing everything possible to prevent them, such as: leaving a "cushion" of space around your car, having an empty space next to you in case you need to move into it suddenly to prevent an accident, always looking even when you have the right of way, letting other drivers know what you intend to do (using signals, brake lights, etc.), predicting and allowing for others to be distracted and make mistakes, being aware of how you feel, the condition of your car, other cars, the road surface, traffic, weather, time of day, mood and alertness of other drivers and not driving when very tired, etc.

diesel fuel: The gas used by most big trucks and a few cars which have diesel engines. It's made from the same crude oil which gasoline is made from, but it's oilier and if not burned completely in the engines its exhaust fumes make more smoke and smog.

dipstick: The narrow, thin, flat long metal stick which sits in a tube going to the bottom of an engine. It's used to measure how much oil is in the engine by showing the oil level at the end of the stick, with a high mark and low mark. Automatic transmission cars have a second dipstick – usually much shorter – used to check the transmission fluid.

disc brake: A brake made of a metal disc (flat plate) on a vehicle wheel, plus a somewhat rectangular-shaped brake pad which pushes against the disc, creating friction against it to make the wheel slow or stop. Disc brakes are more open to the air, so they don't overheat easily like enclosed drum brakes.

divided highway: A highway divided by a center strip of dirt, grass, trees, concrete walls or other barriers that separate vehicles going in different directions.

drive axle: The axle which turns the wheels to push or pull the vehicle.

eighteen-wheeler: A Big-Rig truck (tractor), plus its one or two trailers. The Big-Rig tractor and trailer or trailers usually has a total of eighteen wheels.

eyeball: A slang term meaning to look at or check something with the eyes only (no tools or instruments), to roughly measure or adjust something, or just to make a quick inspection.

eyes – put the eyes in: Slang meaning to get one's eyes and attention properly adjusted to the scenery around one, and adjusted to the action one is about to do. Before a tennis match players must get their eyes and attention adjusted by hitting a few balls. Likewise, a person who drives only occasionally or spends a long day in front of a computer screen must also "put his eyes back in," meaning get his attention farther out, before driving.

fan belt: A circular belt connecting the engine to a fan which by turning keeps air flowing through the radiator even when the car isn't moving.

fluid levels: How full or empty a vehicle's fluids are. Engine oil and radiator water (also known as coolant) are the most frequently checked fluids. Others are brake fluid, steering fluid, transmission fluid and battery water.

fixated: Having one's eyes and attention fixed or stuck, mostly or only on just one thing or area, instead of the attention freely moving over several things and areas, back and forth, up and down, near and far, so one can better perceive all of the areas and things ahead and around oneself.

four-second rule: The minimum safe following distance, measured by four seconds of time, which one should stay back from the vehicle in front,

GLOSSARY

in poor or bad driving conditions. It's also the minimum safe following distance used by large trucks for following vehicles in front.

four-way flashers: Emergency lights which make all four turn signals flash off and on, used when parked dangerously.

four-wheelers: A slang word used by truckers for cars.

friction: The result of rubbing two surfaces against each other. The amount of friction is determined by how much the two surfaces resist being rubbed against each other. The more friction resistance, the faster the rubbing motion and the more rubbing pressure, the more heat and wear.

friction point: (First see the words "clutch" and "friction" above.) In cars and trucks with a manual transmission (stick shift), "the clutch friction point" is the point where the clutch pedal is partly let out and the first contact is made with the two disks, just before the two disks fully lock together. The two disks start rubbing against each other, but they are not fully locked together. At this point, one disks slips a bit and moves slower than the other.

gap: An empty space between objects. As used in this book it's a space between two vehicles which is big enough for a third vehicle to comfortably and safely fit between the two, with room in front of and behind it. A gap can also be the empty space between a parked car and the center line of the road, or the space between road dividers or barrels, where there's still room for a car to go through.

hazard: A potential, possible danger.

hydraulic: Pushed or worked by the force or pressure of a moving liquid, usually a liquid thicker than water, more like a light oil.

hydraulic brakes: Brakes using hydraulic fluid in the brake lines to apply the brakes to slow or stop the wheels.

jackknife: The action of a Big-Rig's trailer skidding sideways and its back end coming toward or up to the tractor. It's similar to the action of folding a pocket knife blade into its case. Jackknifing sometimes results in both the tractor and trailer over-turning.

learner's license: See "permit."

low gear: Usually 2nd or 3rd gear (or "D2" or "D3" in an automatic), used when going down a steep hill to let the engine help slow the car, instead of using the brakes only.

momentum: The tendency for any object in motion (including a car or truck) to continue moving at the same speed. If it's moving at 35 mph, it has the momentum to keep going at 35 mph on a level road, without being given more gas. Once its speed is increased up to 65 mph, it has the momentum to easily continue going at 65 mph on a level road, unless brakes are used, or it hits something or it starts going uphill. Big-Rig trucks, due to their much heavier weight, take longer than cars to gain the momentum needed to get up to a cruising speed of 65 mph.

MPH: Miles per Hour. The speed of travel.

NASA: The U.S. National Aeronautics and Space Administration, which mainly researches and develops air and space flight technology and is also involved in related matters such as monitoring the planet's atmosphere, weather and oceans.

neutral: The point in the transmission where no gears are engaged.

odometer: The dashboard instrument which measures the distance a vehicle travels in miles and tenths of a mile, usually shown just below the speedometer dial.

oil level: How full or empty the engine oil is, checked with the dipstick. It should be kept at or close to the top mark, but not above the top mark. The "top mark" is a line across the stick, usually only one or two inches from the bottom end of the stick.

owner's manual: The small book which comes with a new car, which tells how to take care of it and explains the car's different features and how to use them. If you get a used car without one, an owner's manual can be purchased from a car dealer.

peripheral vision: The widest outer areas of one's field of vision, or the ability to widely see the outer sides of where you're looking, not just straight ahead only.

permit: A temporary and limited driver license (or learner license) given to a person who's studied the rules of the road, passed a written test, and now can drive – but only when accompanied by a fully licensed driver. The permit driver takes a road driving test and if passed, gets a full license.

radiator: A large, narrow, somewhat rectangular box with dozens of thin, flat, metal "fins," sitting in front of the engine. Small pipes run through it, and air flowing around them cools the pipes' hot water from the engine. The cooled water is pumped back through the engine, keeping it cooler, and

GLOSSARY

heat from the engine is partly absorbed by the water which then returns to the radiator to be cooled again.

rev or rev's: See RPM.

RPM: Revolutions Per Minute, also called "revs" for short. It's the speed at which an engine revolves (rotates or turns) its crankshaft. One revolution is one complete, circular, turning motion, such as the hand of a clock from twelve, all the way around the clock back to twelve. How fast the engine runs or turns the crankshaft is measured by the number of complete revolutions the shaft turns per minute of time. That can be as slow as a few hundred RPMs at a parked idle or as fast as several thousand RPMs.

rig: The arrangement of parts. A horse and carriage was sometimes called a rig. Now when we speak of a Big-Rig we usually mean a tractor and trailer combination.

road film: Unburned vehicle fuel (especially diesel), exhaust fumes, bits of motor oil, and tiny bits of tire rubber in the air, which stick to and build up on windows and windshields.

road instinct: The ability to predict what could happen on the road ahead, especially in situations which may require the driver to do something to prevent an accident.

roadwise: A new word to describe someone who has learned to properly look up ahead, focus on what one sees, and to read and predict the road conditions and the traffic ahead.

scan: As used in this book, to glance at quickly.

sixth sense: An extraordinary or super-human perception, one beyond what are considered the five basic human senses of sight, sound, touch, taste and smell.

sleeper: An area for sleeping, behind the driver's and passenger's seats in the extended cab of a Big-Rig truck.

steering axle: The front wheel's axle of a car or truck which allows the wheels to turn and thus enables one to steer the vehicle.

stick shift: A vehicle with a gear shift lever (stick) which requires one to change gears manually (with the hand) by moving the stick to different gear positions, unlike an automatic transmission which changes gears by itself. In a stick shift, the clutch pedal must first be pushed all the way down before moving the stick to a different gear.

tachometer: Also known as a rev counter. It shows the revolutions-per-minute of an engine.

tailgate: The action of a vehicle following too closely for safety behind another vehicle, risking a rear-end collision if the front vehicle suddenly stops or slows quickly.

team driving: Two people sharing the driving of a large truck. One person drives while the other driver can sleep in the sleeper.

three-second rule: The recommended safe following distance, measured by three seconds of time, which one should stay back from the vehicle in front, even in good driving conditions.

tire tread: The grooved outer layer of rubber on a tire, which is in contact with the road.

traction: How well the tires "grab" the road and hold the vehicle steady on it.

tractor: The front part of a Big-Rig truck that has the engine, and which can pull or tow one or two trailers behind it. There are also farm tractors which pull plows and other farm equipment.

trailer: A vehicle without an engine, used to carry loads.

transmission: An enclosed group of vehicle gears between the engine and the wheels. The transmission transfers (transmits) the power and motion of the engine, through the gears, to the wheels.

trip meter: A specialized odometer which can be re-set to zero at the end or start of any trip.

twelve-second rule: The distance, measured by twelve seconds of time, which the driver should be looking ahead at any speed. At 30 mph, it's about one block ahead. At 65 mph, it's about a quarter of a mile ahead. For more details, see the How Far to Look Ahead section of Chapter 5.

two-second rule: The minimum safe following distance, measured by two-seconds of time, which one should stay back from the vehicle in front, at any speed, in good driving conditions. See Chapter 6 – Following Distances, for details on how to use this.

windshield washer: The small water pump which sprays the windshield with water and any cleaner in the water; used together with the windshield wipers to wash off the windshield.

INDEX

ABS, 201
Accelerate, 108, 129, 236
Accident prone, 17
Achieve your goals, 158
Aggression, 126
Aggressive, 36, 52, 65, 113, 126
Aging Population, 3
Aim high, 46, 192
Aim up ahead, 55, 220
Air Brakes, 131-132, 255
Air Force Pilots, 49
Airbags, 10, 121, 196, 201
Airline, 101-102, 157
Alcohol, 17, 155, 183, 251-252
Alertness, 51, 104, 257
Alphabet, 87, 141-142
American Medical Association, 124
Angle parking, 173, 208-210, 212, 227
Anti-lock brakes, 33, 83, 95-97, 206, 255
Anti-skid control, 184
Apprenticeship, 31, 245, 255
Are we there yet?, 8, 84-85
Areas You Know, 187
Athletes Start Young, 26
Athletic and musical success, 7
Athletic development, 12
Attention deficit problems, 176
Authorities, 31, 149
Auto Parts, 77
Auto Salvage, 77
Automatic Response, 87, 100, 157, 168, 177, 182, 204
Automatic Transmissions, 151, 184-185
Automatics, 185-186, 255
Avoid Unnecessary Use of Parking Brake, 236

Back-seat driver, 29
Background scenery, 67
Backing, 112, 170, 173, 186, 207-210, 227, 229, 255
Backing Skills, 112
Bad Driver, 47, 78, 126
Bad instruction, 163
Bad Temper, 126
Basic Math Words, 140
Behavior expert, 197
Best Teacher, 20
Bicycle, 25, 70, 72-73, 88, 107, 111-112, 156, 173
Big picture, 48, 50, 66, 74
Big-rigs, 65, 131-133, 139
Bigger Trucks, 133
Bike, 3, 19, 53, 65, 70-74, 83, 88, 108, 111-112
Bike Riders Looking Ahead, 73
Biting point, 233
Blind corner, 58-59
Blind Spots, 107-109, 137, 197, 219
Bored, 8, 26, 196
Boredom, 8, 90
Boxers, 175
Brain, 3, 9-11, 29-30, 41, 51, 117-118, 175-176, 178, 204, 250
Brain Gym, 176
Brain Pattern, 10-11, 29-30
Brake, 3, 8, 10-11, 20, 36-37, 64-67, 72, 76-77, 79, 95-100, 102-103, 105, 110, 132, 154, 156, 158, 160, 185-186, 193, 195-201, 204-207, 212, 220, 223-226, 236-237, 240-243, 250, 255-259
Brake Harder, 97
Brake Lights, 36-37, 65, 79, 102-103, 154, 256-257
Brakes, 10, 17, 33, 37, 43, 65, 67, 71, 75-79, 81, 83, 95-99, 103-104, 110, 131-133, 161, 177, 197, 199, 204-206, 223-224, 229, 236, 255-260
Braking, 5, 65, 81, 95-99, 133, 189-190,

201-202, 204-205, 217, 220, 225, 229, 255
Bunny Hopping, 235
Buses, 36, 137

California Driver Handbook, 66
California Highway Patrol, 182
Calm, 154, 163, 171, 177
Car Care, 78, 256
Car Centered, 60, 219
Car sick, 203
Cars Kill Kids, 6, 15, 38, 245
Carwise, 75, 78, 146, 256
CB Radio, 256
CD, 122
Cell Phones, 102, 117-121, 252-253
Changing gears, 185, 199, 239
Chatter, 163, 165-166, 177
Chemicals, 80
Child contribute, 39, 123
Child Distractions, 122
Child's car seat, 82
Children Are Closer, 69
Children Looking Ahead, 31, 39
Choosing a car for teenagers, 184
Citizens band radio, 256
Clunker, 36
Clutch, 11, 21, 75, 100, 156, 160, 167, 169, 173, 185-186, 190-191, 195, 197, 199, 201, 205, 208-210, 212, 215, 224-228, 231-237, 239-243, 256, 259, 261
Clutch control, 169, 190-191, 195, 208-210, 212, 215, 225, 227-228, 235, 240-241
Clutch Creep, 225-226, 228, 240-241, 256
Clutch Handling Faults, 235
Clutch Out, 156, 167, 199, 224-226, 232-236, 239-243, 256
Clutch pedal, 156, 185, 226, 231-232, 234-236, 239-240, 256, 259, 261
Clutch Works, 231, 233
Code word, 38
Cold sweats, 94

Collision, 29, 40, 101-102, 104, 106, 119, 121, 129, 189-190, 247, 255, 257, 262
Commentary driving, 33-34, 229
Commercial drivers, 16, 257
Common sense approach, 4, 7
Communicate and ask questions, 153
Communication, one with another, 4
Compass, 90-92
Computer, 25, 51, 53, 62, 94, 96, 116, 156, 203, 245, 255, 257-258
Confidence, 19-20, 55, 149, 158, 164-165, 171, 182, 187, 203-205, 219, 227-228, 233-234, 254
Confident drivers, 5, 19, 34, 254
Congested roads, 252
Contact point, 233
Contribute to your driving, 8
Coordination, 25, 100, 175-176, 178, 181, 196, 219, 227
Correct Passing, 128
Counting Games, 144
Counting Wheels Game, 139
Country Road Lesson, 227
Cover the brake, 204, 257
Crash, 36, 41, 77, 82, 101-102, 120-121, 245
Crazy driver, 214-216
Cruise control, 67, 198, 257
Crumple lines, 78, 257
Cushion of space, 64, 66, 257
Cyclist Wise Drivers, 72

Dangerous Faults, 170, 178, 191
Dangerous situations, 102, 157, 191
Daydreaming, 115-117
Deadly problem, 7
Decision points, 105
Defensive Driving, 5, 101-104, 126, 136, 257
Demonstrate, 42, 76, 87, 112, 140, 156, 173, 178, 190, 202, 209, 223-224, 226, 234, 240
Demonstration, 77, 173, 232
Developing Senses, 5, 83

INDEX

Dirty headlights, 79
Disable a car, 77
Disc brakes, 76, 132, 255, 258
Discover What, 171
Distract the driver, 28
Distraction, 27, 32, 41, 86, 94, 117-118, 120, 122, 163
DMV, 183
Do-or-die, 23
Don't be Distracted By Carsick Kids, 94
Doodling, 115-116
Dramamine, 94
Drilling an action, 157
Drilling can be overdone, 158
Driver Education, 10, 75, 78, 254
Driver improvement course, 151
Drivers Handbook, 192
Driveway, 8, 71, 99, 196-197, 200, 207, 225, 238, 248
Driveway Lesson Zero, 196
Driving Around Busy Mall Parking Lots, 212
Driving in other countries, 247
Driving Instructor, 17, 30, 54, 88, 100, 114, 149, 161, 165, 167, 170-171, 174, 177, 181, 186 187, 189 190, 192, 200, 214, 240, 254
Driving Test, 149, 160, 163, 170, 183, 188, 219-220, 230, 245, 260
Drowsy Drivers, 123
Drunk drivers, 118, 131, 252
Dual control brakes, 161
DUI, 155, 251
DVD player, 26
DWI, 251

Educational game, 98
Elderly driver, 34
Emergency brake, 95
Emergency braking, 202, 217, 225, 229
Emergency code word, 38
Emergency stops, 205
Emergency vehicles, 43, 49, 56, 110
Emphasize improvement, 172
Engine revs, 217, 236, 242

Engineers, 64, 99, 101, 121
Errors, 170, 172
Exact Point Stopping, 205, 227, 229
Exercising, 176
Expectations, 164, 178
Experienced at reading the road, 7
Experienced driver, 9, 50, 55, 60, 100, 136, 166-168, 170, 182-183, 207, 214, 241, 245
Extra Eyes Prevent Accidents, 27
Eye contact, 72, 102
Eyes Moving, 5, 33, 39, 45, 48-50, 53-54, 71, 74, 90, 212, 219, 228

Failed Drivers Taught Me How To Teach Driving, 149
Farmer Counting, 142-143
Fast motions, 34
Fast Moving Trucks Can Deceive, 67
Fast reaction time, 40
Faster Truck, 135
Fear Makes Poor Drivers, 114
Fear of traffic, 30-31, 105
First Lesson, 30, 114, 173, 187, 196, 200, 217, 224-225, 234
Fix It, 172, 192
Fixate, 48-50, 52, 54-56, 106, 113, 122, 198, 212, 218-219, 225, 229, 247
Fixating attention, 50, 52, 190, 228
Fluid levels, 22, 154, 258
Focus Is Seeing Sharply, 40
Focus the eyes on the object, 48
Focus your eyes on what you see, 108, 123
Following Distances, 5, 63, 66, 262
Following Trucks, 66, 133, 259
Foot and eye coordination, 175-176, 181
Football, 37, 41-42, 74, 83, 121-122
Foundation, 125, 145-146
Four-wheelers, 131, 259
Freeway Driving, 92, 116, 127, 135, 163, 217-219, 229
Friction, 76, 156, 190, 226, 228, 232-234, 236, 240-243, 256, 258-259
Friction point, 156, 190, 226, 228, 232-234, 236, 240-243, 259

Fuse box, 77
Future drivers, 2-3, 15, 34, 36, 42, 85, 158
Future Drivers Manual, 2

Game plan, 193
Gas pedal, 11, 98-100, 103, 114, 185, 190, 195, 197, 199-200, 215, 217, 223, 226, 233, 235, 240, 243, 257
Gas to brakes, 99
Gatherer mode, 117
Go-carts, 25
Golfing, 53
Good Example, 5, 22, 115, 118, 121, 203
Goofing off, 160
Google Earth, 91
GPS, 38, 120
Grabbed the steering wheel, 29
Grandparents, 12, 139, 145
Gymnasts, 20, 158

H-pattern, 237-238
Hand-eye coordination, 25
Hand-held cell phone, 120
Hand-over-hand, 201, 203
Handbrake, 10
Harley-Davidson, 252
Head-on collision, 106, 129, 247
Help Wanted, 6, 145
High beams, 107, 134
Highway Patrol, 182, 253
Hill Starts, 243
Hitting the brake, 20, 100, 158
Horn, 17, 36, 52, 102, 107, 124, 137-138, 198
Horsepower, 184, 252
How Cars Stop, 95
How Pilots Focus, 48
How to teach, 6, 8-9, 17, 75, 84, 147, 149-150, 168, 172, 181, 205
Hunter mode, 117
Hunters and gatherers, 116
Hydraulic, 98, 132, 255, 259
Hydroplaning, 76

Ideal Driving Students, 25
Imaginary brake, 99-100
Imaginary path, 57-58
Inexpensive solution, 7
Infrequent driver, 50-51
Instruction Guide, 6, 177
Instructor, 17, 23, 30-31, 33, 54, 88, 100, 114, 149-150, 152-153, 156, 159-161, 165-168, 170-172, 174, 177, 181, 186-192, 200, 202, 205, 214, 216, 234, 237, 240, 254
Instructor interfered, 153
Instructor Needs, 153, 160, 168
Insurance companies, 12, 18
International travelers, 250
Internet, 26-27, 34, 91-92, 116, 138, 175
IPod, 111

Jackknifing, 65, 259
Jumped lanes, 17
Junkyard, 76-78

Keep Your Eyes Moving, 48, 71
Keeping You Safe, 159
Kick down, 186
Knobs and buttons, 122

Landmarks, 89-92
Lane, 16-17, 36, 40, 45, 50, 55, 57-58, 60-62, 65, 67, 72, 86, 98, 113, 127, 133-134, 136, 169, 213-214, 218-220, 250
Lanes and Passing, 5, 127
Largest cause of death, 12
Later Lessons, 163, 166, 205, 228, 237, 241
Laws, 7, 18, 22, 82, 193, 199, 251, 253
Lawsuit, 101
Leading cause of death, 7
Learn from his mistakes, 152
Leave yourself an out, 102
Left and right, 86-88, 98, 102, 108, 191-192, 197, 206-207, 220, 226, 248, 255
Left Turns, 109, 137, 192, 197, 207, 226

INDEX 267

Legal driving age, 9, 17, 25
Lesson Four, 226-227
Lesson One, 25, 70, 188, 218, 223-225
Lesson Three, 226
Lesson Two, 25, 224-225
Lesson Zero, 196
Lessons Plan, 6, 206, 223
Let Me Confess, 251
Let Youngsters See Out, 82
Lets Sleep On It, 174
Licensed Driver, 160, 228, 245, 260
Licensing Age, 182
Light and bright, 23-24, 126, 178, 252
Light-hearted, 23
Location, 38, 89-90, 92-93, 119, 200-201, 220, 232
Long Curves, 61, 219
Long distance vision, 141
Look Ahead, 3, 26, 30, 39-40, 42, 44-51, 53, 55, 58, 60, 63, 71, 73-74, 87, 93, 113, 128, 186, 192, 207, 227-229, 238, 252, 261-262
Look left, then right, then left again, 88, 248

Mack truck, 77, 171
Making Confident Drivers, 5, 19
Massachusetts Driver Handbook, 66
Math words, 140
Mattel electric car, 10
Mayflower, 35, 68
Meaning of New Concepts, 155
Medical student, 9, 31
Mentally visualize, 158
Metrolink, 121
Miles driven, 9, 138
Mindless task, 116
Mirrors, 50-51, 60-61, 66, 107-109, 133-134, 137, 151, 169, 196-199, 207, 229, 255
Misjudging, 73
Motorcycles, 69-70
Motorcycles Near You, 69
MPH, 16, 32, 46, 63-64, 66-67, 73, 83-84, 96, 104, 113, 115, 122, 131-132, 135, 205-206, 216, 225, 229, 253, 260, 262
Multitasking, 115, 117
Mundane things, 171
Music, 7, 12, 26, 39, 77, 116, 122, 158
Musical ability, 12
Musicians, 26
Must drive slow, 114
Mustang, 184

National Sleep Foundation, 125
Natural curiosity, 168
Natural progression, 9, 11, 241
Navigator, 93, 165
Nervous, 19, 30, 33, 37, 44, 100, 103, 114, 137, 161-162, 170, 204-205, 217-218, 236, 243
Neurons, 11
New generation, 12
New student driver, 43
Newspaper, 80, 145, 152, 159
Nine years experience, 18
No-go zone, 137
Non-driver, 39
North, South, East and West, 90

Observing stupid driving, 37
Open space, 11, 44, 82, 210
Optic nerves, 51
Orders and rules, 4
Other Countries, 247, 250
Over-confident Driver, 214
Over-correction, 58
Over-pass, 45, 62, 141
Overheated, 132
Overloaded, 36
Overpowered cars, 253
Overwhelmed, 169, 187, 189, 252

Parallel Parking, 173, 186, 209-211, 220, 228, 240
Parental involvement, 7
Parents' most important job, 15, 251
Parking, 30, 36-37, 54, 81, 95, 98, 119, 123, 141, 173, 186, 196-197, 201,

206, 208-212, 214-216, 220, 223-229, 234, 236, 240-243, 256
Passengers, 3, 7-10, 15, 18, 28, 32, 44, 54, 72, 77, 81, 102, 119, 145, 181, 185, 257
Passing, 5, 7, 16, 118, 127-129, 134-137, 164, 170, 185, 245, 253
Passing Trucks, 135
Pedal extender, 97
Pedestrian, 24, 107, 110, 112, 206, 220, 248
Pep talk, 20
Perfection, 165, 171, 200
Perfectionist, 164
Pickup trucks, 36
Pilots focus, 48
Playing with matches, 15
Point of no return, 104-105
Poor Leg Control, 235
Poor Vision, 46
Post-It note, 122
Potential danger, 17, 33, 259
Potholes, 10, 71, 73-74
Potty training, 153
Power steering, 78-79, 151, 201-202
Practicing, 20, 26, 30, 61, 100, 112, 157, 169, 174, 178, 206, 212, 215, 219, 226, 228, 235, 239
Predict, 17, 34, 36-37, 78, 193, 261
Predicting Others, 34
Prepare to stop, 97
Preventing Accidents, 101
Problems, 21, 27-28, 79, 97, 119, 122, 155, 174-176, 183, 196, 206, 235, 252-253
Professional, 35, 44, 78, 149, 161-162, 165, 167-168, 181, 188, 207, 254
Purpose, 3, 18, 28, 126, 145-146, 182, 224
Purpose of this book, 3
Push-pull-slide, 201-203

Rain, 32, 70, 76, 80, 96, 103, 143
Reading other drivers, 32
Reading the road, 3, 7, 9, 11, 18, 20, 26, 29, 31-33, 45, 123, 139, 174, 190-191
Reassure, 137, 164, 227
Red light, 37, 97-98, 102, 105, 110
Regain a child, 26
Report Even Minor Accidents, 111
Republican President Reagan, 24
Research, 7, 11, 49, 51, 115-117, 124-125
Respect and trust, 4
Rest Assured, 146
Rev-counter, 197, 217
Revolutions Per Minute, 75, 261
Riding as passengers, 3
Right Turns, 109, 137, 192, 197, 206-207, 226
Road conditions, 3, 9, 26, 65-66, 104, 166, 239, 261
Road film, 79-80, 261
Road instincts, 18
Road markings, 32, 128
Road rage, 252
Road repairs, 44
Road Signs, 31-32, 46, 140-141, 155
Road work, 32, 45
Roadwise, 5, 26, 29-31, 38, 78, 135, 146, 261
Rough spot, 174
Roundabouts, 29, 249
RPMs, 261
RV, 128

Safe driving patterns, 9
Sailors, 90, 92, 157
Scanning, 48-49
Scary, 40, 44, 62, 105, 127, 170, 218
Schedule, 36, 104, 125, 138, 162, 178, 188-189
School bus, 33, 95
Science, 9, 51
Scientific, 11-12, 51
Seat Belts, 82, 121
Seating Position, 195
See over the wheel, 21
Sense of Distance, 83-84, 139

INDEX

Sense of Speed, 85, 139
Sense of Time, 85
Series of Small Actions, 168
Shapes, 32, 140
Shared Moments, 28
Sharing the road, 73
Shift lanes, 99
Shifting Sticks, 100
Shoes, 78, 195, 235, 255-256
Shopping malls, 54, 210
Short Lessons, 200
Siblings, 22
Signal, 36, 79, 102-103, 108, 110, 120, 128-129, 138, 169, 191-193, 197-199, 206, 209, 212, 218
Simple exercises, 8, 176
Sing, 94, 144
Sit on your hands, 152
Size does matter, 133
Sketch, 173, 208
Skipping, 175-176
Slang, 157, 258-259
Slaves, 116
Sleep, 4, 27, 36, 50, 117, 124-126, 174, 178, 249, 252-253, 262
Sleep-deprived, 124, 252
Slips the clutch, 233
Slow Vehicles, 47
Slow-moving truck, 98
Slowing Down, 76, 97, 102-103, 109, 196, 212, 214-215, 257
Slowing is better than stopping, 98
Small Things Seem Farther Away, 5, 69
Soccer mom, 35
Soccer Player, 26, 42, 59-60
Sounds of the road, 110
Space cushion, 64, 66, 102, 257
Special times, 8, 28
Speed demon, 215-216
Speed is relative, 215
Sport, 19, 53
Sports car, 35, 98, 184, 253
Spot situations, 34
Stare straight ahead, 118
Start Them Young, 5, 23

Starting Downhill, 240
State Driver Handbook, 18, 83, 155, 193
Steer a bike, 3
Steering into disaster, 8
Steering wheel, 3, 10, 17, 20, 23, 29, 57-58, 81-82, 86, 88, 97, 106, 108, 112, 160, 181, 190, 192, 195-196, 201-203, 207, 209, 228, 239, 242, 248-250, 255
Steering While Turning, 201
Step by step, 8, 168, 182
Stick Shift, 11, 100, 156, 166-168, 173-174, 184-186, 190, 193, 195, 197, 199, 201, 205, 209-210, 212, 215-217, 223-227, 229, 231-233, 238, 240, 243, 256, 259, 261
Stomp, steer, stop, 96-97, 206, 255
Stop sign, 161, 169, 187, 191
Stops Here, 6, 245
Structure and rules, 18
Student Correction, 192
Student Do His Job, 152
Student Driver, 8, 24, 43, 49, 54, 85, 106, 126, 153, 155, 159, 166, 170-172, 174, 188-189, 192, 196, 204-205, 211, 213, 217, 224-225, 242-243
Student Handling, 190
Success, 7, 26, 162, 164
Sunday drive, 104
Survival skills, 3
SUVs, 184, 195
Swerves for no reason, 36
Swerving, 105
Synapses, 11-12

Tachometer, 197, 233, 262
Tailgating, 64
Take a nap, 4, 124-125
Talk, 20, 29-30, 33, 41, 94, 116-118, 120, 138, 154, 163, 165-166, 189, 199, 229, 256
Teach Basic Car Control, 196
Teach Driving, 6, 19, 23, 73, 139, 147, 149-150, 160, 173, 177, 181, 195, 228

Teach one thing at a time, 169-170
Teach to learn more, 21
Teach Your Baby, 1-2, 5, 7, 13, 145-146
Teach Your Child Left, 86
Teach Your Teen, 6, 8-9, 100, 179
Teaching Babies, 12, 32
Teaching Games, 5, 139
Teaching plan, 182
Team players, 22
Tearing of metal, 40, 151, 187
Technical schools, 75
Technology, 120-121, 260
Teen drivers, 7, 15, 120, 131
Teenagers, 3, 7, 9, 19, 25, 77, 120, 125-126, 145, 149-150, 153, 158, 182, 184, 196, 203, 251, 253
Teenagers and sleep, 125
Teens safer drivers, 7
Ten-wheelers, 138
Tennis, 26, 51, 168, 176, 258
Texters, 120
Texting, 115, 120-121
The Sound of Music, 77
Three-Point Turns, 209, 220, 228
Three-Second Rule, 66, 262
Tiger Woods, 7, 26
Tilt steering wheel, 196
Tires, 16, 36, 76, 80-81, 101, 104, 111, 133, 208, 213, 234, 256, 262
Toddler, 11, 15, 153
Touch the brake, 65, 97, 99, 132, 197, 225
Tough love, 246
Tow Vehicle, 127, 219
Toy cars, 11, 19, 25, 112, 158
Toys, 25, 70, 112, 144, 178
Traction, 32, 66, 133, 262
Traffic congestion, 107, 253
Traffic laws, 22
Traffic school, 151
Training wheels, 3, 7
Travel Routes, 93, 109
Trees, 16, 40, 53-54, 59, 90, 227, 258
Tricks of the trade, 21
Tricycle, 25

Truck Blind Spots, 137
TruckerBuddy, 138
Truckers, 136-138, 259
Trucking Guide, 138
Trucks, 5, 19, 32, 36, 66-68, 70-71, 98, 109, 113, 131-139, 152, 170, 254-257, 259-260
Trucks Need More Space, 131
Turning, 17, 37, 41, 56, 71, 92, 107-111, 117, 122, 167, 185, 190, 192, 198-199, 201, 203, 206, 208-210, 215, 219-220, 231, 236, 248, 258, 261
Turning Practice, 219
TVs, 53
Twelve-Second Rule, 45-47, 74, 262
Two different age groups, 9
Two-Second Rule, 22, 63-64, 66, 262

U-Haul, 35
U-turn, 209
Uncoordinated Drivers, 175
Unfixate, 53
UPS, 35, 109
United Van Lines, 35
Unnecessary Talking, 165-166
Uphill, 103, 134-136, 174, 201, 225-227, 234, 240-243, 257, 260
Uphill Starts, 174, 201, 225-227, 240-243, 260
Upset child, 34, 122-123
Upset occurs, 174, 178, 252
Using Shopping Malls, 54

Value Jet, 102
Video games, 19, 25, 203
Visibility, 35, 65-66, 70-71, 102-103, 128, 133, 195
Vision, 41, 46, 58, 66, 68, 79, 113, 141, 260
Visualize, 56-58, 156, 158-159
Visualizing What Needs to be done, 158, 162
Vital driving skills, 7

INDEX

Watch the road, 7, 26, 31, 175
Weaknesses, 113, 117
Weather conditions, 78, 103-104
Web, 10, 37, 92, 145
Whole Scene, 48-51, 62, 190, 198, 246
Why Almost Everyone Learns, 150
Winning, 165, 169
Working models, 75
Working the pedals, 11, 17, 181, 191
Worn Tires Kill, 80
Wrong Side, 23, 106-107, 138, 247-250

Yelling Will Get You Nowhere, 170
You Can help, 78, 118, 141, 145
Your Teaching Plan, 182

www.ingramcontent.com/pod-product-compliance
Lightning Source LLC
LaVergne TN
LVHW051041080426
835508LV00019B/1646